Baseball and Softball Fields

Baseball and Softball Fields:

Design, Construction, Renovation, and Maintenance

Jim Puhalla
Jeff Krans
Mike Goatley

WILEY

John Wiley & Sons, Inc.

Library of Congress Cataloging-in-Publication Data:
Puhalla, Jim.
   Baseball and softball fields : design, construction, renovation, and maintenance / by
Jim Puhalla, Jeff Krans, Mike Goatley.
         p. cm.
Includes index.
   ISBN 0-471-44793-5 (Cloth)
1. Baseball fields—Design and construction. 2. Baseball fields—Maintenance and repair.
3. Softball fields—Design and construction. 4. Softball fields—Maintenance and repair.
I. Krans, Jeff. II. Goatley, Mike. III. Title.
GV879.5 .P85 2003
796.357'06'8—dc21
                                                                              2002153262

Printed in the United States of America
10 9 8 7 6 5 4 3 2 1

Contents

Part II   Renovation and Maintenance

Part III   Ancillary Information

Preface

It has been said that although football reflects America as it is (long meetings interspersed with short periods of violence), baseball reflects America as it would like to be. In a nation that recognizes no limitation on what can be achieved with hard work, creativity, and a little luck, the game of baseball (and its sister sport, softball) represents that vision of unlimited possibilities. In football, no touchdown pass can be more than 99½ yd, no kick can be run back more than 109½ yd. But in baseball, the length of a home run is theoretically infinite. The game itself can last 500 innings, if that's how long it takes for one team to win. The very nature of the game expresses our desire to be surprised and delighted by the achievements of each generation of athletic young men and women.

No wonder it was a baseball field that was first called "Field of Dreams." The shape of the playing area, spreading outward from home plate, suggests our ability to break out of the restraints of modern life, find a gap, and keep rolling forever.

This book has been written by men who admit without apology that they love a well-tended baseball diamond—the deep green of the turf, the smooth skinned areas, the dramatic expansion of the foul lines. Our goal is to share with North America's baseball and softball field managers the knowledge and skills they will need to create and maintain that kind of facility.

Of course, the task of providing those Fields of Dreams is becoming ever more demanding. Construction and maintenance costs have increased steadily in recent years. The rapid growth in athletic participation by women and girls has doubled the use of some facilities and has created the need for tens of thousands of new softball diamonds throughout North America. Greater awareness of the factors that affect safety (and of the potential cost of personal injury lawsuits) has led to greater consistency in the design and construction of new diamonds for softball and baseball.

In our experience, these factors are all having a substantial positive impact on the disciplines of designing, constructing, and maintaining sports fields. If there is no budget for after-the-fact repairs, the field must be built right the first time. Because rescheduling games involves so many headaches due to more games being played at some facilities, fields are being built to remain playable in a wider variety of weather conditions. Even the threat of lawsuits is having a positive effect, calling greater attention to the safety of the facility itself.

THE PURPOSE OF THIS BOOK

It should be noted at the outset that this book is not meant to be a comprehensive scientific and technical reference source on soil science, agronomy, and/or the relation of those academic disciplines to sports fields. That was the goal of our first collaborative effort, *Sports Fields: A Manual for Design, Construction and Maintenance*. For those looking for the kind of in-depth information necessary for full-time professional work in the field, or for a textbook suitable for postsecondary education, we suggest a consideration of that book, which is published by Ann Arbor Press.

This book, on the other hand, is meant to focus sharply on the kind of practical information needed by those who are responsible for the maintenance and management of baseball and softball diamonds, and who may from time to time be involved in the construction of new diamonds or the reconstruction of existing ones. To meet the information needs of these professionals, we briefly consider the critical design elements of baseball and softball fields, review the most commonly encountered problems of baseball and softball diamonds and appropriate solutions to each, and describe the steps for construction or renovation of facilities. We also provide some practical guidance for the design and implementation of maintenance programs in all climatic zones of North America.

We believe that following the principles outlined on these pages will result in fields that are safe, usable in a wide variety of conditions, easy and inexpensive to maintain, visually pleasing, and free of the kind of problems that can compromise athletic performance.

In keeping with established custom, we divide North America into three general growing zones: the *warm season zone,* which includes the sunbelt states of the South and Southwest; the *transitional zone,* which includes Maryland, Virginia, West Virginia, Tennessee, Kentucky, Missouri, and parts of the West and Southwest; and the *cool season zone,* generally composed of the Northern states. Each zone has its own turfgrass maintenance challenges, and we provide information that can be used in developing maintenance and management strategies in each.

It is important to keep in mind that the guidance in this book is not presented as unquestionable, set-in-stone rules that must never be broken. Instead, it is meant to be practical advice that can be combined with the field manager's knowledge of local soil and weather factors to yield safe and playable baseball and softball diamonds.

HOW TO USE THIS BOOK

Part I, "Design and Construction," surveys the principles of field design, including layout, preferred contours, infields, warning tracks, multiple-field layouts, and access for players and spectators. The critical roles of drainage and irrigation are considered, along with the design and installation of systems for each. Part I also includes chapters on the selection of soil for turf and skinned areas, the selection of turfgrass varieties for each climatic zone, and sound construction and reconstruction practices. These chapters are not intended to be a complete course in design or construction, but rather to help the sports field professional serve as an effective interface between the owners of the field and the design and construction specialists hired to work on a project.

Part II, "Renovation and Maintenance," provides guidance on the regular procedures that must be followed to maximize the playability of a field. For our purposes, renovation is defined as the process of restoring a field to its original condition after competition and other stresses have degraded it to some degree, and maintenance is the daily or weekly discipline of keeping a diamond in good order during the competition season. Separate chapters review renovation, skinned area and turfgrass maintenance and management, and field aesthetics.

Part III includes two chapters with important information that does not fit neatly into either the "Design and Construction" or "Renovation and Maintenance" parts of the book. We have included this information because it should prove to be of value to many sports fields managers.

Chapter 10 considers the various auxiliary structures that combine with the field itself to provide the playing environment for a baseball or softball game: fences, backstops, dugouts, and bullpens. Suggestions are offered for selecting, installing, and maintaining these structures to enhance the safety of players and the competitiveness of the game.

Chapter 11 reviews some of the rules and regulations of the game as they relate to the field itself, including some common points of confusion about how the field is to be laid out and constructed. Line and boundary dimensions for fields used by players of various ages, and the names and addresses of governing and sanctioning bodies, are included for the reader's reference.

We take great satisfaction in the thought that this book may play a role in providing a new generation of safe, competitive, and easy-to-maintain fields on which people of all ages can have fun, become more fit, and pursue the dream of athletic excellence.

ACKNOWLEDGMENTS

The authors gratefully acknowledge the contributions of many academic and professional leaders whose advice and counsel have contributed to the completion of this book.

We are appreciative for the advice of the following academic colleagues: Barry Stewart, Wayne Wells, Victor Maddox, Wayne Philley, Wayne Langford, Pat Sneed, Pat Harris, John Byrd, Euel Coats, and David Nagel, all members of the Mississippi State University faculty and staff. Special thanks to Bart Prather, supervisor of MSU athletic fields, and to Richard H. Hurley, for his time and insight in selecting the recommended cool season turf-grass cultivars. Special thanks and appreciation to Donald Waddington, professor emeritus of Pennsylvania State University.

Thanks to David R. Mellor, director of grounds for the Boston Red Sox, for contributing information and photographs on field aesthetics and skinned area maintenance, and to Tom Burns of the Texas Rangers for advice on warm season turfgrass maintenance.

Thanks to James Dailey Puhalla for his assistance with the development of the architectural drawings used in this book. Thanks also to Henry Pearce for his editorial assistance in crafting a consistent style from copy contributed by the three authors and for his help in organizing and managing the project.

Special thanks to our colleagues at Mississippi State University, the staff of Sportscape International, Inc., and our wives and families for their patience during the writing of this book. All of these people have tolerated our preoccupation with this manuscript for the past two years.

PART I

Design and Construction

If you are a sports field manager, grounds supervisor, or administrator in charge of maintaining baseball or softball fields, you may approach this part of the book with a very basic question: Why should I care about principles of design and construction? That's a fair question. Presumably, the fields you are charged with managing have already been designed and constructed. Someone else—a person with sound knowledge of these principles, it is hoped—has developed a design concept for each field and supervised its construction in such a way that the result is a facility that is easy to keep playable.

Before you skip this part of the book and go on to the later sections on renovation and maintenance, consider this: Many of the daily challenges you face in preparing the diamond for competition are profoundly affected by the decisions made by its designers sometime in the past. The more you know about how these decisions were made (and about any errors made during the design process), the better prepared you will be to take the steps necessary to adequately support competition.

For example, field managers will be able to make better decisions about field renovation and/or maintenance based on a sound knowledge of field design. If the skinned area drains toward the outfield grass, the challenge is to keep a lip from forming in that area so water can flow freely into the grass. If the skinned area drains toward the foul lines, then the grass in that area must remain flat for water to flow off the playing surface.

Design problems with an athletic field are most likely to be identified in detail when the facility becomes such a headache that reconstruction is required. Over the past 22 years, reconstruction work on dozens of baseball and softball fields has revealed that just about every one of those fields had design flaws resulting in a number of common problems.

First of all, almost all had a problem with standing water in the infield.

Second, the problem of standing water was nearly always caused by poor grading.

Third, although some of the facilities had some sort of installed drain system, the system did not work as intended.

The one thing the fields did not have in common was the way they were graded. Each field had been designed and constructed, it seems, with a completely different set of grading standards.

Finally, the fields nearly always had in common the only practical and effective solution for their problem: regrading the field to provide for positive surface runoff of water.

Probably more than any other sport, baseball is sensitive to field conditions and especially to water. Skinned areas (areas of the diamond that are intentionally kept free of vegetation to promote uniform ball response) have a tendency to turn into little lakes at the first cloudburst. Play must then be delayed until the field dries out naturally or until drying agents or other materials can be applied to soak up the wet spots and allow play to go on.

Of course, many field managers are intimately involved in the process of designing and constructing new baseball and softball diamonds. Under these circumstances, you have the option of simply leaving this work to professionals hired for the purpose. However, it is worth considering that if these people make mistakes (and, sadly, sometimes they make serious ones), you will be the person responsible for cleaning up after those mistakes—sometimes for years to come.

If, on the other hand, you have taken time to familiarize yourself with the basic principles of field design and construction, you will be in a position to ask questions, make suggestions, and warn against errors. So the time invested in the first five chapters of this book can pay huge dividends in time, money, and headaches.

Of course, some readers will be architects, engineers, or others whose work includes the design of fields and the supervision of their construction. These professionals will be well aware that to successfully design and construct a baseball or softball diamond requires careful attention to the subtleties of survey, design, and grading. For them, the initial chapters of this book will probably prove to be the most useful.

Chapter 1 considers the design of the field in terms of its contours and layout. Chapter 2 provides information on field irrigation, drainage, and covers. Chapter 3 looks at the soils used for both turf and skinned areas. Chapter 4 discusses the selection of turfgrass for baseball and softball diamonds, and Chapter 5 reviews construction and reconstruction practices.

Other elements such as fences, dugouts, and bullpens are considered in Chapter 10.

Chapter 1

Field Design

1.1 INTRODUCTION

In this chapter, we will consider the design of baseball and softball fields from the perspective of the field and surrounding areas. The discussion includes such design elements as contour plans, warning tracks, and access to the field for players, spectators, and equipment. It also considers the design of both skinned and grass infields, and alternative methods of laying out multiple-field complexes.

The chapter begins with the most important single factor affecting the playability of a baseball or softball diamond: contouring. If, for example, a field is not sloped enough to facilitate surface drainage, water puddles will eventually be a problem. On the other hand, if the field has too much slope, playability will be affected by unpredictable ball response and the field will have a disorienting effect on players. If the contours are not uniform, the result will be an uneven surface and heavy rainfall may produce ruts. If the facility is not correctly designed and constructed in the first place, reconstruction will be required to achieve positive surface drainage.

1.2 SURVEY AND LAYOUT

Professionals engaged in the design and construction of athletic fields are frequently called upon to fix fields that are plagued by wet spots, ruts, or other problems. In many cases, a quick examination of the facility shows that it was constructed without the benefit of a thorough survey. Sometimes the original planners just thought it looked level. In other cases, the field started out as a mowed area used for practice or informal play and then was needed for games.

To avoid problems with the field contours, it is essential that any new construction or reconstruction project begin with a thorough survey of the site. Intuition and the naked eye will not provide sufficient understanding of the topography of the area; only a careful survey will accomplish that end.

(Note that the process of surveying includes shooting topographic elevations, measuring the dimensions of the area, and noting such features as streams, structures, roadways, and the like. All are important to the design of a solidly performing diamond.)

In surveying and laying out a baseball or softball diamond, it is best to proceed according to this sequence: First, survey the boundaries of the area, making sure there is sufficient room for the playing field, including foul territory. As a general rule of thumb, it is wise to survey about twice the area of the field itself. Next, using the measurements taken of the area, make a drawing, on which you will mark elevations. Then establish a grid pattern on your drawing, and place markers on the ground to match the grid pattern on the drawing. In designing a new field, it is customary to survey the site using a 50 ft grid pattern. This is sufficient to establish the existing contours of the site where the field will be constructed. Shoot elevations and mark them on your drawing, establishing a benchmark at a permanent point, such as a curb or a sewer lid. (All elevations are stated in relation to the benchmark.) A computerized surveying instrument called a "total station" records all measurements and elevations and allows them to be downloaded to a computer.

(In planning for the reconstruction of an existing field, it can be helpful to shoot the elevations of the key points on the diamond; simply shooting on a grid pattern will miss the most important points that are critical to good playability. Be sure to take measurements to existing backstops, dugouts, fences, and other structures, and include these measurements on your drawing. A surveying worksheet used for shooting necessary elevations for a reconstruction project is presented in Chapter 5, Figure 5.20.)

Using the information from the survey, make a new drawing of the area to scale, and mark on it all the measurements, elevations, and other information on the topography of the area. Then lay out the field or fields, using dimensions such as those in rule books or those given in Chapter 11 of this book.

In laying out the field, it is important to consider its *orientation,* the relationship of the field to the points of the compass. Although many fields are simply oriented to the available space, some official rule books for baseball and softball recommend laying out the facility so that a line drawn from the tip of home plate through the pitcher's plate and second base points in an east-northeast direction. This orientation prevents the batter and catcher from looking into the sun as they stand at the plate and positions most of the fielders so that their eye line to the batter is not directly into the setting sun. You may want to establish the orientation for your field based on the time of year and the time of day when the field is most typically used.

It is also important to reserve space for the dugouts, backstop, surrounding fence, and other peripheral elements. All too often, a failure to plan for these structures forces the builders to install them in an awkward and unsuitable fashion, which may compromise player safety and disturb a well-planned drainage scheme.

Table 1.1 suggests minimum space requirements for baseball and softball fields, with

Table 1.1. Space Requirements

Type of Field	Distance to Center Field Fence (ft)	Acres	Sq Ft[a]
Baseball:			
90 ft Bases	400	4.5	195,000
80 ft Bases	315	2.8	123,000
70 ft Bases	275	2	90,000
60 ft Bases	215	1.5	64,000
Softball:			
60 ft Bases	200	1.4	60,000
65 ft Bases	275	2.4	105,000

[a] Numbers are rounded to the nearest 1000 sq ft.

Table 1.2. Square Footage of Skinned Area and Grass Area

Type of Field	Distance to Center Field Fence (ft)	Skinned Area (sq ft)	Grass Area (sq ft)
Baseball:			
90 ft Bases–95 ft Arc			
With Grass Infield	400	11,550	120,500
With Skinned Infield	400	18,300	113,750
80 ft Bases–80 ft Arc			
With Grass Infield	315	8,400	74,500
With Skinned Infield	315	13,650	69,250
70 ft Bases–70 ft Arc			
With Grass Infield	275	6,800	53,550
With Skinned Infield	275	10,700	49,650
60 ft Bases–50 ft Arc			
With Grass Infield	215	3,850	39,500
With Skinned Infield	215	6,700	36,650
Softball: (Skinned Infield)			
60 ft Bases–60 ft Arc	200	8,350	31,500
65 ft Bases–65 ft Arc	275	9,300	61,450

sufficient space around the playing field for fence lines, dugouts, spectator seating, and swales.

Table 1.2 displays the square footage of the skinned area and the grass area for common-size baseball and softball fields, including foul territory.

1.3 DESIGN CRITERIA FOR NEW CONSTRUCTION

The criteria that follow are based on the authors' experience with fields that were not properly designed. They are divided into two groups: the fundamental issues that allow the field to perform well under a variety of weather conditions, and the safety issues that allow players to use the field with minimal risk of injury. Fields may sometimes be built without following these guidelines, but planners should keep in mind that departing from them may compromise the safety or playability of the diamond. Although following the guidelines may seem inconvenient, failure to follow them will almost always cause substantial problems later.

1.3a Fundamental Issues

One of the most important considerations in designing a field, whether a single field, a multiple-field complex, or an addition to an existing sports complex, is to treat each field as an individual drainage unit. No field should be expected to drain away more water than that which falls on it. This is the reason for surveying beyond the playing area itself. Even if a field is built with correct contours, water running onto the field from an adjacent area can seriously compromise playability in rainy conditions.

Second, the infield should be higher than the rest of the field. To keep the infield playable, it is important that no water drains onto the infield from the outfield or the sideline areas.

COMMON DESIGN ERRORS (AND SOLUTIONS)

INCORRECT FIELD CONTOURS

Sports field contours are expressed as percentage of slope. Any slope that is less than 1.0% (except for baseball/softball infields, which should be 0.5%) or more than 2.0% is considered incorrect. The preferred slope for sports field grass areas is 1.25% to 1.75%. The optimum slope for baseball/softball field skinned areas should be between 0.5% and 1.75%.

A baseball or softball infield should never be the lowest point on the field—it should be the highest point, to enhance surface drainage.

If a contour is not even and consistent, it is incorrect. A field with a 1.5% slope should be graded evenly with a 1½ ft difference in grade over a span of 100 ft.

FAILURE TO ISOLATE FIELDS AS DRAINAGE UNITS

No field should be expected to drain away more water than that which falls on it. Even if a field is built with correct contours, water running onto the field from another field or an adjacent area can seriously compromise playability in rainy conditions.

The preferred design isolates each field as an individual drainage unit by using swales and/or catch basins around the field, or by making the field higher than its surroundings.

INSUFFICIENT CLEARANCE AROUND FIELD

Fields that are designed or constructed with insufficient clearance will have inherent problems: Out-of-bounds areas may be too small for the safety of players, spectator areas may be cramped or unsafe, and surface drainage around a field may not work as intended.

Consider space requirements in the planning stages. Making sure there is enough space around each field before construction begins will prevent it from being "locked in" by other fields, parking lots, roads, buildings, and the like.

FAILURE TO PROVIDE SUFFICIENT ACCESS

A well-designed sports field includes access roadways for players, spectators, maintenance equipment, and heavier renovation equipment, including large trucks. Parking lots should be centrally located to provide easy access, especially for elderly and disabled fans.

Third, the highest point on the infield is the pitcher's mound, and the infield slopes away from the mound in all directions. (The height of the pitching plate, or "rubber," is specified by the sanctioning body for each level of competition. See Chapter 11 for heights established by sanctioning bodies.)

Fourth, the base lines should be as level as possible. Although a slight grade may be used on some fields to enhance drainage, sanctioning bodies typically specify level base paths. When the base lines are not level, the overall contours of the infield can be disturbed, which may result in ineffective surface drainage.

Fifth, differences in grade should be continuous and uniform from contour line to contour line. Ideally, the slope should be set at about 0.5% for the infield, 0.5% to 1.5% for the skinned area, and 1.0% to 2.0% for the outfield. These percentages will allow surface water to run off the playing area and into catch basins or swales outside the boundary lines or to lower-lying areas surrounding the field.

Sixth, to facilitate mowing, areas outside the fences should have a maximum slope of 3:1. That is, for every 3 ft measured horizontally, the grade goes up or down a maximum of 1 ft. The generally accepted maximum slope for pedestrian walkways is 1 in. per foot. (This is, by the way, the maximum slope recommended for wheelchair access under codes related to the Americans with Disabilities Act, ADA.)

Seventh, be sure that sufficient space is left for player and spectator access to the field, in the form of walkways and driveways. Where appropriate, plan for parking at the closest possible point. (This planning will also enhance your ability to get service and maintenance vehicles to the field later.)

Finally, a good field design should take account of two important concepts. "Cutting" refers to the removal of soil when the grade must be lowered, and "filling" means adding soil where the grade must be raised. The best designs balance the amount of soil to be cut with the amount to be filled. This balance minimizes the amount of new material that must be transported onto the site or the amount of existing soil that will have to be trucked away.

1.3b Safety Issues

In designing the diamond, a number of safety issues must be considered. One of the most obvious is the distance from the foul lines to the dugouts, grandstands, and other fixed objects. As a general rule, a minimum clearance of 25 ft is recommended for Little League and softball fields, with twice as much for baseball at the high school level and above. Because players must run through this area looking upward to track foul balls, the greatest possible clear area should be allowed. (However, softball sanctioning bodies recommend no more than 30 ft from the home plate to the backstop and outside the foul lines. See Chapter 11 for the recommended clearance for each level of baseball and softball.)

If possible, catch basins should be located outside the fences surrounding the playing area to prevent player injury. If the presence of grandstands requires the installation of catch basins inside the fences, they should be placed as close as possible to the fences or grandstands. In such circumstances, a flat grid with small openings should be used to minimize the risk of injury.

Obviously, there should be no obstructions in the field of play (including foul territory). Such obstructions include bullpens, although many fields now in use were built with bullpens inside the fences in foul territory.

In designing a competitive baseball or softball field, it is always wise to have the latest copy of the rule book of the organization that governs the particular level of play. Contact the appropriate sanctioning body included in the list of addresses given in Chapter 11.

1.4 FIELD DESIGNS WITH PREFERRED CONTOURS

Baseball and softball diamonds are more complicated to design than any other type of sports fields, largely because they consist of three distinct parts that must be integrated for the diamond to perform successfully. In discussing field design, we refer to these three parts as the *outfield* (used here as commonly understood), the *skinned area* (the groomed dirt portion of the field where the infielders customarily stand during play), and the *infield* (the area enclosed by the base paths). Even where the infield is skinned, as on a softball diamond, for design purposes the infield is distinguished from the skinned area where the infielders position themselves.

The following drawings illustrate three designs—or "grading plans"—for baseball and softball diamonds. Note that the full-field designs continue past the actual playing field and include some of the surrounding area. This is because failure to properly contour these areas can cause water to run onto the field.

1.4a   The Outfield

The most important design principle for an outfield is that it must not drain toward the infield. Figure 1.1 shows one of the simplest and most common field designs. The outfield slopes downward from the second and third base lines to the outfield fence at a rate of approximately 1.0%. (We consider this 1.0% slope to be the minimum acceptable slope,

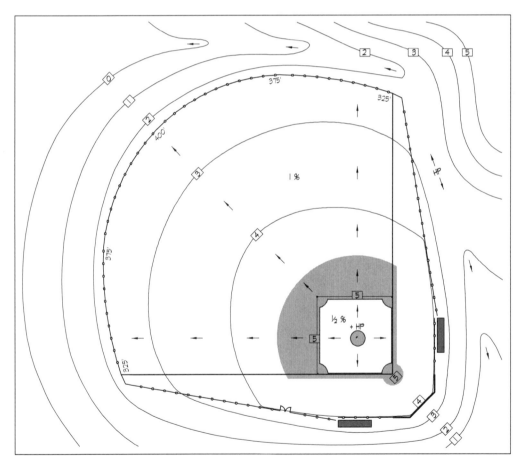

Figure 1.1. The simplest and most common (good) field design—elevations noted in feet. In order to maintain a consistent slope, remember to include spot elevations for the outfield fence. (See Figure 1.4 for spot elevations of the skinned area.)

and we recommend 1.25% to 1.5% whenever possible. Probably, 1.75% is the maximum; a 2.0% slope becomes visibly noticeable.) The most obvious advantage of this design lies is the simplicity of its contours, which makes it fairly easy to build. For instance, in constructing this field, grade stakes can be set on a 50 ft grid pattern, which is easier than finding exact contour lines through the outfield.

The most common complaint about this design is that it slopes downward from the infield to the fence; with a 1.0% slope, the outfield fence will be about 3 ft lower than the infield. Naturally, if the slope is increased, this difference becomes even greater. Another disadvantage of this design is that the entire skinned area drains into the outfield. That means water must pass through the circle at the grass edge. This edge often becomes clogged with dirt as a result of competitive play, grooming the field, and runoff, creating a "lip"—a sort of dam that retains water on the skinned area.

(Figure 1.4 shows detailed skinned area and infield contours for the full-field design in Figure 1.1.)

Figure 1.2 is an improved design, crowned from second base through center field to the outfield fence. The center crown directs water toward the boundaries and away

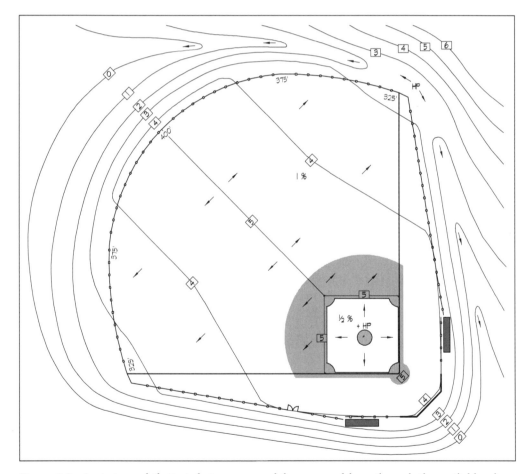

Figure 1.2. An improved (better) design, crowned from second base through the outfield—elevations noted in feet. In order to maintain a consistent slope, remember to include spot elevations for the outfield fence. (See Figure 1.5 for spot elevations of the skinned area.)

from the center of the field. The strength of this design is its handling of runoff. There is a shorter path for runoff from the outfield; water flows to the foul lines rather than all the way to the outfield fence. The skinned area also drains toward the foul lines, creating two exit points, behind first and third base. It is easier to keep these exit points draining effectively than to maintain the entire grass edge between the skinned area and the outfield.

The main disadvantages of this design are related to the crown. Because of the shape of the contours, grade stakes cannot be set on a 50 ft grid pattern for construction, because that grid pattern may not locate the crown precisely. The crown will also cause the outfield fence to slope away from center field toward the foul lines; in relation to the batter, the fences will be lower at the foul poles than in dead center.

(The skinned area and infield detail for this design is provided in Figure 1.5.)

The design illustrated in Figure 1.3 draws from the strengths of each of the first two layouts—we have referred to them as "good" and "better"; consider this one our "best." In this design, a crown has been developed from second base about one-third of the way

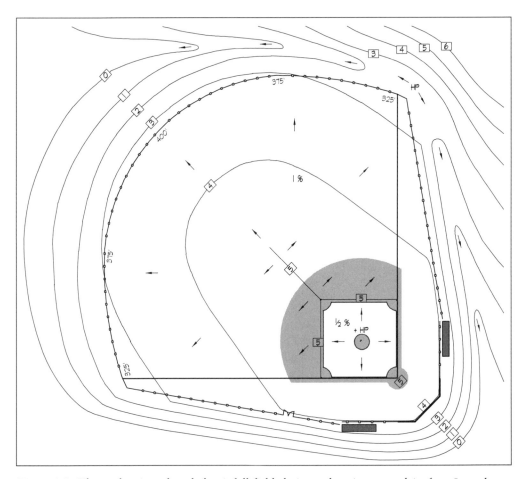

Figure 1.3. The authors' preferred (best) full-field design—elevations noted in feet. In order to maintain a consistent slope, remember to include spot elevations for the outfield fence. (See Figure 1.5 for spot elevations of the skinned area.)

to the outfield fence. This crown allows water to run off the heart of the field toward the foul lines. In the outer half of the outfield, runoff is toward the fence. This design sheds water effectively because it establishes the shortest paths for drainage throughout the field. With a 1.0% slope, it also allows the fence lines around the entire field to be nearly level. (With a 1.5% slope, the fences will be lower at the foul poles.)

The main disadvantage of this design is that it is more complicated to build. Grade stakes for construction will have to be placed on each contour line.

(The skinned area and infield detail for this design are shown in Figure 1.5.)

1.4b The Skinned Area

In all likelihood, the most common reason for a field to be chronically unplayable is that its skinned area was poorly designed. It is surprising how often field planners fail to give this portion of the diamond the attention it deserves; at any given moment, all but three of the defensive players are standing on the skinned area. Because of the critical nature of the slope on a skinned area, spot elevations should be included in the design in order for the skinned area to drain properly. Even a small error can have troublesome consequences in terms of playability. Refer to Figure 5.2 for more details of infield and skinned area design.

One reason to pay such careful attention to the contours of skinned areas is that these areas must rely entirely on positive surface drainage to shed water. Installed drain systems are not effective for skinned areas. Although such systems can effectively drain the turf areas of the baseball diamond, they typically work poorly in the sand/clay soil used for a skinned area. Under normal circumstances, water moves too slowly through skinned area soil and into the drain structures. In most cases, positive surface drainage is the only practical way to prevent standing water on a skinned area.

Figure 1.4 is a simple skinned area contour scheme designed for use with the overall field design in Figure 1.1. This design has a downward slope from the second and third base lines to the outfield. The design is relatively easy to build, and it works adequately in medium-to-dry climates.

However, as mentioned in the preceding section, this design has a disadvantage in that infield water must drain into the outfield through the circled grass edge. As that water runs off, it carries loose soil from the skinned area, which is then deposited in the grass edge. The deposited soil forms a sill or "lip," preventing proper drainage and holding the water in the skinned area. The circled edge must be given constant attention to avoid this problem. (For guidance on removing this lip at the grass edge, see Chapter 6, Section 6.2, "Skinned Area Renovation," and Chapter 7, Section 7.3f, "Grass Edge Maintenance.")

Figure 1.5 shows a skinned area design that includes a crown, for use with the full-field designs in Figures 1.2 and 1.3. As mentioned earlier, this design channels runoff to exit points at the foul lines behind first and third bases, rather than toward the outfield. Because water does not have to flow through the circled grass edge to leave the infield, the puddling and maintenance headaches associated with the dirt lip in the grass edge are eliminated, making this a preferred design for moderately rainy and very rainy areas.

1.4c The Infield

Keep in mind that for design purposes, the term *infield* refers only to the area inside the base paths. The pitcher's mound is the highest point of the infield (in fact, of the entire field), with the rest of the infield sloping away in all directions toward the base paths, as

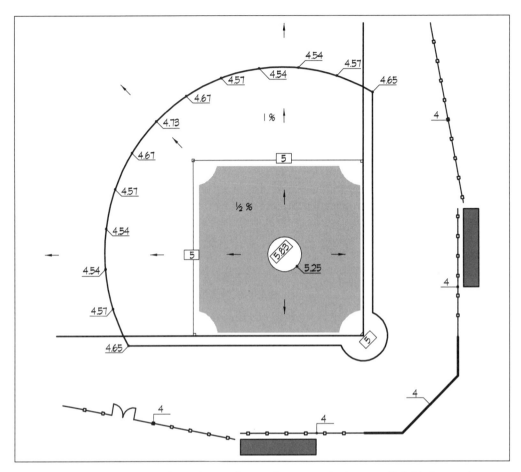

Figure 1.4. A simple (good) skinned area design, for use with the overall field design shown in Figure 1.1—elevations noted in feet. (See Figure 5.2 for spot elevations of the infield grass and foul territory around the infield.)

shown in Figures 1.4 and 1.5. Spot elevations for the top and bottom of the mound, as well as for the bases, must be included for an infield to drain properly.

A problem with this design should be noted. The height difference between the pitcher's plate and home plate is fixed by sanctioning bodies. In Figures 1.4 and 1.5, because the entire infield slopes away from the pitcher's mound, the bottom of the mound is already 3 in. above home plate, so the height of the mound itself will seem 3 in. shorter. This is a matter of perception; the height difference between pitcher and batter will remain the same, but the pitcher may feel that the mound is lower than it should be.

Figure 1.6 is an alternative infield design that eliminates this perception. By raising both the pitcher's plate and home plate by 3 in., this design creates the illusion of a higher pitcher's mound, restoring the perception of the correct mound height and helping to keep the heart of the infield as dry as possible. It is important to note that this alternative design does not change the relative height of the pitcher and the batter. On the other hand, it is somewhat more complicated to build, because a number of critical elevations must be taken.

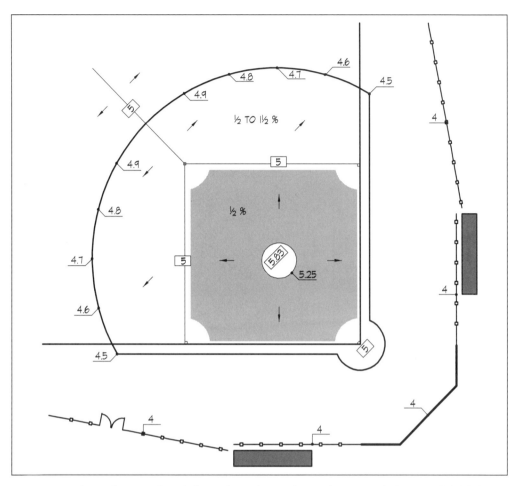

Figure 1.5. The authors' preferred (best) skinned area design, for use with the overall field designs shown in Figures 1.2 and 1.3—elevations noted in feet. (See Figure 5.2 for spot elevations of the infield grass and foul territory around the infield.)

The design shown in Figure 1.6 can be used to replace the grass infield design in Figure 1.4 or Figure 1.5 to create a field that is superior in both aesthetics and performance. This crowned infield design is also well suited to softball, as the pitcher's plate and home plate are level.

1.4d The Pitcher's Mound

According to the *Official Baseball Rules*, published by the *Sporting News* and followed for professional, collegiate, and high school play, the regulation pitcher's mound is a circle 18 ft in diameter. The mound itself is to have a flattened top area that is 5 ft wide and 34 in. from front to back. This flattened area extends 6 in. in front of the pitcher's plate, or rubber, and is elevated 10 in. above home plate. From the point 6 in. in front of the pitcher's plate, the mound is to slope toward home plate at the rate of 1 in. per foot for the first 6 ft, then gradually slope the remaining 4 in. The center of the mound is 59 ft from the white point of home plate and 18 in. in front of the pitcher's plate. Figure 1.7 shows

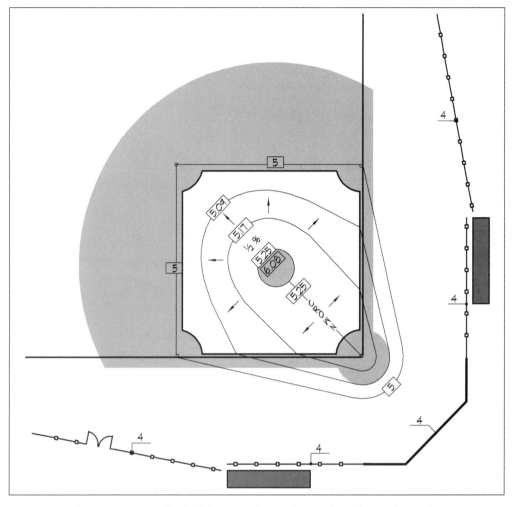

Figure 1.6. Alternative crowned infield design with raised mound and home plate—elevations noted in feet.

the appropriate slope for a pitcher's mound. (A simple tool for achieving the correct slope on a pitcher's mound is shown in Chapter 5, Figure 5.6.)

1.5   SKINNED INFIELDS

Many baseball and softball fields still in use (especially in parks) feature skinned infields (which are sometimes called "dirt infields"). These infields have a continuous skinned playing surface all the way to the grass arc where the outfield begins. Skinned infields are recommended for softball fields and are required for some softball tournament play. When correctly maintained, skinned infields can also work well for baseball fields and under some circumstances may be preferred to grass infields, which require more maintenance and more involved renovation. If the facility has a limited maintenance staff, a skinned infield is easier to keep playable, because it requires less attention to matters such as lip buildup and removal.

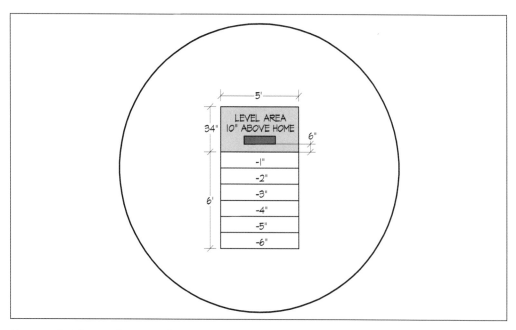

Figure 1.7. The regulation pitcher's mound. The diameter of a regulation pitcher's mound is 18 ft, with the center of the circle 18 in. in front of the front edge of the rubber.

A skinned infield that has grass in foul territory has greater visual appeal than a skinned infield that has a dirt surface all the way to the dugouts. This is especially obvious in a completely skinned regulation (90 ft bases) baseball field, which has some 25,000 sq ft of skinned surface, better than half an acre. Figure 1.8 shows an example of the typical skinned infield (without grass in foul territory) and an alternative and superior design with grass in foul territory, which allows for improved appearance and playability. The grading plan is the same as shown in Figures 1.4 and 1.5. For softball, use the infield grading plan shown in Figure 1.6 to keep the pitcher's plate level with home plate.

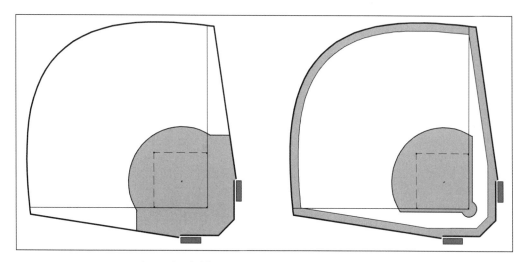

Figure 1.8. Skinned infields, typical design (left) and superior design (right).

1.6   BASES

The selection and installation of bases is sometimes an afterthought in the design and construction of a baseball or softball diamond. However, the wise designer will give careful consideration to the type of bases to be installed, because impact with a base by sliding players is one of the most common causes of injuries. (It is worth noting that many equipment catalogues now imprint a warning on the pages with bases. These warnings typically say, "Be advised that sliding into a base represents a clear and present danger. Injury may occur.")

The style of base that has been considered "standard" has a rubberized or plastic cover over a layer of foam padding and is anchored to the ground by a center post. The post is meant to be inserted in a matching sleeve, which is installed in a concrete square placed in the soil. (For information on making these concrete squares, see Chapter 5, Section 5.2i.) These bases are still in widespread use, but are usually sold with the warning that they are not impact- or energy-absorbing.

To diminish the incidence of injury, manufacturers have developed a variety of bases with designed-in safety features. One style of base has tapered sides, so that a sliding player will slide up and over the base with reduced risk of injury. Other bases are designed to flex when a player slides, or to break free of their anchors upon impact.

Many fields still include bases that are anchored by straps to metal pins hammered into the ground. These bases are easy to remove and replace, but they have some important disadvantages. They are difficult to position precisely, and they can be moved out of place by a fielder's foot. More important, because a sliding player's foot can slide under the base and make contact with the metal anchor, injuries are not uncommon. For these reasons, we do not recommend this type of base.

Double bases at the first base location are sometimes used for younger players and for adult recreational play. These bases have a regular white base in the normal position, with an additional orange base projecting into foul territory. To avoid a collision, base runners are instructed to touch the orange base whenever a fielder is standing on the white base.

1.7   HOME PLATE AND PITCHER'S PLATE

Home plates and pitcher's plates are both manufactured from rubber or from wood with a rubber or plastic coating. A wide variety of systems are used to position and anchor these structures.

Traditionally, the most common type of plate has featured a group of steel spikes that fasten to the bottom of the plate and are hammered into the ground. Others have a single square post that fits into a sleeve in a concrete pad. This pad remains in the ground when the bases are removed.

From the standpoint of installation or replacement, a superior type is designed to be installed directly into the ground, without the need for posts or other anchoring systems. Home plates made to such a design (sometimes called "bury-in" home plates) have an advantage in that they will not curl up at the corners and thus do not present the safety hazard of catching the spikes of a player sliding into home. These plates are typically 3 in. thick, so they remain flat and rigid through long use. (See Figure 1.9.)

A corresponding type of pitcher's plate is a four-sided box, manufactured around a polyvinyl chloride (PVC) or aluminum tube, as shown in Figure 1.10. These pitcher's plates have two important advantages. First of all, they extend downward into the soil

Figure 1.9. A "bury-in" home plate requires no posts or anchoring system and has a safety advantage over other types, because it will not curl up at the corners.

and so require no posts or spikes. Second, because each side of the box is a full-size pitcher's plate, when the plate wears out the box can be removed from the ground, rotated, and reinstalled. (Manufacturers suggest that all four sides of these boxes can be used, but experience shows that rotating them one-quarter turn still leaves some wear exposed. These structures give better service if only the two opposite faces are actually used.)

Figure 1.10. A four-sided pitcher's plate can be rotated 180° and reinstalled to provide a new surface for the pitcher.

1.8   WARNING TRACKS

Many sanctioning bodies now strongly urge the use of warning tracks (a feature that warns players that they are running out of room and is usually made of a granular material) to give players a warning when they are approaching a solid structure (usually a fence) or the out-of-bounds area when no fence is used. Although many fields are constructed without warning tracks, the additional margin of safety provided by a warning track indicates the wisdom of constructing one wherever budgets permit.

1.8a   Dimensions

There is no "standard size" warning track; rather, recommended warning track widths are based on such factors as the distance from home plate to the backstop, the distance from the foul line to the dugout, and the age and ability of players. Although warning track dimensions are not always included in rule books, the distances from home plate to the backstop usually are. For instance, for softball fields, the rule books recommend a minimum of 25 ft and a maximum of 30 ft from home plate to the backstop. An 8 ft warning track, therefore, would tell a catcher that he or she had crossed two-thirds of the distance to the backstop. Table 1.3 shows recommended warning track widths for fields of different sizes. (Also see Chapter 11, Section 11.3, "Line and Boundary Dimensions," for field dimensions recommended by various sanctioning bodies.)

Figure 1.11 illustrates how appropriate warning track width is related to field dimensions. The smaller field on the left has less space around the infield for a warning track than the regulation field on the right. If the same warning track width were used on both fields, the one on the left would have only a few feet of grass in foul territory.

1.8b   Other Warning Track Design Criteria

A major decision to be made in the design of a warning track is the depth of the surfacing material. The depth of the material is dependent on the budget, the type of underlying soil, and whether a filter cloth is used between the soil and the warning track material itself. The appearance of weeds on the warning track can compromise footing, and 4 in. to 6 in. of material is usually sufficient to prevent weeds from being a serious problem. In addition to reducing weeds, installing filter cloth under the surfacing material can prevent the intermingling of underlying soil with the surfacing material. When filter cloth is used, 4 in. of surfacing material is usually sufficient to prevent the cloth from surfacing; once exposed, it can catch on dragging equipment or present a tripping hazard for players. To prevent weeds from coming through, preemergent herbicides can be applied before the warning track material is installed. (For more on the use of herbicides for warning track maintenance, see Chapter 7, Section 7.4, "Warning Track Maintenance.")

Table 1.3. Recommended Warning Track Dimensions

Distance from Home Plate to Backstop[a]	Recommended Warning Track Width	
	Foul Territory[b]	Outfield Fence
25 ft	8 ft	12 ft
30 ft	10 ft	12 ft
40 ft	12 ft	15 ft
50 ft	15 ft	15 ft
60 ft	15 ft	15 ft

[a] The distance from the foul lines to the dugout is the same.

[b] Includes backstop fence and foul line fence.

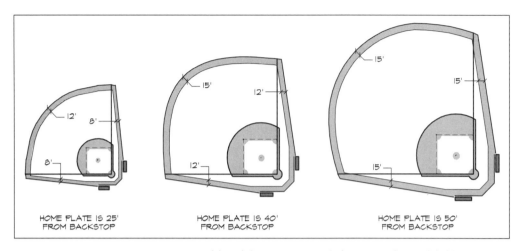

Figure 1.11. Appropriate widths of the warning track for variously sized fields.

In designing a field, it is important to specify that when final grade is achieved, the warning track should be level with the grass.

As with skinned areas, installed subsurface drainage systems usually are not effective on a warning track; because components of the material bind together, water filters through too slowly to allow drains to have much effect. It is more useful to make sure the final grade provides for positive surface drainage.

Warning tracks are sometimes installed with edging material (such as lumber, plastic, or aluminum, normally used for shrub bed edging) between track and turf. This practice is not recommended, because these materials are next to impossible to keep flush with the finish grade and may pose a hazard to players. (See Figure 1.12.)

Figure 1.12. The use of lumber or other edging materials to separate the warning track from the grass is not recommended, because it may represent a hazard to players.

1.8c   Choosing Warning Track Material

Because the purpose of a warning track is to warn players that they are running out of room—basically a safety function—the material should be chosen with that purpose in mind. The best materials have a noticeably different texture than the turfgrass next to them; it is the difference in texture that warns players they are approaching the edge of the playing area. Warning track materials should also be firm enough to prevent players' feet from slipping or sinking in.

Warning tracks are typically constructed from a granular material such as crushed brick or crushed blast furnace slag. In selecting these materials, it is important to choose one that has particles of many different sizes, including some fine particles; these materials will bind together when thoroughly settled, resulting in firm footing for the players. It would be next to impossible to specify a standard particle size distribution for warning tracks. However, a good rule of thumb is to specify a granular material with aggregates no larger than $\frac{5}{16}$ in. and enough small aggregates (passing a 100 sieve screen) to cause the material to bind. The best way to verify how well a particular material performs for warning track applications is to visit a field where that material is already in use.

Crushed red brick materials (sometimes mixed with sand and/or clay) are popular for warning tracks because of the contrasting color, which enhances the appearance of the field. However, these materials are not available at a reasonable cost in all areas. A field designer is advised to check with local suppliers to learn what similar materials are available in his or her locality.

An additional method of warning track design, one which began with designers of professional facilities and has now trickled down as far as high school diamonds, is to construct the warning track like an all-weather track, with rubber chips installed over a concrete or asphalt base. This type of warning track has the advantage of remaining level without maintenance or renovation, and it also stands up to a wide variety of weather conditions. The greatest disadvantage of all-weather tracks is their cost.

In designing and constructing a field that will have an all-weather warning track, it is very important to carefully design the field contours so that the warning track will not obstruct positive surface runoff from the field and so that the track itself will drain. If the turfgrass areas next to the track are not carefully designed and installed, settling of the topsoil can expose the edges of the all-weather surface, presenting a tripping hazard to players and serving as a dam that interrupts surface drainage.

1.9   MULTIPLE-FIELD LAYOUTS

In recent years, the growing popularity of amateur sports leagues has led to the construction of hundreds of multiple-field complexes throughout North America. In designing this type of facility, it is important to follow the design criteria discussed in Section 1.3a. Two of these criteria merit consideration. First of all, it is critical to treat each field as an individual drainage unit. In far too many cases, multiple-field complexes are designed in such a way that water drains from one field across another or from parking areas onto playing fields. In the vast majority of situations, a field cannot remain playable with water draining onto it from outside its boundaries.

The second critical consideration is to ensure adequate slope. Many complexes are being built with fields so level that moderate rainfall does not drain away. Minimum slopes of 0.5% for the infield and 1.0% to 1.5% for the skinned area and the outfield should be maintained on each field. Outside the playing areas themselves, mowable slopes are a maximum of 3:1. Access slopes are a maximum of 1 in. in 1 ft.

In most cases, the designer of a multiple-field complex has less control over the orientation of the fields than the designer of a single field. Many complexes (especially those built for younger players) feature "four-plex" fields, with players facing in all directions during competition. Under these circumstances, the designer should at least give thought to whether some of the fields will be used for playoff competition or other special uses, and plan the orientation of those fields with an eye to the position of the sun during the time of day when critical games will be played.

1.9a Shared Outfield Complexes

A common approach to multiple-field layouts for younger children is to place four home plates at the corners of a square, with the outfields of the four fields overlapping. This layout can be used for younger players (especially in peewee and Little League minor leagues), because they seldom hit the ball out of the infield and the danger of high-speed collisions is minimal. (See Figure 1.13.)

An advantage of this design is the very efficient use of available space. However, the designer should ensure that there is enough space in the common outfield to support safe

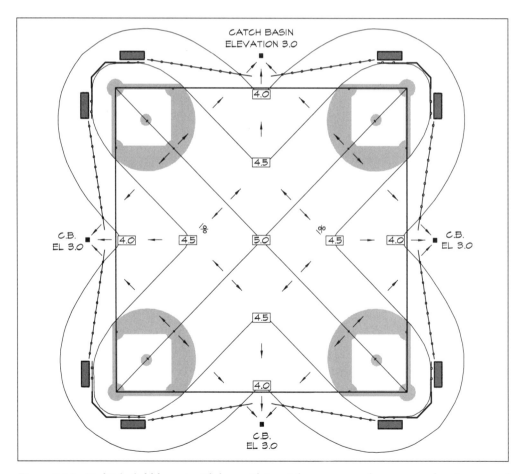

Figure 1.13. Multiple-field layout with home plates at four corners of a square—elevations noted in feet.

play. In the complex illustrated in Figure 1.13, for instance, Little League size fields with 60 ft base paths are laid out with the home plates 300 ft apart. As a rule of thumb, plan to separate the home plates by a minimum of five times the length of the base path for the age group that will use the facility.

1.9b Back-to-Back Complexes

Many complexes, especially for older players, are designed with the home plates of four fields back-to-back. (See Figure 1.14.) This layout works best when working with a fairly level existing grade. Constructing this type of complex on a sloped site would require a great deal of excavation to provide sufficient level space for the four fields. Back-to-back complexes allow for fairly efficient use of space but can present a hazard when pop-ups in foul territory stray into another field or into the spectator area of another field. This design should be used for experienced players, and as much space as possible should be left between the backstops. The complex illustrated in Figure 1.14 shows four Little

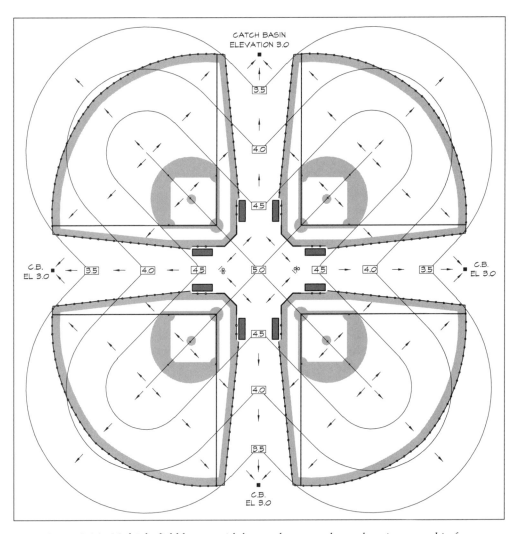

Figure 1.14. Multiple-field layout with home plates together—elevations noted in feet.

League or softball sized fields with 150 ft between home plates and foul lines 106 ft apart. We recommend even more clearance when space permits.

In addition, overhanging backstops should be used, wherever possible, to prevent pop-ups from going backward onto the next field. Some installations are now being constructed with screens over the spectator areas for this purpose.

This back-to-back design is obviously preferred for players of Little League age and older, who routinely hit the ball into the outfield. However, because each field has a full outfield, it requires substantially more space to lay out four fields in this fashion; if the two layouts shown in Figures 1.13 and 1.14 have the same size fields, then the back-to-back layout would take up almost twice as much space.

1.9c Discrete-Field Complexes
A discrete-field complex features fields that are not laid out symmetrically in four-field groups. These fields are designed "discretely" (or individually), unlike those that share outfields or have back-to-back home plates.

For fields built on uneven terrain, a discrete-field complex makes more efficient use of space. For example, the complex shown in Figure 1.15 was designed to accommodate a number of fields, ranging from Pony League to peewee, in addition to a football field. The complex is 30 ft higher in the center than at the corners, but each field is designed with appropriate contours for effective surface drainage and no field drains onto any other. Swales surrounding the fields channel runoff into lower-lying areas. (If the site had been more level, it would have been necessary to use catch basins in various areas to intercept water from the swales.)

1.10   VEHICULAR, PLAYER, AND SPECTATOR ACCESS

Access to the field is important not only for players and spectators, but also for maintenance and renovation equipment. Throughout the year, the maintenance staff must be able to move in equipment for mowing and other routine operations. When the season is over, renovation equipment must move in to get the field ready for the next season. Unless access is properly planned, pedestrian and vehicular traffic may be forced to pass over muddy areas or hilly terrain and may even compromise the playability of the field itself.

1.10a Vehicular Access and Parking
As a general rule, each field should have a road or pathway adequate to allow a single-axle dump truck to enter the field. This access should be about 12 ft wide, and the surface should be stable enough to support the weight of the vehicle without rutting. Ideally, vehicular access should allow entry to the field at a point near the skinned area, because this is where the most intensive maintenance is required during the season and where the greatest amount of renovation work will take place after each season. If vehicles must enter the field through the outfield, important maintenance or renovation work may have to be delayed in wet conditions.

In planning for vehicular traffic into a new field or complex, access roads or paths should be nearly level side to side, with a maximum slope of 8.33% in the direction of travel. It is critical that any construction of these roads take into account the overall drainage plan for the field or complex and that they not restrict runoff. This access should always be planned as a part of the design process for the fields themselves, and not simply inserted after the grading plan is established.

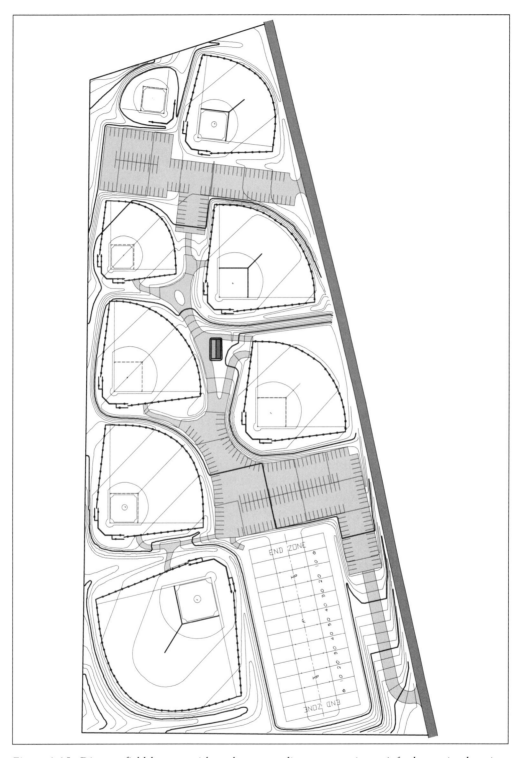

Figure 1.15. Discrete-field layout, with each contour line representing a 1 ft change in elevation. Note that each field is treated as an individual drainage unit. Vehicular, player, and spectator access is provided to each field, with parking for about 40 cars per field.

In planning parking areas for parks and recreation fields, a good rule of thumb is to have a least 40 parking spaces per field. Fields designed for the youngest players may very well need more parking, inasmuch as both parents and grandparents turn out eagerly for games. As most fans realize, cars parked too close to the field have a good chance of being struck by foul balls. If parking is 100 ft from the playing area, the chance of a baseball reaching parked cars is relatively small, but it should be noted that occasional stray fouls still present the possibility of damage or spectator injury.

1.10b   Player Access

Obviously, players can reach the field using the same road or path that vehicles use. For entry to the playing area itself, players should be provided with a separate entrance, either near the dugout or directly into it. To prevent foul balls from passing through these entrances and into the spectator areas, a gate can be installed in the fence, but this arrangement creates the possibility of a hazard if the gate is left open. Another option is to install fences that overlap, so that players walk around sections of fencing; this method removes the possible hazard of an open gate. (See Figure 1.16 for an example of this arrangement.)

Some planners may be tempted to install a single entrance to be used both for maintenance vehicles and for player access. However, the gates suitable for vehicles are typically so large and heavy that their use for player traffic is not recommended. If these gates are frequently opened and closed, as they would be when used for player access, the chances

Figure 1.16. Overlapping fences eliminate the need for gates. (Photo courtesy of Don Uber, Sportscape of Texas, Inc.)

increase that they will be inadvertently left open or that the constant opening and closing will cause excessive wear and tear.

Provisions should be made for scorekeepers' tables on some fields, especially those used for play at the high-school level and above. These tables should be located near the infield or in a press box behind the backstop or on top of the dugout. Umpires' changing rooms and equipment storage rooms should also be provided.

1.10c   Spectator Access

An important part of planning the field is providing areas from which spectators can watch the game. Many coaches and umpires prefer not to have spectator areas behind the backstop, where they can cause a distraction. In fact, some field supervisors have installed screens on the backstop to discourage the congregation of fans in this area. We recommend that dugouts be installed along the base paths close to the backstop, with spectator areas farther down the baselines. It is also advisable to provide a pedestrian pathway behind the backstop so that spectators can move from one side of the field to the other without struggling over obstacles. If there are no bleachers, a sufficiently large and flat area should be provided to allow spectators to sit on the grass or in folding chairs to watch the game.

1.10d   Access and Parking for Those with Disabilities

With the passage and enactment of the Americans with Disabilities Act (ADA), accommodation for the special physical needs of disabled spectators and participants was mandated by law. Any newly constructed or reconstructed facility is required to provide access for those with disabilities, including access to seating areas, rest rooms and concession areas, and parking.

In planning walkways, ramps, and other access structures to be used by disabled persons, the maximum allowable slope is 8.33% (1 in. of rise per lateral foot, or a 1:12 slope). However, many people with disabilities find it very difficult to maneuver on a pathway this steep, and the guidelines published by the federal government recommend a slope of between 1:16 and 1:20. Passageways used by disabled persons should be at

Table 1.4. Number of Accessible Parking Spaces Required Under Federal Law

Total Parking in Lot	Required Minimum Number of Accessible Spaces
1 to 25	1
26 to 50	2
51 to 75	3
76 to 100	4
101 to 150	5
151 to 200	6
201 to 300	7
301 to 400	8
401 to 500	9
501 to 1000	2% of total
1001 and over	20 plus 1 for each 100 over 1000

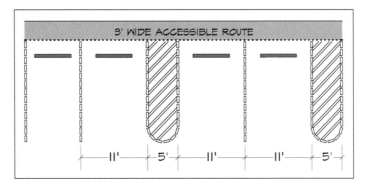

Figure 1.17. A universal parking space design layout.

least 36 in. wide. On ramps designed to provide this access, a level landing is required at the top and bottom, as well as after every 30 in. of rise. These landings are to be as wide as the ramp and at least 60 in. in length. If a ramp changes direction at a landing, the landing is to be at least 60 × 60 in. in size. In addition to the ramps used by spectators with disabilities, a flat and level area must be provided for their use while they are watching a game.

Federal law also mandates parking for disabled persons; spaces should be provided as close as possible to the field and to handicapped ramps. The law dictates the number of spaces that should be reserved for handicapped parking and requires one "van-accessible" space 16 ft wide for each eight accessible spaces. All spaces reserved for disabled persons are to be marked with the familiar signage, and the van-accessible spaces are to be specifically marked as such. (The published requirements for parking for persons with disabilities are shown in Table 1.4.)

An alternative to the traditional method of setting aside parking spaces for disabled persons is the application of what is called "universal parking design." This scheme is based on the concept of designing all accessible facilities in such a way that both cars and vans can use them. Universal design recommends that all spaces be 132 in. (11 ft) wide, with a 60 in. access aisle next to every space. (Laying out two spaces, one aisle, two spaces, another aisle, and so on, ensures that each space is adjacent to an access aisle.)

Among the advantages of this universal design system is that no special signage is needed for van-accessible spaces, because all accessible spaces can accommodate a van as well as a passenger car.

Figure 1.17 shows a universal parking scheme that can be used for both cars and vans.

Finally, in designing parking for those with disabilities, it is critical that all spaces be as level as possible. A slight slope, which may not be noticed by the typical spectator, can represent a substantial difficulty for a person with a disability.

Chapter 2

Irrigation, Drainage, and Covers

2.1 INTRODUCTION

In this chapter, we will consider the management of water on a field. We will begin by considering the design and development of irrigation systems, then turn our attention to the drainage systems required to remove excess water. Finally, we will look at the various types of covers used to protect the field or to enhance the quality of the turfgrass culture.

2.2 IRRIGATION SYSTEMS

2.2a Automatic Systems and Their Components

An automatic irrigation system is a network of pipes and pop-up sprinklers, controlled by automatic valves, that supplies water to the playing field or other designated area. To fully understand the operation of an automatic irrigation system, it is necessary to consider the various components of such a system and the role each plays in irrigating the field.

Pipe

The pipe running from the irrigation system's point of connection (POC) into the service line to the zone control valves is called the "continuous pressure main line" or simply the "main line." It is common practice to use solvent-welded polyvinyl chloride (PVC) pipe at a depth of 18 in. below the surface for pipe sizes up to 4 in., and 24 in. below the surface for pipes larger than 4 in. Gasketed pipe is sometimes specified, it should be placed deeper—36 in. below the surface for pipes larger than 4 in. is usually considered reasonable. However, higher system pressures may lead the designer to specify deeper installation to hold the pipe securely in place.

The nonpressure pipes that connect the control valves to the sprinkler heads are referred to as "lateral lines." These lines can be installed at a depth of 12 in., which is standard for the industry.

Poured-in-place concrete "thrust blocks" are sometimes specified where pipe connections must be especially solid. For instance, thrust blocks are typically specified at all changes in direction on all gasketed pipe, for main line pipes of more than 2 in. in diameter, and on long runs when the system will have higher-than-normal pressure. See Figure 2.1.

Specifying the proper pipe sizes helps to maintain the correct water velocity and to minimize friction losses throughout the system. Water flowing through pipes experiences

Figure 2.1. Thrust blocks at points where the pipe changes direction will protect the system against shifting, which can cause leaking joints.

considerable drag or friction from the pipe itself; when the velocity of the water increases, the pressure loss resulting from friction increases. If the pipe used for the system is too small, the operating pressure will be much lower for the heads at the end of the zone than for the heads closest to the valve serving that zone. There should be no more than a 10% variation in pressure among all heads in a zone.

PVC pipe is also commonly used as sleeves for the irrigation system's pipes and wires where they pass under walkways, driveways, and roads. A good rule of thumb for sleeve sizing is to specify sleeves two times the size of the pipe being sleeved.

Sprinklers, Nozzles, and Swing Joints

A sprinkler head consists of three major components: the main body, the nozzles through which water flows outward, and the swing joint at the bottom of the body, which maintains the sprinkler's connection to the lateral lines.

Sprinkler heads have been gradually downsized over the years, primarily for safety purposes. Newer heads have a small surface diameter and a protective thick rubber cover that makes them a very safe alternative to the older-style sprinklers. Many of today's safer heads also have a heavy-duty body cap that will withstand the pressure of the large equipment now being used in routine maintenance. Most newer gear-driven rotary sprinkler heads should be installed right at the finish grade of the turf. See Figure 2.2.

Figure 2.2. A properly installed sprinkler head will be flush with the finish grade of the turf.

Irrigation experts recommend a rotary sprinkler with a large nozzle selection, where the largest nozzle has a radius of about 1½ times that of the smallest nozzle. A nozzle is chosen to fine-tune the flow of water out of the system. The experienced irrigation system designer uses correct nozzle sizes to obtain "matched precipitation."

Swing joints can be fabricated on-site by the installers of the system or can be manufactured parts provided by the supplier. Manufactured full-circle-swing joints cut down on installation time and are often more dependable. Correctly installed, a full-circle-swing joint provides flexibility and resists breakage when large mowers or other heavy equipment rolls over the sprinkler. Figure 2.3 shows a manufactured swing joint.

Figure 2.3. Manufactured full-circle-swing joint detail. A full-circle-swing joint allows the system to absorb the weight of mowers and other pieces of equipment without damage to the system.

Valves

In an irrigation system, there are two basic types of valves: shut-off valves and sprinkler valves. Shut-off valves ("gate valves" or "ball valves") are used in a continuous pressure main line to temporarily turn off the water to the entire system or a section of the system. Sprinkler valves deliver the water from the continuous pressure main line to the sprinklers. In the discussion of sprinkler systems, when the term *valve* is used alone, it usually refers to an automatic control valve.

Automatic control valves are used in conjunction with automatic controllers or timers to deliver preset amounts of water to the turf at designated times. Because these valves can be precisely controlled, an automatic system allows the sports turf manager to efficiently schedule the delivery of the right amount of water to each zone.

Placement of the valves should be planned with maintenance and safety in mind. These valves are usually installed in subsurface boxes, and for a baseball or softball field they should be installed near the out-of-play fence. Two or three 1 in. valves can be installed in a valve box, whereas valves larger than 1 in. are usually installed one valve per box.

Controller

The controller (or "timer") is the part of an automatic sprinkler system that determines when a valve will turn on and how long the valve will operate. The controller sends a low-voltage signal through buried wires to the automatic control valve, which then opens for a predetermined amount of time. When the predetermined watering time is completed, the controller turns off the valve.

Controllers should be placed in an easily accessible location, in a lockable room or waterproof enclosure. Some irrigation systems require a pump to maintain adequate water pressure. A controller chosen for this type of system includes a pump start feature. As with any electrical equipment, to prevent injury from high-voltage electrical shock, it is essential to specify the installation of a proper ground wire to the controller. Consult local codes for the grounding requirements in a specific area.

Wires

In an automatic sprinkler system, low-voltage direct burial wire is used to carry the signal from the controller to the automatic control valves. The most frequently used wire for commercial applications is single-strand, heavy-gauge direct burial copper wire. The irrigation designer or a supplier can specify the necessary wire size when the system is being designed.

We recommend that the wire be buried in the same trench as the main line, taped to the underside of the pipe. This will help to protect the wire and make it easier to locate. Furthermore, a wire taped to the pipe can serve as a tracer wire to locate the main line should it become necessary to do so.

Wherever control wire will be exposed, it should be installed in a protective conduit. Waterproof wire connectors should be used to connect the valve's solenoid wires to the low-voltage irrigation wire. Where permitted by local code, wire nuts can be used for connections that are not exposed to moisture.

Backflow Prevention

To protect a potable (drinking) water supply from contamination, most states and municipalities require the installation of *backflow prevention* devices on all plumbing systems that are connected to the public water supply. In planning or installing a sports field irrigation system, consult the local water company to determine the backflow devices required and their proper installation.

2.2b   Automatic Irrigation System Design Basics

Because each baseball or softball field has its own dimensions, it is next to impossible to describe a "typical" irrigation plan for all fields. For instance, the distance from home plate to the outfield fence varies from field to field. The distance between the heads can vary from 47 ft to 67 ft, depending on the number of rows needed to reach the outfield fence from the infield arc, the water pressure at the field's edge, and the type of head used.

The variation in distance between the heads can even be greater in foul territory around the infield. The distance between the foul lines and the out-of-play fence dictates the spacing of the heads, which should be laid out to provide head-to-head coverage. For example, if the width of the grass area from the base line to the dugout is 20 ft, the heads must be set no more than 20 ft apart; heads with greater spacing would cause puddling on the base paths. A field that has 50 ft of grass between the base line and the dugout must have heads that are set 50 ft apart.

Because of the technical complexity of automatic irrigation system design, most sports fields designers assign the task of developing the irrigation system to a specialist, who may be a design subcontractor or an employee of the irrigation system supplier. It is probably a mistake to try a do-it-yourself approach to irrigation system design without the appropriate experience and training. The cost of employing a specialist is easily justified by the potential cost of correcting problems in a poorly designed system.

In spite of the challenges of matching an irrigation system design to the specific dimensions of a field, there are a number of general rules for irrigation system design that apply to nearly every baseball or softball diamond. To properly supervise those who will design and install a system, a field manager or designer should have at least a passing knowledge of these principles.

The first (and probably the most obvious) rule is that heads must be spaced uniformly throughout the area to be irrigated. In reviewing an irrigation system design, it is important to measure the distance between heads and to make sure there are no areas on the field that are too far from a head to receive adequate watering. Conversely, heads that are too close together will contribute to puddling or wet spots on the field. It is a good idea to get the manufacturer's specifications for the system components (especially the heads) and to make sure they are designed to perform as the design intends. These specifications indicate the coverage that can be expected at an established water pressure; if your field's water pressure varies substantially from that specified by the manufacturer, you may not get the irrigation efficiency you expect.

A second general principle is that the grass infield of a baseball diamond is the hardest area of the field on which to achieve good distribution uniformity. No matter how carefully the heads are placed, some areas of the infield will inevitably receive more water than others, especially in windy conditions. To ensure adequate and uniform irrigation of the infield, supplemental hand watering will be necessary. To support a hand-watering operation, a well-designed irrigation system should include a quick-coupler valve in the grass behind the pitcher's mound. The quick-coupler valve can also be used to hand water the skinned area for dust control purposes.

Irrigation systems are typically designed with a series of "zones." In irrigation system design, a zone is a subsystem of several heads controlled by a single valve for each zone.

Figure 2.4 is an example of an automatic irrigation system design for a baseball field with 90 ft bases, a 355 ft distance to center field, and 60 ft between the base lines and the dugouts. This design requires water pressure of 75 psi at field edge and yields a pressure of 60 psi at the base of the sprinkler heads. The average precipitation rate for this system is 0.35 in./hour for full-circle heads, 0.7 in./hour for half-circle heads, and 0.29 in./hour

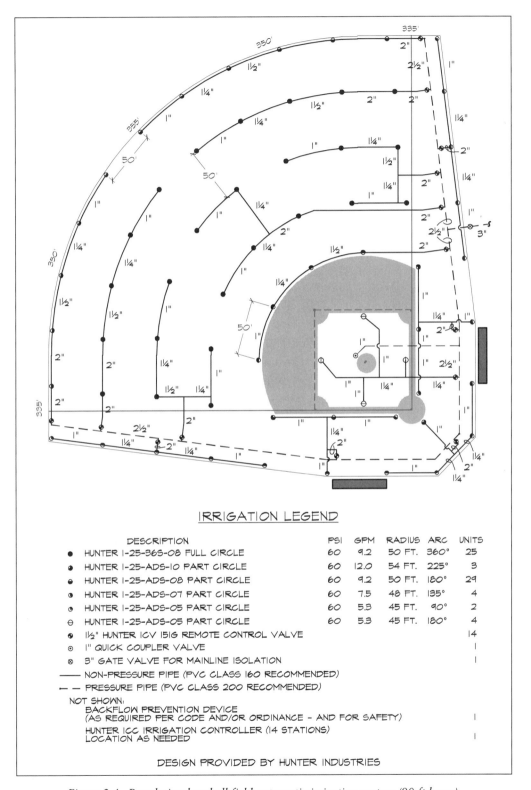

IRRIGATION LEGEND

DESCRIPTION	PSI	GPM	RADIUS	ARC	UNITS
● HUNTER I-25-36S-08 FULL CIRCLE	60	9.2	50 FT.	360°	25
◑ HUNTER I-25-ADS-10 PART CIRCLE	60	12.0	54 FT.	225°	3
◐ HUNTER I-25-ADS-08 PART CIRCLE	60	9.2	50 FT.	180°	29
◔ HUNTER I-25-ADS-07 PART CIRCLE	60	7.5	48 FT.	135°	4
◔ HUNTER I-25-ADS-05 PART CIRCLE	60	5.3	45 FT.	90°	2
⊖ HUNTER I-25-ADS-05 PART CIRCLE	60	5.3	45 FT.	180°	4
⊚ 1½" HUNTER ICV 151G REMOTE CONTROL VALVE					14
⊙ 1" QUICK COUPLER VALVE					1
⊗ 3" GATE VALVE FOR MAINLINE ISOLATION					1
—— NON-PRESSURE PIPE (PVC CLASS 160 RECOMMENDED)					
– – PRESSURE PIPE (PVC CLASS 200 RECOMMENDED)					

NOT SHOWN:
BACKFLOW PREVENTION DEVICE
(AS REQUIRED PER CODE AND/OR ORDINANCE – AND FOR SAFETY)   1

HUNTER ICC IRRIGATION CONTROLLER (14 STATIONS)
LOCATION AS NEEDED   1

DESIGN PROVIDED BY HUNTER INDUSTRIES

Figure 2.4. Regulation baseball field automatic irrigation system (90 ft bases).

for the infield. The run time for 1 in. watering is 2 hr, 51 min for full circle heads, 1 hr, 26 min for half-circle heads, and 3 hr, 28 min for the infield.

Figure 2.5 shows an automatic irrigation system for a softball field or a Little League baseball field (with a skinned infield). Bases are 60 ft, center field is 220 ft, and the distance from home plate to the backstop is 25 ft. For a Little League field with a grass infield, install four sprinkler heads in the infield.

This design requires water pressure of 75 psi at field edge and yields a pressure of 60 psi at the base of the sprinkler heads. The average precipitation rate for this system is 0.43 in./hour for full-circle heads and 0.82 in./hour for half-circle heads. Run time for 1 in. watering is 2 hr, 20 min for full-circle heads and 1 hr, 13 min for half-circle heads.

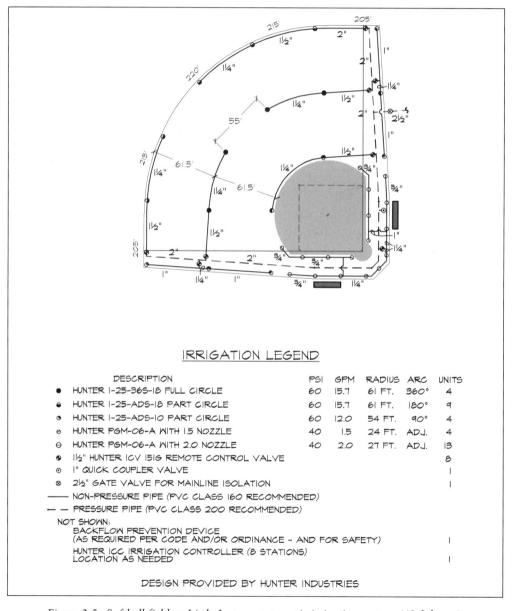

IRRIGATION LEGEND

	DESCRIPTION	PSI	GPM	RADIUS	ARC	UNITS
●	HUNTER I-25-36S-18 FULL CIRCLE	60	15.7	61 FT.	360°	4
◕	HUNTER I-25-ADS-18 PART CIRCLE	60	15.7	61 FT.	180°	9
◔	HUNTER I-25-ADS-10 PART CIRCLE	60	12.0	54 FT.	90°	4
⊖	HUNTER PGM-06-A WITH 1.5 NOZZLE	40	1.5	24 FT.	ADJ.	4
⊖	HUNTER PGM-06-A WITH 2.0 NOZZLE	40	2.0	27 FT.	ADJ.	13
◐	1½" HUNTER ICV 151G REMOTE CONTROL VALVE					8
⊙	1" QUICK COUPLER VALVE					1
⊗	2½" GATE VALVE FOR MAINLINE ISOLATION					1
——	NON-PRESSURE PIPE (PVC CLASS 160 RECOMMENDED)					
— —	PRESSURE PIPE (PVC CLASS 200 RECOMMENDED)					

NOT SHOWN:
BACKFLOW PREVENTION DEVICE
(AS REQUIRED PER CODE AND/OR ORDINANCE - AND FOR SAFETY)   1

HUNTER ICC IRRIGATION CONTROLLER (8 STATIONS)
LOCATION AS NEEDED   1

DESIGN PROVIDED BY HUNTER INDUSTRIES

Figure 2.5. Softball field or Little League automatic irrigation system (60 ft bases).

2.2c Portable Irrigation Systems

Portable irrigation systems are those that are placed on the field long enough to irrigate each area and are removed once the job is complete. Portable systems are used on many fields, often because their initial cost is less than that of an automatic system. However, because portable systems require a good deal more labor to operate, their overall long-term cost of operation may end up being higher.

Traveling (Reel) Irrigators

There are two types of traveling irrigators in common use. One type of traveling irrigator consists of a rotating sprinkler attached to a hose, propelling itself along a wire. The maintenance staff pulls out the wire and stakes it to the ground. The sprinkler then follows the wire across the surface of the field, using water pressure to drive an internal winch mechanism. When this type of traveling irrigator reaches the end of the wire, it turns itself off. The same process is then used to irrigate another portion of the field.

The other type of traveling irrigator (a "reel" unit) has a sprinkler head at the end of a long hose. The hose is pulled out and placed on the turf. When the water is turned on, the unit gradually retracts the hose, drawing the sprinkler through the area to be irrigated and winding up the hose on a reel.

The wire type of traveling irrigator is small enough to be moved easily around the field by hand, whereas the reel type is much larger and heavier and requires the use of a tractor to place it in the area to be watered.

Traveling irrigators require a considerable amount of labor to continually move the setup and must be actively supervised to ensure uniform and adequate irrigation. Watering is usually restricted to the daytime hours, because traveling equipment is vulnerable to vandalism (or even theft) if unattended or left out at night.

There is an important point to be noted concerning the use of traveling irrigators on a baseball or softball field. These irrigators work fine on large, rectangular areas (such as football fields), where the entire area can be irrigated in a series of parallel passes. But on a baseball field, with its characteristic shape, it is nearly impossible to achieve uniform watering with a traveling irrigator. If this type of equipment is used, the staff must be prepared to perform a good deal of hand watering on areas not reached by the traveling irrigator.

Quick-Coupler Systems

Quick-coupler systems have a series of underground pipes with quick couplers (sometimes called "quick connects") that are permanently installed flush with the ground. (City water systems usually provide all the water pressure required to operate the system, but where pressure is low, booster pumps may be needed.) Hoses or sprinklers can then be attached directly to the system.

Quick-coupler systems have one important advantage for baseball and softball fields. Because of the difficulty in achieving uniform irrigation around the infield and adjacent foul territory, a quick-coupler hose connection can allow the staff to hand water these areas with minimal extra work or inconvenience. Installing these hose connections around the outside of the field also allows the maintenance staff to hand water any dry areas that are not adequately irrigated by the field's overall system.

To operate the system, a hose connection or a direct-connection sprinkler head is inserted into the valve and given a half turn *to the right*. (This is different from the procedure used with most valves, and one of the weaknesses of the quick-connect system; many valves are damaged by being forced in the "normal" direction.) Turning the valve to the right opens it and locks it into position.

Using a quick-coupler system requires attention to some important characteristics of these irrigators. Each sprinkler (or group of sprinklers) must be operated for the same amount of time to achieve uniform irrigation of the field. It is important to follow the installer's (or the manufacturer's) instructions on the number of sprinklers that can be operated at once. Using too many sprinklers at once causes a drop in pressure and results in uneven watering.

(It should be noted that portable systems being installed today must have the same type of backflow prevention device required for automatic systems. See Section 2.2a for more on backflow prevention.)

2.3   INSTALLED DRAIN SYSTEMS, SWALES, AND CATCH BASINS

Before considering installed drain systems, an important distinction in terms should be noted. The phrase "internal drainage" is sometimes used to denote installed drain systems. But for the purposes of this discussion, "internal drainage" is used to describe the passage of water through the soil and away from the playing surface, and installed drain systems are planned structures designed to carry water away from the field through buried pipes. In a well-designed system, internal drainage works together with the installed drain system to provide a playable surface.

2.3a   Installed Drain Systems

An installed drain system is a system of pipe drains or strip drains designed to collect and remove water from the surface or the soil profile.

Ideally, a baseball or softball diamond should be designed to provide for positive surface drainage, so that water will run off the entire field without the need for an installed drain system. However, a field that has less than 1.25% slope (or has a history of wet spots) may require an installed drain system in order to remain playable in a variety of weather conditions. For example, a diamond built using sand-based soil can be designed with little or no slope if an installed drain system is included in the design. An installed drain system usually performs well on a sand-based field. On the other hand, a native soil field with little or no slope, especially one with high percentages of silt and clay, can present problems for an installed drain system. The reason is that water must pass through the soil to reach an installed drain system before it can be removed from the field, and native soils with high percentages of silt and clay can slow the movement of water through the soil. Yet it is probably true that in almost any type of soil, an installed drain system will improve the removal of water and allow greater playability in a wide range of weather conditions. Where the budget allows, an installed drain system is usually a good investment. (Remember that this principle applies only to turf areas; installed drain systems are not effective for skinned areas.)

2.3b   Types of Installed Drain Systems

Sand-Filled Trench Drains
Most people, when thinking of installed drain systems, think first about traditional subsoil pipe drain systems, the type used most often. However, we have chosen to look first at sand-filled trench drains, because we regard this type as having greater potential usefulness on a wide range of fields. Sand-filled trench drains are comparatively narrow and shallow structures, designed to intercept and remove surface water as it moves across the field. The trenches are typically 3 in. to 4 in. wide and 12 in. deep, and are filled to the

surface with coarse to very coarse sand (0.5mm to 2.0mm.). Because these drains are filled all the way to the surface with sand (and have no topsoil above them), they are able to collect and carry away surface water.

Perhaps the most common type of sand-filled trench drain features the strip drain, which is a cloth-wrapped plastic or fiber structure about 1 in. wide and 4 in. to 6 in. deep. A strip drain is placed in the bottom of the trench and extends halfway to the surface. (Figure 2.6 shows the design detail of a strip drain system.) Other sand-filled trench drains are constructed similarly, but may have only a single perforated drainpipe in the bottom of the trench.

In addition to their application as part of an overall installed drain system for a baseball or softball field, these sand-filled trench drains are also effective in solving drainage problems such as wet spots on a field that was originally built without sufficient slope to promote surface drainage. These drains can be installed in a section of the field as shown in Figure 2.7, or even throughout the entire turf area, to drain an otherwise soggy playing surface.

The sand-filled trench drain is the most affordable type of installed drain system, and it provides immediate benefits in water removal. However, there are some important points to consider in regard to such systems. First, these drains have a limited life span, although there is no precise way to calculate their effective life. Over time, materials like silt, clay, and organic matter will be introduced into the sand through water movement, earthworm activity, and maintenance practices. Sometimes these materials are unwittingly introduced into the sand when sod is installed over the trenches, inasmuch as sod grown in native soil carries with it a layer of silt and clay soil. For new or reconstructed fields, the planner can avoid this problem in one of two ways. Either a washed sod can be installed, minimizing the amount of native soil introduced into the sand, or the sand-filled trench drains can be installed after the sod is rooted. Many planners instinctively resist the idea of cutting trenches in new sod, but the narrow trenches used for these systems will quickly fill in, becoming invisible within a matter of a few months. If the turf is being established by seeding or sprigging, this issue is avoided altogether, but special attention to irrigation will be required to ensure full germination and establishment over the sand-filled trenches.

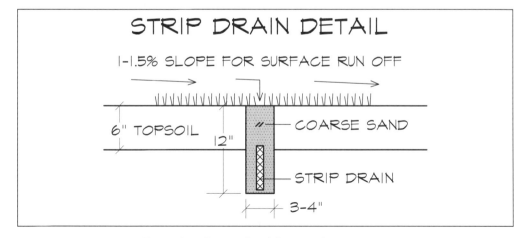

Figure 2.6. Design detail for strip drain systems.

Figure 2.7. Installing strip drains in a section of the outfield. These sand-filled drains can be used to correct spot drainage problems, or installed throughout the entire turfgrass area of a field for improved surface drainage.

Subsoil Pipe Drains

The traditional type of drainage system for a baseball field is a pipe drain system, which is more appropriately called a "subsoil pipe drain" system. The reason for this distinction is that these systems are designed to remove water from the subsoil of the field, rather than from the surface, as is the case with sand-filled trench drains. In the past, these subsoil pipe drain systems typically were constructed of foot-long sections of clay tile pipe, which were either covered with felt paper or packed with coarse sand to prevent the system from filling up with silt and clay. Today's subsoil pipe drain systems use more modern and economical thermoplastic pipe (most supply yards refer to it as "sewer and drain" pipe). This thermoplastic pipe has two or three rows of holes and is designed to be placed with the holes down on top of a 1 in. bed of gravel. The subsoil pipe drain trenches are filled with gravel to a level about 6 in. beneath the surface and then filled to the surface with topsoil.

The trenches for subsoil pipe drains are typically wider and deeper than those for sand-filled trench drains and are usually 12 in. to 18 in. wide and 2 ft to 3 ft deep. The installation of topsoil for the final 6 in. of backfill allows for seeding over the trenches. Subsoil pipe drain trenches are too wide to fill to the surface with sand, which would cause unstable footing for players.

These subsoil pipe drains traditionally have been the most commonly installed type, partly because planners have been most familiar with them. However, pipe drain systems have some inherent drawbacks that make them less than ideal for sports fields built on native topsoil. (For information on the use of subsoil pipe drain systems on amended sand fields, see the following section on soil types.) Because pipe drain systems remove water from the subsoil, they work at a very slow rate—as low as 0.01 in. per hour. Before the water can reach these systems, it must pass through heavy topsoil or subsoil, which typically has a very slow percolation rate. This slow percolation rate means that subsoil pipe drains have little effect in draining the surface of a field.

Another disadvantage of subsoil pipe drains is that the soil above the trenches must become fully saturated before water begins to move downward into the gravel. (This occurs

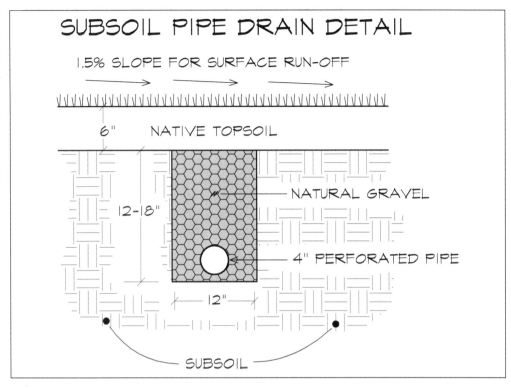

Figure 2.8. Design detail for subsoil pipe drain systems. Note that pipe drain systems placed under native topsoil growing media typically remove water only from the subsoil. They can work effectively to remove surface water if the surface layer is an amended sand medium that is continuous to the soil surface.

because the layering of topsoil over gravel creates a false—or "perched"—water table.) Conversely, in drought conditions, pipe drains also can dry out the soil immediately above the trenches. As mentioned earlier, filling the wide pipe drain trenches to the surface with sand may help drain the playing area, but might adversely impact turf growth and traction.

Figure 2.8 shows the design detail of a subsoil pipe drain system.

2.3c Drainage System Considerations for Common Soil Types

Native Topsoil Fields
As suggested in the preceding section, designing an effective drainage system for any field requires an understanding of the drainage characteristics of the soil used to build the field. The native topsoil in most parts of North America falls into the category of "heavy soil," meaning it has a high percentage of fine sand, silt, and clay. On fields built with heavy soil, water movement is primarily across the surface, and downward percolation is too slow to allow subsoil pipe drains to work effectively. In a few areas, the native soil is high in sand content, but this sand is typically much too fine in texture to permit effective percolation, and water movement tends to be across the surface on these fields as well. In either case, to be effective, a drainage system must be designed to intercept runoff at the surface and so should rely on sand-filled trench systems.

Sand-Based Fields

An increasingly common practice, particularly for fields with higher construction and maintenance budgets, is the construction of a sand-based field. The sand used for these projects is coarser than that typically found in sandy native soil and is amended with peat or other organic materials.

On a field constructed of amended sand, the water flows downward through the profile at a greater rate (typically at least 5 in. to 10 in. per hour). This, of course, is the primary reason for building a sand-based field in the first place. When the amended sand has been correctly blended to percolate as it should, subsoil pipe drain systems can work very efficiently. (For further information on amended sand fields, see Chapter 3, "Soil.")

2.3d Layout of Installed Drain Systems

Having considered the types of installed drain systems and their suitability in various soil types, the discussion now turns to the process of laying out the trenches in which they will be placed.

In addition to the previously noted advantages of sand-filled trench drains, a further advantage of these systems relates to the way they are laid out. Sand-filled trench drains can be laid out in either of two ways: perpendicular to the direction of surface runoff or at a 45° angle to runoff. Either orientation can work effectively, but the designer should give some thought to the type of construction equipment that will be used before settling on a layout.

If the drains are installed perpendicular to the direction of runoff, proper installation will require laser-guided equipment. This is because the drains will have to slope downward to keep the water flowing through them, but this downward slope of the drains is independent of the slope of the field itself. Achieving this independent slope requires the precision of laser equipment.

A much easier (and less expensive) way to install sand-filled trenches is at 45° to the direction of runoff. Trenches laid out this way can be installed at a consistent 1 ft depth from the field surface, because the contours of the field itself will provide the drains with adequate slope to keep them working. This type of installation can be performed with standard trenching equipment.

In sand-based fields, the planner has a good deal more flexibility in designing installed drain systems. Because these fields drain downward through the profile, drains can run in any direction, as long as they have sufficient downward slope to a collector drain.

The next question to be addressed is the distance between drains. In most cases, drains should be laid out on 10 ft to 20 ft centers. A field with relatively less slope (less than 1%) should have drains that are closely spaced. A field with greater slope can drain adequately with more widely spaced drains. In regions with heavy rainfall, or where soils tend to hold water, drains can be placed closer together.

Sand-based fields are typically constructed according to one of several published standards, such as the United States Golf Association's (USGA) *Method for Putting Green Construction.* The USGA standard recommends placement of drains on 15 ft centers. Other standards recommend closer spacing when the surface is level.

Having planned for the layout of the drains on the field, the designer will then need to provide for sufficient collector drains to carry the water to a storm sewer or other outlet. Because these collector drains will carry the water from a number of individual drain structures (sometimes called "laterals"), they will have to be large enough to provide adequate movement. Collector drains are typically made up of solid-wall pipe, 4 in. to 8 in. in diameter, and are often laid out in a continuous loop around the outside of the field with a minimum of three outlet points. At these outlet points, the collector drains should

Figure 2.9. An adapter (black fitting) *is used to tie strip drains into collector drains* (white pipe).

tie into catch basins. From the catch basins to the storm sewers, piping 10 in. to 18 in. in diameter is installed. (For more information on catch basins, see Section 2.3h.)

For subsoil pipe drain systems, standard sewer and drain fittings can be used to tie the laterals into the collector drains. Where strip drains are used, the manufacturer of the strip drains can supply adapters to make the connections to the collector drains. (See Figure 2.9.)

2.3e   Common Problems of Installed Drain Systems

In planning and installing these drainage systems, two common problems must be prevented: a heavily compacted subbase that slows the movement of water into the drain system and the destruction of the pipe by crushing when heavy equipment is being moved across the surface.

Although it can be argued that these difficulties are construction problems, rather than design errors, they most frequently result from faulty specifications provided by the designer of the drainage system. For example, many plans and specifications call for a "compacted subbase." Many excavators understand these specifications to call for the use of a sheepsfoot roller or vibrating roller. When this sort of equipment is used, the subbase becomes so heavily compacted that water passes through the topsoil but stops at the subbase. The uncompacted topsoil will become fully saturated during a heavy rain because the subbase is so compacted that there is nowhere for the water to go.

For the designer, preventing this problem is very simple. Specifying that the excavator "avoid overcompaction of the subbase during rough grading" and "scarify subbase before installing topsoil" will alert the contractor to the drainage dynamics at work in the field system and help to ensure proper operation of the drainage system.

2.3f   Examples of Installed Drain System Design

Figures 2.10 through 2.12 show installed drain system designs for use with field designs shown in Chapter 1. All of these designs can be constructed either with subsoil pipe drains or with sand-filled trench drains. All three of these designs have the advantage that the trenches can be laid out at a consistent depth because they follow the field contours, sloping downward toward the collector drain. Moreover, the drains are installed at a 45° angle to the direction of the flow of the surface water. This is especially helpful for sand-filled trench drain systems, which work by intercepting surface runoff.

(The reader may notice that drain lines are shown running through the skinned area of the field and may remember the warning that installed drain systems do not work effectively on these areas. In the designs shown, the drain lines in the skinned area are in place to provide a continuous flow of water from the turf area of the infield. For completely skinned [dirt] infields, these drain lines can be eliminated altogether.)

2.3g   Other Drain System Design Elements

Two other elements are sometimes used in the design of installed drainage systems: filter cloth and gravel beds. Although these elements can be of value, each also has potential drawbacks that the designer should consider before including them in his or her specifications.

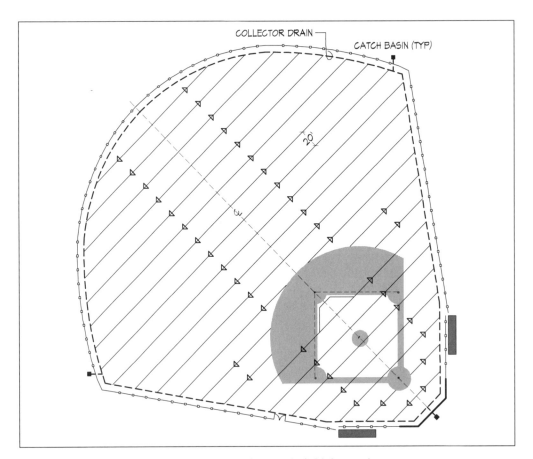

Figure 2.10. Installed drain system for simple field design shown in Figure 1.1.

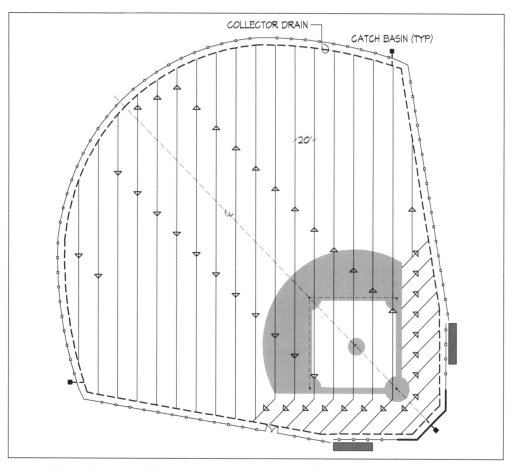

Figure 2.11. Installed drain system for improved field design shown in Figure 1.2.

Filter Cloth

Filter cloth is a synthetic spun textile material that is sometimes specified as part of an installed drain system. This material is used in two ways: to prevent the migration of fine soil particles into the pipe or to separate two layers of different soil materials. To prevent the infiltration of fines into drainpipes, rectangular sheets are used to line the trenches in which drainpipe will be laid. Drainpipe can also be purchased with a tubular "filter sock" already installed. When the goal is to separate two soil layers, large sheets of filter cloth are rolled out on top of the first layer, and then covered with the other material. Some designers even specify multiple layers of filter cloth—on the subbase, as well as between the layers of material installed above. The filter cloth on the subbase can also keep the rootzone from mixing with the subsoil, a very important consideration in areas where the freeze-thaw cycle of a soil can substantially change the soil profile.

It is important to keep in mind that there are different types of filter cloth. Some grades strain out the fines but allow water to pass through. Other types (called "impermeable") hold back water as well as fines. Impermeable filter cloth is typically used in the construction of roads but is not recommended for baseball or softball diamonds, where the passage of water should not be restricted. In specifying filter cloth, ask the supplier for the

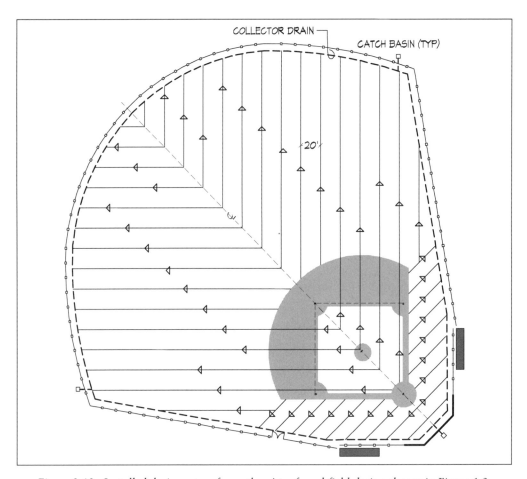

Figure 2.12. Installed drain system for authors' preferred field design shown in Figure 1.3.

manufacturer's specifications on permeability. Use the material with the highest permeability, which is stated in a percentage.

Sports fields professionals are not unanimous on the effectiveness of filter cloth. One objection is that as it strains out fines that would otherwise reach the drains (which is, of course, the exact purpose of a filter), the filter cloth itself may become clogged. When that happens, the material may slow the passage of water into the drain system or between layers of the soil profile. For this reason, some specifying bodies, such as the USGA, do not recommend the use of filter cloth.

An application in which filter cloth can have a substantial positive effect is in lining trenches for drains meant to collect runoff from the surface, rather than from the soil profile itself. In this situation, the filter cloth prevents fines from moving laterally from the soil into the trenches and keeps the drains clear to handle water flowing downward from the surface.

Gravel Beds

A gravel bed is a layer of gravel placed below the growing medium and meant to assist in the rapid movement of water out of the soil and into an installed pipe drain system.

Although this method seems like a promising way to improve drainage, it creates a perched (false) water table, because the water will not move downward into the gravel layer until the topsoil or sand-based growing medium is completely saturated. This actually results in a waterlogged playing surface in wet weather. Although common sense may indicate dictate that a gravel bed would help to keep the surface drained, research at several universities has clearly shown that layering fine-textured material over coarse material creates a perched water table. The only place where this practice is recommended is in USGA specifications, where it is actually *meant* to create a perched water table, holding moisture in a sand-based growing medium that would otherwise dry out too fast.

2.3h Swales and Catch Basins

Swales

Swales are valley-like excavations, wider than they are deep (as opposed to ditches, which are deeper than they are wide). Swales are used to direct the flow of surface water away from a field, toward a catch basin or lower-lying area. They can be used outside the field to collect and carry away runoff from the playing surface and also can be used to prevent water from reaching the field from adjacent areas.

When swales are included in the design of a field, it is important to remember that they have a tendency to stay wet longer than the surrounding areas. Because vehicles and pedestrians may need to cross over these structures to reach the field, this tendency to remain wet must be kept in mind. For vehicular traffic, culverts can be installed to allow access without the problems of rutting or getting stuck, which can result when vehicles must cross through the wet area of the swale. Another way to allow traffic to cross a swale is to install an "interceptor drain" at the bottom. This is a pipe drain filled to the surface with stone, gravel, or coarse sand. Interceptor drains are adequate for pedestrian traffic and for light vehicles such as mowers, but heavier equipment (including cars) will crush the pipe at the bottom, so culverts should be used to provide access for these vehicles. Figure 2.13 shows the design detail of an interceptor drain system.

Catch Basins

Space limitations sometimes make it impossible to design sideline contours that are sufficient to shed the necessary amount of water from the playing surface. This problem is frequently caused by the presence of sideline grandstands or by hilly surrounding terrain. Under such circumstances, it may be necessary to install catch basins. A catch basin is a hollow structure installed in the ground, with an open grate at the surface to allow runoff to enter the system. Catch basins also serve as "junction boxes" for the underground pipes of a drainage system. Collector drains carry water from the field drainage system into the catch basins, and larger discharge pipes then carry the water out of the catch basins and away from the field area to storm sewers or other exit points.

As a general principle, the fewer catch basins included in a drainage system, the deeper in the soil the collector drains will have to be. The drainage system designs shown in Figures 2.10 through 2.12 each have three catch basins, one near each foul pole and one behind home plate. For these systems, the deepest points of the collector drains would typically be 2 ft to 3 ft deep for sand-filled trench drain systems, and 3 ft to 4 ft where subsoil pipe drains are used. If the same system were built with a single catch basin, the collector drains would have to be 5 ft to 6 ft deep by the time they reach the catch basin.

The catch basin itself is made up of a cylinder of pipe or a prefabricated concrete structure with openings at the appropriate depths for the collector drains, and at a greater depth for the discharge pipes. The grate at the top of the catch basin can be flat, and

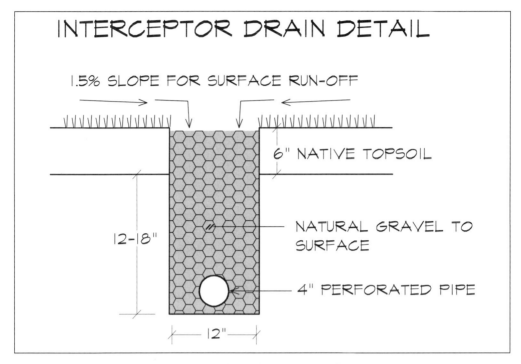

Figure 2.13. Design detail for interceptor drain systems.

designed to be mounted flush with the surface of the ground, or can be convex (domed). Flat grates are to be preferred for most applications because of their greater safety for traffic. It is important to consider that some settling is likely to occur around the catch basins after installation, and that this settling can leave the entry point of a catch basin exposed above the soil. Careful planning is required to ensure a safe installation that will easily admit surface runoff. The designer should include in the specifications for the system the requirement that the installer continue checking around the catch basins until full settling has occurred.

In laying out catch basins, select locations just outside fences, where they will be shielded from the playing area. We do not recommend placing catch basins on the playing area itself. However, some situations occasionally encountered by the designer may require such an installation. For instance, grandstands can disturb the contours of the area, and placing a catch basin right in front of the stands can often help to drain potentially swampy areas. Another situation that may dictate the installation of catch basins on the playing area is the reconstruction of an existing field in which surface contours are insufficient to carry away runoff. Where such an installation must be made, place the catch basin as close to the fence or grandstands as possible and use a small grate to protect players, or cover the catch basin grate with plywood and carpet for each game.

2.4   COVERS

When most people think of covers for a baseball diamond, they think of the rain protection covers placed on high-profile fields when a rain delay is declared. But there are a variety of types of covers used for different purposes, and this section briefly reviews these types. It also considers the effect of covers on the health of turfgrass and the cultural management practices required in connection with their use.

2.4a   Rain Covers

Rain covers, the best-known type of sports field covers, are meant to allow rainfall to drain off the field without soaking into the playing surface—particularly the infield and skinned areas. (See Figure 2.14.)

Rain covers are made of weatherproof plastic, typically reinforced with nylon or other fiber material for strength and durability, and are available in both light and dark colors. Dark covers obviously absorb more solar energy and thus make the underlying soil warmer, whereas light covers reflect more sunlight and warm the turf less. Some covers are dark on one side and light on the other, allowing the turf manager to install the cover "dark side up" when the temperatures are cooler and "light side up" in hotter weather.

Rain covers can be very effective in preventing water from soaking into the field. However, it is important to remember that the cover gets the water to the edge of the covered area. The runoff still must be channeled away from the field to prevent wet areas in the outfield or in foul territory. Some fields are built with systems of strip drains or small catch basins (typically 4 in. plastic basins) at the edge of the areas that will be covered, to assist in drainage. This practice can make a substantial improvement in the overall condition of a covered field, because the runoff from the covered area does not have to be accommodated by the uncovered areas. We recommend strip drains rather than catch basins for this purpose, because catch basins require much more maintenance to prevent their becoming a safety hazard or affecting ball response. For instance, in colder areas, freezing and thawing of the soil can cause catch basins to lift, requiring that they be dug up and reinstalled.

Figure 2.14. Rain cover in place on the infield and skinned area at the home field of the minor-league Toledo Mudhens. Note the puddles on the warning track at left, which the rain cover is designed to prevent. (Photo courtesy of Jeff Limburg, head groundskeeper, Fifth Third Field, Toledo.)

Although rain covers can be a big help in ensuring the playability of a field, it is important to know how a particular field reacts to being covered. For example, turfgrass areas can be slippery right after a cover is removed, because the cover traps some water underneath. Whenever possible, rain covers should be removed sufficiently in advance of play to allow the field to dry adequately.

Rain covers should be used to ensure a playable surface for one game only and should not be left on the field more than one day at a time. Leaving a cover in place for extended periods increases the risk of certain diseases, particularly of those caused by water-loving fungi such as *Pythium*.

2.4b Turf Enhancement Covers

A second type of cover, a "turf enhancement cover," is designed to keep the soil warm in cold weather. Such covers can also be used to stimulate seed germination or to protect the turf from winter injury and offer the additional benefits of causing quicker green-up in the spring and keeping the turfgrass green longer in the fall.

Turf enhancement covers are very lightweight and transparent, typically made of spun synthetic fabric. These covers are designed to be porous and translucent so that air, water, and sunlight can pass through to the turf beneath. Because of their porosity, turf enhancement covers can be left in place for weeks or months at a time, or even over an entire winter. (However, it should be noted that *Pythium* blight can still occur under a porous cover, so a preventive application of a fungicide specific to *Pythium* may be advisable when the cover will be left in place for an extended period.) With turf enhancement covers, as with

Figure 2.15. This test plot shows the difference between bermudagrass that has been covered for the winter (and is still lush and dark green) and bermudagrass that has been left exposed to cold weather, and which is dormant and light brown.

rain covers, color is a consideration in determining how long a cover can be left in place. Black covers cannot be left on the turf as long as white covers, which have less impact on the quality of light reaching the turf.

The use of turf enhancement covers for winter protection of bermudagrass turf has become increasingly common in recent years. Covers can reduce the winter dormancy period of bermudagrass and provide earlier green-up the following spring. The cost of covering an entire field can be substantial, but the potential for loss of turf from winterkill can require remediation steps that are more costly still. (See Figure 2.15.)

In northern climates, turf enhancement covers are sometimes used to assist with the establishment of seeded fields when the seeding is performed late in the fall. (See Figure 2.16.) However, it is important to remember that a covered field can be vulnerable to snow mold if the cover is left in place all winter. Under these circumstances, a preventive application of a fungicide specific to snow mold is a good idea.

2.4c Turf Protection Covers

The third type of cover is a "turf protection cover." Such covers are used to protect the turf in heavy traffic areas, such as the points at which teams enter and exit the facility. They can also be used to protect the turf during events like graduations and concerts, when large numbers of people will stand or sit on the field. Turf protection covers are typically made from a porous, nonwoven synthetic fabric, which allows water, air, and limited sunlight to reach the turf. The primary purpose of these covers is to protect the turf from heavy traffic and from extreme compaction. (See Figure 2.17.)

Figure 2.16. *Establishment of a late fall seeding in the cool season zone can be improved with turf enhancement covers. At left, the cover has been peeled back to show the germination that has occurred beneath. (A preventive snow mold fungicide should be applied before covering the turf for the winter.)*

Figure 2.17. A turf protection cover is used to prevent damage from short-term heavy traffic at special events such as concerts or, as in this case, at batting practice. (Photo courtesy of Jeff Limburg, head groundskeeper, Fifth Third Field, Toledo.)

Because of their porosity, turf protection covers can be left in place for a few days at a time, but because they restrict sunlight from reaching the turfgrass, they should not be left in place for extended periods.

Turf protection covers are sometimes used in combination with plywood for greater protection of the turf from mechanical stresses.

Research has been conducted at the University of California-Riverside to evaluate various types of covers in combination with plywood.[1] The most effective combination was found to be ¾ in. plywood over two layers of geotextile fabric. The next most effective was plywood over one layer of geotextile fabric. Plywood over geotextile plus a commercial product called "Enkamat" was less effective still, but more effective than plywood alone, and all tested options were better than no cover at all. (The UC-Riverside study also showed that lightly watering the turf helped to enhance turfgrass recovery.)

---

[1] S. T. Cockerham, R. A. Khan, G. H. Pool, R. Van Gundy, and V. A. Gibeault, "Events Traffic on Sports Fields: Protection and Recovery, *California Turfgrass Culture* 44, nos. 1 & 2 (1994): 6–7.

Chapter 3

Soil

3.1   INTRODUCTION

On most sports fields, soil is expected to perform a single function: to serve as a growing medium for turfgrass. Soil operates as a medium for turf growth by trapping nutrients and water and making them available to the roots of the plants, by providing space for air to reach the roots, and by serving as an anchor for those roots. On a baseball or softball diamond, of course, the soil of the skinned areas is expected to fulfill an equally critical function: to provide a uniform hard surface with predictable ball response. Soil used for the skinned area must be uniform in texture to allow predictable ball response, solid enough to provide good footing, and loose enough at the surface to allow sliding by base runners. In this chapter, we will consider how different soils are used for these two functions, as well as how to select appropriate materials for each.

3.2   TURFGRASS SOIL

Turfgrass soil is expected to serve as a medium for the passage of water, nutrients, and air to the roots of the plants. Because of this function, its quality as a growing medium is judged by its ability to hold these substances and release them in a controlled fashion to satisfy the growth requirements of the turf. High-quality turf soil has enough organic material to allow it to absorb and then slowly release moisture and nutrients. It must also have the right blend of different-sized mineral particles to allow air to pass through to the roots of the plants. The organic material in the soil also helps to provide "stability," which for our purposes means the ability of the soil to provide good footing under a variety of weather conditions without collapsing into slippery mud.

In order to specify soil that will work effectively as a growing medium for turfgrass growth, it is important to understand three critical issues: soil physical properties, the effects of various soil amendments, and the special characteristics of sand-based rootzones.

3.2a   Physical Properties of Turfgrass Soil
The physical properties of soil that influence its ability to support plant growth are texture, porosity, structure, and strength.

Soil Texture
In regard to the physical properties of soil, *texture* refers to the size of its particles, or its relative coarseness or fineness. Texture is determined by the relative proportions of sand, silt, and clay particles in the particular sample of soil. Sand, silt, and clay have different

particle size diameters; grains of sand range from 2.0 mm to .05 mm, silt particles are from .05 mm to .002 mm in diameter, and clay particles are less than .002 mm.

Soil that is made up of particles of a wide variety of sizes can be said to have a greater (or "nonuniform") distribution of particle size. If most of the particles in a sample are about the same size, it is considered to have a very narrow ("uniform") particle size distribution. The classification of particle sizes is shown in Table 3.1.

In terms of internal drainage (drainage through the soil), a key factor is permeability, which is the rate at which water passes through the profile. For example, permeability is very high in sand with particles of 0.15 mm to 2.00 mm—as high as 15 in. to 20 in. per hour. When "fines" (microscopic particles of finer sand, silt, and/or clay able to pass

Table 3.1. Particle Size Distribution and Sieves of the Standard Screen Scale

USDA System of Classification		Sieve No.	Sieve Opening (millimeters)	Approx. Opening (inches)
Gravel >2 mm		2½	8.00	
		3	6.72	¼"
		3½	5.66	
		4	4.76	
		5	4.00	
		6	3.36	⅛"
		7	2.83	
		8	2.38	
Sand	very coarse 1–2 mm	10	2.00	
		12	1.68	¹⁄₁₆"
		14	1.41	
		16	1.19	
	coarse 0.5–1 mm	18	1.00	
		20	0.84	¹⁄₃₂"
		25	0.71	
		30	0.59	
	medium 0.25–0.5 mm	35	0.50	
		40	0.42	¹⁄₆₄"
		45	0.35	
		50	0.30	
	fine 0.1–0.25 mm	60	0.25	
		70	0.21	¹⁄₁₂₈"
		80	0.177	
		100	0.149	
		120	0.125	
		140	0.105	¹⁄₂₅₆"
	very fine 0.05–0.1 mm	170	0.088	
		200	0.074	
		230	0.062	
		270	0.053	¹⁄₅₁₂"
Silt 0.002–0.05 mm		325	0.044	¹⁄₆₀₀"
Clay <0.002 mm				

through a 100 sieve screen) are added, the permeability may be reduced to as little as 0.01 in. per hour. Obviously, particle size distribution can make a huge difference in the effectiveness of internal drainage, and thus in the ability of a particular field to remain playable. Because native clay-based topsoil includes fine sand, silt and clay, the movement of water will be slower through this kind of soil than through sand.

In selecting soil for a baseball or softball field, there is a trade-off between permeability and stability. Coarse soils (those with few fines) are the most permeable. However, coarse-textured soils have proven to be too unstable for most sports fields, because it is the fines that bond the soil particles together. Stability is gained by adding fines to the mixture, but these fines also reduce permeability and slow internal drainage. The challenge is to find the percentage of fines that can be added before internal drainage is slowed to the point at which the turf becomes waterlogged.

Obviously, there are an infinite number of possible combinations of sand, silt, and clay to make up a soil. To describe the texture of soil, scientists with the United States Department of Agriculture (USDA) have developed a system that divides soils into 12 groups, called "textural classes," based on percent compositions of sand, silt, and clay. The range of particle sizes for each class is illustrated and defined by a triangle diagram called the "soil textural triangle" (also conceived by USDA soil scientists), shown in Figure 3.1. It is important to keep in mind that these textural classes refer to soils with various combinations of sand, silt, and clay. For instance, soil in the textural class "clay" will nearly always have silt and sand in the mixture as well.

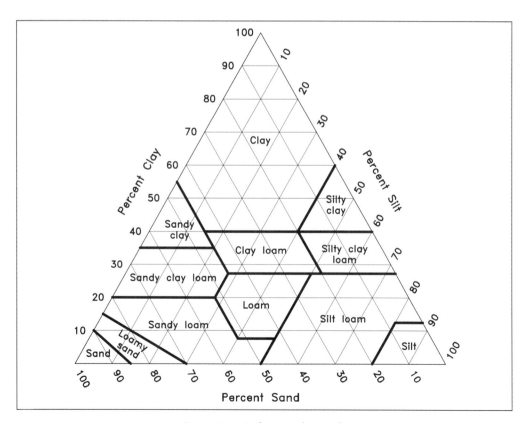

Figure 3.1. Soil textural triangle.

The textural class of a soil can be used to predict a wide range of soil chemical and physical properties, including porosity and soil strength. In sports turf applications, soil texture cannot be relied upon as the sole source of information for determining the suitability of a soil. Other considerations, such as water percolation rate, macro- and microporosity, and soil reaction, are also important. These factors should be individually analyzed by a testing laboratory, not just assumed on the basis of the soil texture class. However, soil texture class determination is still an essential first step in evaluating a soil for sports turf use.

Soil Porosity

Soil porosity is the ratio of open space (pores) to the total volume of a particular sample of soil or other material. Porosity is an important physical characteristic of soil, because it is through the pores that water, air, and nutrients reach the roots of the turfgrass. Soil porosity is expressed as a percentage; a porosity of 50% indicates that one-half of the soil volume consists of pores and the other half consists of solids. Pores are of two types: macropores (large pores that are drained free of water by gravity) and micropores (smaller pores that are not drained by gravity).

The pore characteristics (macropore or micropores) of a particular soil play a critical role in that soil's ability to drain. For instance, some sandy soils have a low porosity; whereas some clay soils have a high soil porosity. This comparison seems to suggest that clay soils drain better than sandy soils. However, experience shows that sandy soils have a higher percentage of macropores than heavy clay soils. So, although a clay soil may have a higher overall porosity, the higher percentage of macropores in a sandy sample allows it to drain more effectively. Ultimately, it is the pore *size,* not total pore *space,* that determines the suitability of a particular soil for a baseball or softball field. Sandy soil drains freely and allows water, air, and nutrients to reach the roots; heavy clay soil holds water, restricting the passage of air to the rootzone and limiting the ability of the plants to take up nutrients.

In considering a particular sample of soil for sports field use, it is vital to know the percentages of macropores and micropores. A testing laboratory will provide these values upon request.

The porosity of soil can be improved by the addition of certain inorganic amendments (most typically sand). For information on the use of amendments, see Section 3.2b.

Soil Structure

Another physical characteristic of soil, and one that affects its porosity, is *soil structure.* Soil structure is the combination or arrangement of soil particles into aggregates, which are clusters of individual particles. Aggregates are separated from adjoining aggregates by "fractures," or channels through the soil. (Figure 3.2 shows a cross section of a soil layer with particles formed into an aggregate.) Widespread aggregate formation results in a well-structured soil that allows for better internal drainage as well as for turfgrass root systems to function properly.

Aggregate formation is caused by the penetration of roots into the soil, by cycles of wet and dry weather, and by freezing and thawing. All of these mechanisms cluster soil particles into aggregates. Of all the plants that promote aggregate formation, grasses are the most effective. Grasses regularly deposit organic residue in the form of decaying leaves and roots, and this depositing of organic material contributes to aggregate formation and good soil structure.

Unfortunately, the mechanical stresses associated with player and vehicular traffic on sports fields tend to destroy good soil structure, collapsing the fractures through which air, water, and nutrients must pass.

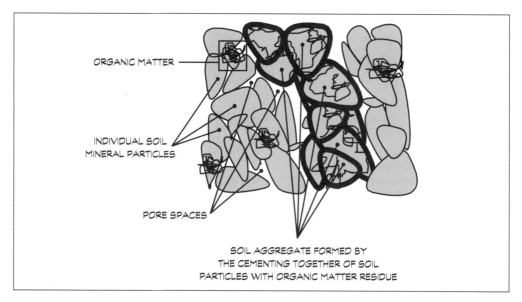

Figure 3.2. Soil aggregate formation.

Soil structure can be promoted by the addition of organic amendments such as peat. For more information on the use of these materials, see the following section on organic amendments.

Soil Strength

As used in reference to sports field soil, *strength* is the ability to resist displacement by an external force, such as imposed by the cleats of athletes' shoes or the tires of maintenance equipment. Good soil strength is necessary to anchor the roots of turfgrass firmly in the soil and to prevent "divoting." Good soil strength allows players to perform with minimal concern for stable footing.

The strength of a soil is determined by a number of the characteristics already discussed, including structure and texture, as well as by moisture content. For example, dry sand has little strength, as anyone who has walked on a beach has observed. As a playing surface, dry sand provides very poor traction and stability. However, the same sand, if it is kept moist (as by the breaking of waves on the beach), has greater strength, better traction, and more stability. On the other hand, heavy clay soil has better soil strength (and provides excellent traction) when it is dry. But if dry clay gets wet, it becomes slippery and provides poor traction. As these simple examples show, in sports turf management, soil selection and moisture control are critical factors in determining soil strength.

In soils underlying sports fields, all of these physical characteristics must be considered. A heavy clay soil may have good strength and structure, but may also have a high compaction tendency and poor natural porosity. A sandy soil has high porosity, but poor structure and strength. Obviously, no single soil type has all the necessary characteristics for a successful sports field. Optimum plant growth requires consideration of compromises, like blending or topdressing, to achieve a soil that will help turf remain playable in a variety of conditions. The only reliable way to predict how a certain soil will perform is to have it tested by a laboratory.

3.2b   Amendments for Turfgrass Soils

Amendments are materials mixed into a soil to improve its performance as a growing medium for sports turf. Amendments can enhance the turf culture either by improving drainage or by increasing water-holding capacity, thus allowing improved root penetration and resisting compaction. In addition to the type of amendment used, effectiveness depends on the amount added, the properties of the soil being amended, and the uniformity of the soil/amendment mixing operation. Soil amendments can be classified as "organic" or "inorganic."

Organic Amendments

Organic amendments are typically added to soil to improve its nutrient-holding capacity and to improve soil structure and internal drainage by promoting the formation of soil aggregates. Organic amendments that are added to sand-based soils will improve the water-holding capacity of that soil. The most popular organic amendments for sports field soil are peat, sawdust, and various waste or by-products, such as sewage sludge, manure, and compost. The choice of organic amendments usually depends on the texture of the soil; fine-textured organic amendments are better for amending coarse-textured soil, and coarse-textured organic amendments are preferred for fine-textured soil. Organic amendments are usually added at a rate of 10% to 20% by volume.

One of the most widely used organic amendments is peat. The most common forms of peat are fibrous and sedimentary. For sports field applications, fibrous peat is preferred because sedimentary peat may contain excessive silt and clay. The most popular form of fibrous peat is sphagnum peat moss, which can be used with both fine- and coarse-textured soil. In fine soil, sphagnum peat moss increases permeability, and in coarse soil it helps to hold water in the soil profile.

Sawdust is sometimes used as an organic amendment. Sawdust can effectively amend sports field soil, provided that it is well rotted and is mixed with compost at a rate of one to one. It is important to avoid using fresh sawdust, because the process of decay in this material will rob the soil of nitrogen needed for plant growth.

Another common organic amendment is compost. With the growing concern about waste-hauling costs and landfill space, many municipalities have gone into the soil amendments business, marketing organic by-products like composted grass clippings, leaves, and tree branches. In some parts of the country a material called "mushroom compost" is available and is becoming a popular soil amendment. Mushroom compost, which is the material used for commercial cultivation of mushrooms, usually consists of straw, manure, and peat moss. Because of the presence of manure (and fertilizer added for the cultivation of the mushrooms), mushroom compost can add substantially to the nutrients in the soil, helping to support turfgrass growth.

Like most turf management practices, the use of organic amendments has both advantages and disadvantages. Adding organic amendments to sand allows for better water retention, but may restrict permeability. These materials have the opposite effect in heavy clay soil, where they increase permeability and enhance internal drainage. As discussed earlier, under "Soil Structure," the binding together of soil particles to form aggregates is most desirable for improving permeability. In heavy clay soil, organic amendments facilitate this binding process, acting as a cementing agent and helping to hold soil particles together.

However, as previously observed, soil structure breaks down when players are put on the field. Compaction caused by foot traffic tends to break down the soil structure, resulting in wet, muddy soil that fails to drain effectively. Under these circumstances, the water-holding characteristic of organic amendments (generally considered to be one of their chief advantages) turns into a disadvantage.

Laboratory testing of the soil/amendment mixture can allow the planner to know how it will perform in use and whether the addition of organic amendments is advisable.

Inorganic Amendments

Inorganic amendments are materials of mineral composition. These amendments are typically used to improve porosity (in the case of sand), to enhance the ability of the soil to absorb or retain moisture (in the case of calcined clay or calcined diatomaceous earth), or to improve the nutrient-holding capacity of sandy soils (in the case of materials like zeolite).

When using sand to amend native heavy clay soil, which typically includes about 65% silt and clay, the objective is to add enough sand so that the sand particles are touching each other. The result is called "bridging"—air spaces (pores) are created within the soil profile.

To achieve bridging, the total sand content of the mixture should be at least 70%. In the case of topsoil with 35% sand and 65% silt and clay, a mixture of 1.5 parts sand and 1.0 part topsoil would be needed to reach 70% total sand content (1.5 parts new sand plus 0.35 part sand already in the topsoil = 1.85 parts total sand ÷ 2.5 parts sand and topsoil = 74% sand).

This seems like a lot of sand to add, and some field designers have made the mistake of thinking that less sand would do the trick. However, it is important to be aware that adding less sand, resulting in a sand percentage below 70%, may actually *slow* internal drainage. Unless enough sand is added to achieve bridging, there is no net increase in the macropores, or pores that will drain freely because of the force of gravity. In addition to the effects on drainage, adding insufficient sand may make the soil harder and may create "hydrophobic" soil, which resists the passage of water into the soil profile.

The best sand for use as an inorganic amendment for heavy soil has particles of uniform size, with most of the particles falling into the "coarse" range (0.5 mm to 1.0 mm). Medium and fine sands (0.1 mm to 0.5 mm) are less effective for modifying native soil, because the smaller particle size does not produce bridging as effectively. It should be noted that these sands have their own uses in sports turf culture; medium and fine sands are preferred for constructing and topdressing sand-based fields. For more information on sand-based fields, see Section 3.2c.

Another group of materials used to amend turfgrass soil includes calcined clay and calcined diatomaceous earth. (The term "calcined" refers to a process of firing the material to harden it. Such materials are typically processed into a granular form for installation.) The addition of calcined materials to native topsoil provides a variety of benefits to the soil, most of them related to water-holding capacity.

Whereas organic amendments hold moisture in the soil, sometimes making it too wet, calcined inorganic amendments have the opposite effect. Because they draw moisture out of the pore space in the soil, these amendments help the field return faster to a playable condition after a rain. In very dry conditions, on the other hand, the most effective calcined amendments will retain water applied through irrigation, then release that water slowly to the root system of the plants. However, researchers are finding that some calcined materials have very high water-holding capacities but do not readily release this water for plant use. If the goal is to increase the plant-available water, it is wise to check the available research on the product under consideration. (Because of the water-holding and release characteristics of calcined materials, they are sometimes blended into skinned area soil to help it dry quickly in rainy weather and to prevent dustiness in dry weather. For more information on their use in skinned area soil, see Section 3.3d.)

Inorganic amendments are sometimes applied to existing turf by topdressing after core aeration, by "drill and fill" operations with deep-drill aerators, or by direct injection using "dry-ject" equipment. When applied by these methods, inorganic amendments form a vertical column through the soil, providing a channel for water percolation and improving the internal drainage of the field. To have the desired effect, the columns must be filled all the way to the surface. These methods also typically promote rooting, as the turfgrass roots spread into the vertical channels to reach the increased soil oxygen in the columns. Sand and calcined materials are sometimes mixed together to be applied by these methods.

Several other inorganic materials are used as amendments for sand-based fields, and a brief description of these materials and their use is given in the next section. However, sand and calcined materials are by far the most common inorganic amendments for native heavy soil fields.

3.2c   Sand-Based Fields

A relatively new form of sports field is the sand-based field, sometimes referred to simply as a "sand field." These fields are all built from an amended sand, not simply pure sand, which would be unsuitable for sports competition. For this reason, such facilities are referred to here as "sand-based" or "amended sand" fields. These fields have several key advantages over native soil fields. The primary advantage of a sand-based field is its high permeability, which promotes surface water removal by internal drainage. A second, equally important, advantage is that a properly designed and installed sand-based rootzone will resist a field's worst enemy: compaction. When correctly specified and tested, a sand-based field will not compact enough to restrict internal drainage.

It is important to be aware of some of the disadvantages of sand-based fields. The primary problem is stability; unless soil or another amendment is added to firm up the surface, players' cleats will sometimes tear through the turf and into the loose sand base. (This is especially true of cool season turfgrasses, which are less tightly knit than the bermudagrass used in the South.)

Other potential problems of sand-based fields include cost, the lack of knowledgeable professionals to design and build such a facility, and heavy maintenance requirements. The cost of constructing a single sand-based field, with all recommended extras like installed drain and irrigation systems, amendments, and so forth, can easily approach a half million dollars. In most areas, there are few designers and contractors with the expertise to build an effective sand field, and their unusual acumen may come at a high price. Furthermore, it is almost impossible for the typical groundskeeping crew to adequately maintain an amended sand field; it is usually necessary to hire a professional turfgrass manager, because maintaining a sand field is as much an art as a science.

Size Range Distribution of Sand

By far the most critical factor in the design of a sand-based field is the selection of a sand with an appropriate size range distribution. Sand particles range in size from 0.05 mm to 2.0 mm (see Table 3.1), and this extremely wide range of sizes represents one potential problem with the use of sand. The largest sand particles (very coarse) are up to 40 times larger than the smallest (very fine) sand particles.

Be wary of sand that is being sold as "well graded." This phrase suggests that the product is high-quality sand, but in fact it refers to sand with a wide range of particle sizes. That kind of sand is desirable for making concrete, but doesn't work well for the rootzone of a sports field. A field built of sand with a wide size range distribution will compact more readily, may be prone to drought, and will be difficult to irrigate properly. The reason is that the smallest particles fill in the pore spaces between the largest particles, a process called "interpacking." This problem is especially troublesome where traffic is heaviest, because the weight of players and vehicles makes the interpacking worse. Eventually, the compaction of the sand causes reduced water permeability and poor drainage in the affected areas.

Strength (Surface Firmness) of Sand-Based Rootzones

Strength, or "surface firmness," is the ability of a field to resist mechanical stresses applied by players' feet and maintenance equipment. In the case of a sand-based field, these stresses can disturb the uniformity of the sand layer. Sand layers tend to lack firmness, a special problem when the turf cover becomes thin or nonexistent. Footing and traction can quickly deteriorate under these conditions. As mentioned earlier in this chapter, keeping the sand moist will provide greater strength, better traction, and more stability.

Sand fields sometimes lack firmness because of the rounded shape of the particles, their lack of cohesion, and their low moisture-holding capacity. Layers constructed from angular sand particles have enhanced stability, but this characteristic is rare because natural weathering quickly rounds off their edges. Most suppliers do not even think of testing for this characteristic.

The surface strength of sand is enhanced by the addition of silt or clay particles (fines), which are usually added in the form of topsoil. This step improves cohesiveness and moisture retention. However, the increased strength of a sand layer achieved by adding fines must be balanced against the disadvantage of the practice—it reduces the sand's permeability.

The addition of a surprisingly small percentage of topsoil results in a substantial reduction in permeability. The reason is fairly simple: The added fines fill the pore spaces through which water drains. The result can be a mix that works like a heavy clay soil (sometimes draining as little as $\frac{1}{100}$ of an inch per hour). This effect can be seen on sand fields with as little as 15% clay-based soil added.

For amending sand in a baseball field, loam soil (preferably sandy loam) is a better choice than heavy clay topsoil, because loam soil has less silt and clay content. Sandy loam should be added at a rate of 5% to 20% of the mix by volume. Before specifying any form of soil as an amendment for a sand-based field, it is wise to have the material analyzed by a reputable lab to determine how it will affect the final mix.

A variety of organic and inorganic amendments are added to sand to improve its stability and water-holding capacity. Among these are organic amendments like peat and compost, and inorganic materials like calcined clay or diatomaceous earth, zeolite, interlocking synthetic mesh elements, and synthetic fibers. (For further information on the characteristics and use of each of these materials, we suggest that you consult our general text, *Sports Fields: A Manual for Design, Construction and Maintenance*, Ann Arbor Press, 1999).

3.3   SKINNED AREA SOIL

Whereas the soil used as a growing medium for turfgrass must possess a number of properties related to the passage of air, water, and nutrients to the roots of the plants, the soil used to construct the skinned areas of a baseball diamond must meet an entirely different set of demands. Skinned area soil does not have to support the growth of plants, but it must provide uniform ball response and good traction, and must be able to remain playable at widely different moisture levels. The primary difference between topsoil used as a growing medium for turfgrass and the soil used to construct skinned areas is that skinned area soil has less organic matter. Because it will not be expected to support plant growth, skinned area soil does not need the nutrient-holding capacities typically found in turfgrass soil.

To provide a playing surface with optimum playability, we prefer a mixture of about 60% sand, 20% silt, and 20% clay. These percentages should be considered a guideline, rather than a firm specification; skinned area soils with different amounts of sand, silt, and clay can work effectively, depending on the particle size and other characteristics of the sand. Diamonds that will be covered during rain typically use more silt—as much as 30%—and less sand. Some suppliers stock and sell a material specifically formulated for skinned areas. They may describe the product as "skinned area soil," "baseball diamond mix," or even "base path soil." Materials suppliers can usually blend soils at the request of the field designer. In any case, the designer must understand how the sand, silt, and clay affect the playability of the finished skinned area.

3.3a   Properties of Skinned Area Soil

In choosing soil for the skinned areas of baseball or softball fields, soil properties like texture, porosity, strength, and surface evaporation must be considered somewhat differently than they are in specifying soil for turfgrass culture.

It should be remembered that skinned areas must deal with water through positive surface drainage, not by percolation downward through the soil. As we have observed, subsurface drain systems work poorly on skinned areas, because water takes too long to move through an effective skinned area soil to the underground drainpipes. Sandy soil would be preferred if percolation were the goal, but the presence of finer-textured soil particles (silt and clay) is necessary to create a firm surface. As mentioned earlier, without the fines from silt and clay, the surface is too loose, like a beach. However, skinned area soil with too much clay is also undesirable, because it can dry as hard as concrete.

Soil strength, a soil's ability to adhere or hold together when horizontal or vertical pressure is applied, is a critical factor in traction. That makes it especially important for skinned areas. Higher percentages of silt and clay particles increase the strength of soil, whereas increasing the sand content reduces its strength. Variations in soil moisture levels also change the strength of a particular sample of soil. An effective way to enhance the strength of a skinned area soil is by mixing in conditioners such as calcined clay or calcined diatomaceous earth. These conditioners make the soil strength more consistent by improving the soil's ability to absorb moisture in wet weather.

Surface evaporation, or the ability of a soil to release moisture into the air, is another important property of skinned area soil. The reason is obvious: The more quickly the soil dries out, the more quickly play can resume. Some soils dry more quickly than others; before selecting a skinned area soil, the designer is advised to perform evaporation tests on the available mixes. (Instructions for two easy-to-perform evaporation tests are included in Section 3.3b.)

3.3b   Tests for Skinned Area Soil

To be sure that a skinned area will perform effectively, the field designer should subject samples of skinned area soil to several tests before approving it for installation.

The first test to which the soil should be subjected is "particle size analysis," which must be performed by a qualified testing laboratory. All of the soil used in the skinned area of a baseball or softball diamond should pass through a ⅜ in. wire screen. A minimum of 97% should pass through a number 8 sieve, and of the remaining 97%, at least 60% should pass through a number 140 sieve.

Although particle size analysis is recommended before the installation of any skinned area soil, such analysis is not sufficient to tell the planner how well the material will perform. It is a good idea to compare two or more different soils with similar particle sizes by doing some further testing of material samples. There are two simple evaporation tests that a field designer can perform personally that will help to predict the performance of particular soils.

The first is a cup test. To perform this test, punch four or five ⅛ in. holes in the bottom of several 8 oz plastic cups, then fill each cup three-quarters full with the different soils to be tested. Slowly pour water into each cup until it reaches the top. Allow the water to drain away through the holes in the bottom of the cup, and see how long it takes the various samples to become firm enough to offer some resistance when a finger is pushed into the soil. The soil that firms up first is the one that will return to playable condition most quickly. A typical good sample will firm up in two days. A less desirable sample may take six or seven days. (Figure 3.3 illustrates this cup test.)

A second simple evaporation test is the "bucket test." Fill a bucket with each soil to be tested, then dump each sample on the ground, tamping it lightly—just enough to make the sample hold together in a mound. Use a watering can, or a hose with a watering wand, to gently but thoroughly soak each sample. Then, as in the previous case, compare the samples in regard to how long it takes each soil to firm up.

Another good practice is to visit the supplier's stockyard before accepting any skinned area soil. Look closely at the undisturbed piles of material to see the size of the gravel that is visible in each. Choose the soil with the smallest gravel particles, preferably ¼ in. or smaller. (The best time to visit the stockyard is shortly after a rain, which exposes the gravel.)

Figure 3.3. This easy-to-perform cup test allows for the comparison of skinned area soils. The soil that firms up fastest will become playable most quickly after a rain.

It is also wise to visit some ball fields in your area to inspect their skinned area soils under different weather conditions. Visit a field during rainy weather to see how the skinned area soil drains and how quickly it dries. Go during a dry period and see how easily it is prepped before a game and how dusty it can become. Don't limit yourself to visiting only the highest-profile facilities in the area; many lower-budgeted facilities have skinned area soils that work well and were installed at a very competitive cost. When you find a field that performs well, ask where the skinned area soil came from. Finally, remember that in all too many cases the color of the skinned area soil has been regarded as the most important criterion in its selection. Color is important for aesthetics, but should be regarded as secondary to the selection of material that offers the best overall performance.

3.3c Pitcher's Mound and Batter's Box Soil

As anyone who has ever maintained a baseball or softball diamond would agree, the pitcher's mound and batter's box present a special challenge. Each pitcher scrapes and kicks at the dirt to customize the surface to his or her liking, and this process goes on at least twice an inning throughout the game. Batters dig in at the plate, disturbing the soil and making a hole that base runners must slide across when they approach the plate.

To withstand the special stresses on these areas, only clay-based soils provide the necessary soil strength. Sand- and silt-based soils are easily disturbed by stresses during competition, and the result is deep holes that present a safety hazard, as well as holding water and compromising playability. Although native heavy clay soils can perform fairly well in these spots, some manufacturers have introduced clay-based soil products for pitcher's mounds and batter's boxes. These products include additives with special binding properties and are specifically designed to resist the stresses applied by the cleats of pitchers and batters.

To maximize playability, these products should be specified for batter's boxes (as shown in Figure 3.4) and for an area 3 ft to 4 ft wide, extending 6 ft to 7 ft in front of the pitcher's plate. For younger players, this distance can be reduced to as little as 5 ft, as long as the pitcher's forward foot lands on the rectangle of processed material. (A photograph showing the installation of these products on the pitcher's mound (Figure 5.7) can be found in Chapter 5, "Construction and Reconstruction.")

3.3d Conditioners and Drying Agents for Skinned Area Soil

One way to enhance the ability of the skinned area to withstand weather is to use conditioners and drying agents. Although the same materials may, on some occasions, be used as conditioners and as drying agents, there is a difference, which should be understood if the field manager is to get the full benefit of each.

A conditioner is a material designed to be mixed into the soil, or spread across the entire skinned area, to improve its ability to remain playable in a wide variety of weather conditions. A drying agent is a product meant to be applied to wet soil in order to soak up some of the excess water and allow play to continue. Drying agents are usually used as spot treatments where wet areas may compromise playability.

Most commonly used conditioners are either calcined clay or calcined diatomaceous earth products. (As mentioned earlier, these materials are also used as the basis for amendments in soil used to grow turfgrass. Typically, the products used for conditioning skinned area soil have larger particle sizes than those used for turfgrass soil amendment.) When applied in the off-season, these conditioners are typically tilled into the top 3 in. to 4 in. of the skinned area soil. During the season itself, they are spread over the surface or mixed into the top 1 in. of the soil with the use of a pulverizer, a weighted nail drag, or a solid-tine aerifier.

Figure 3.4. Installing clay-based material in batter's boxes. The boxes are excavated to a 4 in. depth, then 3 in. of material is installed, tamped, and covered with skinned area soil to surface level.

Some high-profile facilities also take the additional step of spreading conditioners in an even layer up to ⅜ in. thick on top of skinned area soil that has already had conditioner mixed into it. When used this way, the conditioner becomes the playing surface of the skinned area. This is an effective practice, but may be too costly for most facilities.

Calcined conditioners also help to fight compaction, because skinned areas with conditioners incorporated in the soil will loosen more easily and uniformly when a nail drag is used on the surface. Conditioners also allow the skinned area to support tractor weight faster than unconditioned skinned areas, so a maintenance staff can get onto the field to drag it much faster after a rain.

An additional benefit of calcined conditioners is that they allow the maintenance staff to rake soil out of the edge of the grass area when it has accumulated there. Dragging and players' cleats can cause this kind of accumulation, which can prevent surface runoff and lead to the formation of wet spots. Soil without conditioners usually can't be raked out and can be removed only by cutting out a strip of sod or by blasting the soil out with a high-pressure water hose. As far as some field managers are concerned, that quality alone makes these products worth the price, because it allows quick and easy removal of the grass-edge lip before it builds up enough to cause problems.

Because conditioners absorb so much water, they also make the skinned area much less slippery. Slipperiness is a primary factor considered by umpires in deciding whether to call a game because of rain. If they see players slipping, they will stop the game. It is not unreasonable to expect that once or twice a season, a skinned area with conditioner will allow play to continue when an unconditioned skinned area would not. Of course, that also means it's a little *safer* for the players on the skinned area.

A final benefit of skinned area conditioners is that they help with dust control during the summer, because they hold water in the soil longer. In most of the country, it should be possible to wet the soil thoroughly in the morning and play on it all day without having to stop and rewater. For facilities that have games going on from morning until night, that can be a substantial benefit.

In addition to skinned area conditioners, the designer should consider the use of drying agents. As mentioned earlier, these materials are spot treatments, spread on wet portions of a skinned area to soak up standing water and are used in the maintenance of the field. Some drying agents are also calcined clay or diatomaceous earth products, but they differ from conditioners in that drying agents have finer particles to allow more rapid absorption of water.

Another group of drying agents are organic products, such as those manufactured from corncobs. These drying agents can effectively soak up enough water to let a game go on, but they should be removed before the next rain. If left in place, organic drying agents will be mixed into the soil through routine nail dragging and other maintenance processes. This can cause more serious problems, such as making the soil gummy and compacted. Eventually, the affected portion of the skinned area may have to be completely excavated to get rid of the gummy mess that organic drying agents can leave.

When the removal of a drying agent after a game may not be possible, the use of fine-textured calcined products is recommended, because they can be left in place without causing the soil to become gummy. In fact, they perform like conditioners, helping to prepare the skinned area for the next spell of rainy weather.

Chapter 4

Turfgrass Selection

4.1 INTRODUCTION

Player performance and safety are largely determined by the quality of the turf surface. This surface quality, in turn, is determined in large part by the species and cultivar chosen for the field. The choice of turfgrass has important and long-lasting effects; once a decision has been made as to species/cultivar and the turfgrass established, changing to an alternate type is time-consuming and costly.

The selection of a turfgrass species and cultivar can be relatively straightforward when it is based on your own personal experience and knowledge of what turfgrasses have been grown most successfully in your area. In the absence of this type of detailed knowledge, you must rely on other sources of information. This chapter provides that kind of useful information to help you select turfgrass species and cultivars for a baseball or softball field.

4.2 DEFINITIONS OF KEY TERMS

In selecting turfgrass for a baseball or softball field, you will be required to make two choices in sequence—first the species, then the cultivar. A turfgrass *species* is a class or group of turfgrass plants having broad, yet similar, characteristics and traits. A species is identified with a two-word Latin designation, such as *Poa pratensis*. This name is referred to as the scientific (or Latin) name, and it is always printed in an italic font or underlined to signify an italic font. Turfgrass species are also given a common name, such as Kentucky bluegrass. Both names are important for referencing a turfgrass species, but the Latin name is preferred because it is unique to the particular species and less ambiguous, given that more than one common name is usually associated with a single species (Table 4.1).

A turfgrass *cultivar* is a subclass of a species, and multiple cultivars are common within a single species. The cultivar designation should always be used in context with the species name, and can precede the species name (such as Merion Kentucky bluegrass) or follow the species name (Kentucky bluegrass cv. Merion). Turfgrass cultivars within a single species are usually quite similar, but can differ significantly in terms of their performance or suitability for a particular application. Commercial and public turfgrass breeders have developed a large number of cultivars for each of the most popular turfgrass species. Cultivar evaluations are conducted at many state universities under the guidelines of the National Turfgrass Evaluation Program (NTEP)[1] or independently by the universities themselves. All

---

[1] For more information on the National Turfgrass Evaluation Program, contact USDA/ARS, Beltsville Agricultural Research Center, Beltsville, MD 20705 (NTEP information is located at www.ntep.org).

Table 4.1. The Latin and Common Names of the Cool Season and Warm Season Turf-grasses Best Suited for Baseball and Softball Fields

Temperature Class	Latin Name	Common Name
Cool Season	*Poa pratensis*	Kentucky bluegrass English meadow grass June grass smooth-stalked meadow grass
	Lolium perenne	perennial ryegrass English bluegrass ray grass
	Festuca arundinaceae	tall fescue fescue
Warm Season	*Cynodon dactylon*	bermudagrass couch grass devil's grass dogtooth grass Bahama grass wire grass

of this information is available to the public and is a resource for increasing your knowledge of the performance of individual cultivars.

4.3   CRITERIA USED IN TURFGRASS SELECTION

Several criteria are useful in the selection of turfgrass for a baseball or softball field. The first and most important is climatic adaptation, the biological adaptation of a turfgrass species or cultivar that allows it to survive as a perennial in a particular area. The ability of a turfgrass cultivar to survive as a perennial is essential for its optimum performance in sports turf. The use of perennial turfgrass avoids the expense of yearly reestablishment. More important, a perennial turf will develop mature and self-sustaining plant morphology, creating tillers, stolons, rhizomes, branched roots, and lateral stems, which become integrated into a "knitted sod." Without this characteristic, the turf is weak and susceptible to wear, divoting, and other stresses.

Zones of turfgrass adaptation in the United States have been widely published in various books and other publications. In this text, we have included maps that divide North America somewhat differently than those used in other books, including our own text, *Sports Fields: A Manual for Design, Construction and Maintenance*. These new maps are based on regional average temperatures measured over long terms (typically decades). Unlike older maps that simply divide North America into three distinct zones, those presented in this book are separate maps showing where cool season turfgrasses can be successfully grown (Figure 4.1) and where warm season grasses can be successfully cultivated (Figure 4.2). On each map, the "Primary Zone" (dark gray) shows where the particular species can most readily be established as a perennial; the "Secondary Zone" (light gray) indicates areas where these species can be established, but with greater difficulty; and an unshaded area shows parts of the country in which these species cannot be grown perennially at all.

The two separate maps were needed to reflect the differences in biology of cool and warm season turfgrasses that form the basis of their perennial nature. Cool season turfgrass tolerates heat poorly, but has excellent cold tolerance. Warm season turfgrasses have poor cold tolerance, but excellent tolerance to high temperatures. Cool season turfgrasses can tolerate one or two days of extremely hot weather, but three or four weeks of extremely high temperatures can result in the thinning or widespread death of these grasses. In the case of warm season turfgrasses, their ability to tolerate cold temperatures depends only on how cold it gets. For example, two or three weeks of mildly cold weather can be survived by most warm season turf, but even a single night of extreme cold can kill the same turf (an occurrence known as "winterkill").

On the cool season map, the divisions into three areas are based on a temperature threshold of 86°F (30°C) and the number of days each year that the daily high reaches or exceeds that temperature. In the Primary Zone, there are typically fewer than 90 days each year above this threshold; in the Secondary Zone, between 90 and 120 days; in the unshaded area, more than 120 days.

Primary Zone (dark gray)—Regions with 90 days or fewer per year of air temperature above 86° F. Suitable for Kentucky bluegrass, perennial ryegrass, or mixtures of the two.

Secondary Zone (light gray)—Regions with 90 to 120 days per year of air temperature above 86° F. Suitable for tall fescue, Kentucky bluegrass, or mixtures of the two.

Rest of the country (white)—Regions with greater than 120 days per year of air temperature above 86° F. Not suitable for any cool season turfgrass species.

Zones of adaptation based on the Plant Heat-Zone Map published by the American Society of Horticulture, 7931 East Boulevard Drive, Alexandria, VA 22308.

Sports turfgrasses best adapted to the Primary Zone are Kentucky bluegrass, perennial ryegrass, and mixtures of the two. In the Secondary Zone, the best-adapted grasses are tall fescue, Kentucky bluegrass, and mixtures of these species. No cool season sports turfgrasses are adapted to the unshaded area of the map; turfgrass selection for this area should be based on the warm season map. For information on the morphology of cool season turfgrasses and the implications of this morphology for sports turf, see Table 4.2

Unlike the cool season map, the warm season map is based only on the average minimum low temperature (the lowest single reading taken during the year). The Primary

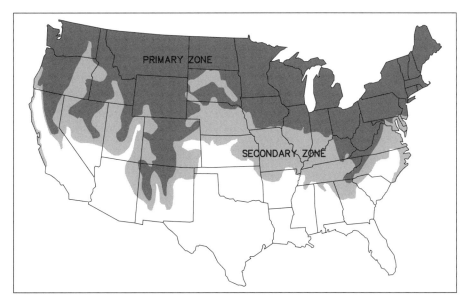

Figure 4.1. Cool season turfgrass zones, based on high-temperature exposure.

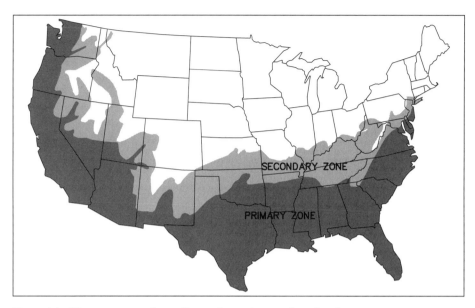

Figure 4.2. Warm season turfgrass (bermudagrass) zones, based on low-temperature exposure.

Zone has an average minimum low temperature of greater than 0° F. The Secondary Zone has an average minimum low temperature of –10°F to 0°F, and the unshaded area has an average minimum low temperature of less than –10°F.

Primary Zone (dark gray)—Regions with average minimum low temperature values greater than 0° F. Suitable for all seeded or vegetative bermudagrass cultivars.

Secondary Zone (light gray)—Regions with average minimum low temperature values ranging from –10° to 0° F. Suitable only for cold-hardy bermudagrass cultivars.

Rest of the country (white)—Regions with average minimum low temperature values less than –10° F. Not suitable for any bermudagrass cultivars.

Zones of adaptation of bermudagrass cultivars based on the United States Department of Agriculture map entitled *Plant Hardiness Zones of the United States and Canada*. Misc. Publ. 814 (Washington, DC: USDA, 2001).

Table 4.2. Morphology, Description, and Implications of Kentucky Bluegrass, Perennial Ryegrass, and Tall Fescue as Turfgrasses for Baseball and Softball Fields— Cool Season

Species	Morphology	Description	Implications
Kentucky bluegrass	Determinate rhizomes; tillers	Internode elongation below the soil surface; high shoot density	Excellent shear and traction strength; excellent recuperation potential; excellent resiliency
Perennial ryegrass	Long vertical leaf extension; lignified leaf tissue; tillers	Rapid leaf regrowth; durable leaf tissue; high shoot density	Enhanced surface smoothness; excellent wear tolerance; excellent resiliency.
Tall fescue	Lignified leaf tissue; tillers	Durable leaf tissue; high shoot density	Excellent wear tolerance; excellent resiliency

Table 4.3. Morphology, Description, and Implications of Bermudagrass as a Turfgrass for Baseball and Softball Fields—Warm Season

Morphology	Description	Implications
Indeterminate rhizomes	Above- and belowground lateral stems	Excellent shear and traction strength; excellent recuperation potential
Leaf blade and sheath elongation	Rapid regrowth	Excellent surface recuperation potential
Adventitious roots	Deep and highly branched root system	Excellent sod strength, traction, and firmness
Lignified stem and leaf tissue	Durable leaf and stem surface	Excellent wear tolerance
Multiple branching at nodes	High shoot density	Excellent resiliency
Internode elongation	Elongation of above- and belowground lateral stems	Excellent recuperation potential

In the warm season Primary Zone, all seeded and vegetatively propagated bermudagrass cultivars are suitable for use. In the Secondary Zone, only the cold hardy vegetative cultivars are recommended. In the unshaded area, bermudagrass cultivars are not recommended, and the cool season selection map should be used.

The cool season map shows the areas in which three species and multiple cultivar choices can be established as perennials. On the other hand, the warm season map indicates the areas for growing only one species (bermudagrass), although this species includes multiple cultivar choices. Bermudagrass is the only warm season species choice because of its unique morphology and cosmopolitan range of adaptation (Table 4.3).

4.4   THE MAPS

To determine the turfgrass best suited for your fields, find your location on each of the two maps presented in Figures 4.1 and 4.2; you will have to look at both maps, because in some areas, both warm and cool season grasses can be grown as perennials. If this is the case in your location, then you have a choice of using cool or warm season turfgrass on your fields.

An area in which both cool and warm season turfgrass can be grown is said to be an "overlap zone," or a "transition zone." In such areas, the climate transitions from cool to warm, or vice versa, from one year to the next. Because of the wide shifts in weather from season to season, these overlap zones are the most difficult areas in which to manage turfgrass. (Note that there are some small areas, such as East Central Utah, Eastern Colorado, and West Central Kansas, that do not fall within the perennial growing areas for either cool season or warm season turfgrass. Obviously, it is possible to establish turfgrass in these areas, but as in an overlap zone, either cool season or warm season turfgrass would be an option.)

4.4a   Warm Season Turfgrass Selection

In the warm season zones, bermudagrass is the only practical choice for sports fields, and the manager's choice is limited to a particular cultivar. In the warm season Primary Zone (the zone in which bermudagrass can be most easily grown as a perennial), the manager's first decision is whether to use a vegetatively propagated or seed propagated type. The vegetative types either lack seed for propagation because they are sterile, or they require vegetative propagation to maintain their true-to-type turf characteristics. Vegetative cultivars typically have high shoot, stolon, and rhizome density, robust growth, and a deep fibrous root system. On the other hand, seeded cultivars, although they have similar morphology, lack the vigor and density of the vegetative cultivars. If the decision is based only on the quality and vigor of the established turfgrass, the first choice would be the vegetative cultivars. However, these cultivars cost more, so budget constraints may justify the use of seeded cultivars. To achieve genetic diversity, it is a good idea to choose two or three cultivars and have them blended in equal proportions.

Once the choice of a seeded or vegetative type is made, the next step is the selection of a particular cultivar. Some cultivars are established more successfully in the Primary and Secondary zones. In the Primary Zone, our recommended vegetative choices are Tifway, Tifway II, TifSport, MS-Pride, and MS-Choice (Bull's-eye). Within the group of vegetative types, MS-Choice (Bull's-eye) was developed specifically for athletic field use. This cultivar has highly lignified leaf tissue, durable stolon and rhizome structures, minimal seedheads, dark green color, and a uniquely compact and prostrate growth habit, all of these features making MS-Choice (Bull's-eye) a top vegetative recommendation. In the warm season Primary Zone, the recommended seeded cultivars are Princess, Savannah, Blackjack, Sultan, SunStar, Riviera, Yukon, and Transcontinental. (If a seeded type is chosen, we suggest you look into the commercial availability of seed for your choice before putting its name into the specifications. Some seeded types are low seed producers, so their seed supply can quickly run out. Specifying a seeded cultivar that is not available can disrupt the construction schedule and cause an unnecessary delay.)

In the Secondary Zone for warm season turfgrass, our recommended choices are Midiron, Midlawn, Vamont, and Quickstand. All of these are vegetative cultivars with excellent cold hardiness. Among seeded cultivars, only Riviera, Yukon, and Transcontinental provide the desirable level of cold hardiness. Cold hardiness may not be needed every year, but when the climate does become unseasonably cold, a cold hardy bermudagrass cultivar will survive better.

For recommendations of bermudagrass cultivars for various warm season applications, see Table 4.4.

In the rest of North America, bermudagrass is not recommended.

4.4b Cool Season Turfgrass Selection

Managers in cool season zones may choose among three species, mixtures of these species, and a selection of cultivars within each species (Table 4.2). In the Primary Zone, a monostand of Kentucky bluegrass, and a mixture of Kentucky bluegrass and perennial ryegrass (known in the trade as a blue/rye mix), are the options. The composition of a seed mix by weight may vary from 50% to 70% Kentucky bluegrass, with the rest perennial ryegrass. The proportion of Kentucky bluegrass and perennial ryegrass in a mix will be determined by your relative location within the cool season Primary Zone. Kentucky bluegrass has excellent cold tolerance; perennial ryegrass has moderate cold tolerance. For this reason, a lower proportion of perennial ryegrass should be used in the northern regions of the cool season Primary Zone. Consult with an experienced field manager or a university extension specialist to help you determine the appropriate blue/rye mix for your area.

A monostand of perennial ryegrass is not recommended. Although this species can perform very well for baseball and softball fields, perennial ryegrass is especially susceptible to some diseases, and a monostand can be quickly wiped out by an outbreak of one of these diseases.

Table 4.4. Selected Bermudagrass Cultivars Best Suited for Baseball and Softball Fields in Zones Indicated on Warm Season Map (Figure 4.2.)

"Vegetatively Propagated Only" Bermudagrass Cultivars	Seeded Bermudagrass Cultivars
Primary Zone—Select one cultivar from the list.	**Primary Zone**—Select two or three cultivars and make a seed blend in equal proportions.
Bull's-eye (MS-Choice) MS-Pride Tifway Tifway II TifSport	Princess Savannah Blackjack Sultan SunStar Yukon Riviera Transcontinental
Secondary Zone—Select one cultivar from the list.	**Secondary Zone**—Select at least two of these cultivars and have them blended in equal proportions.
Midiron Vamont Midlawn Quickstand	Riviera Yukon Transcontinental

In the cool season Secondary Zone, the best options are tall fescue, Kentucky bluegrass, and a mixture of these species. In this zone, long periods of high temperatures are common, and tall fescue is a heat- and drought-tolerant species. A monostand of Kentucky bluegrass or tall fescue, and a mix of Kentucky bluegrass and tall fescue, are options. However, Kentucky bluegrass and tall fescue mixes are not widely used, because these species can segregate over time, resulting in localized patches of Kentucky bluegrass and tall fescue. These segregated colonies cause poor field uniformity and reduced player performance and safety. The manager should keep in mind that new and improved turf-type tall fescue cultivars are being developed, and these cultivars may perform better when mixed with Kentucky bluegrass. Consult an experienced field manager in your area or a university extension specialist to help you determine the suitability of a Kentucky bluegrass and tall fescue mix.

In the rest of the country, cool season species are not recommended.

Once the manager has decided on a species or mix of species, the next step is cultivar selection. The list of cultivars for each cool season turfgrass is lengthy; there are 150+ tall fescue cultivars, 250+ Kentucky bluegrass cultivars, and 150+ perennial ryegrass cultivars. For information on the attributes of these cultivars, consult NTEP data or visit your state's cooperative extensive service web site. As a starting point, we have complied a list of recommended cool season cultivars (Table 4.5). As with seeded bermudagrasses, determine the commercial seed availability of the various cultivars before making a selection. It is also wise to use blends of two or more of your top choices, rather than planting a single cultivar, to ensure that the turf will exhibit the strengths of each.

4.4c Transition or Overlap Zone Turfgrass Selection

As mentioned earlier, the overlap or transition zones are the areas of the United States where the zones of adaptation for cool season and warm season turfgrasses overlap. In these locations, a manager may choose either a cool season species or bermudagrass for sports field applications.

Table 4.5. Selected Kentucky Bluegrass, Perennial Ryegrass, and Tall Fescue Cultivars Best Suited for Baseball and Softball Fields in Zones Indicated on the Cool Season Map (Figure 4.1.)[a]

Kentucky Bluegrass		Perennial Ryegrass		Tall Fescue	
Primary Zone—Select one cultivar from three of the four groups listed and make a seed blend in equal proportions.		Primary and Secondary Zones—Select two to five cultivars from this list and make a seed blend in equal proportions.		Primary and Secondary Zones—Select two to five cultivars from this list and make a seed blend in equal proportions.	
Group 1	**Group 2**	Brightstar II	Seville II	Gazelle	Scorpio
Odyssey	America	Riberts 629	Nexus	Rembrant	Jaguar III
Midnight	Unique	Allstar 2	Premier II	Millennium	Olympic Gold
Liberator	Brilliant	Integra		Dynasty	Crossfire II
Rugby II	Apollo	Amazing		Falcon III	Wolfpack
Total Eclipse		Pizza 22		Plantation	Rebel
Nuglade		Applaud		Coyote	Sentry
		Churchill		Masterpiece	Watchdog
Group 3	**Group 4**	Charismatic		Shenandoah II	Dominion
SR2109	Preakness	Gator III		Tarheel	
Moonlight	Livingston	Fiesta III			
Princeton 105	Plush	Paragon		*Note:* For a Kentucky bluegrass/ tall fescue mix, select two to five Kentucky bluegrass cultivars from Group 4 and mix with two to five tall fescue cultivars.	
Glade	Eagleton	Jet			
Wildwood	SR2000				
Secondary Zone—Select two to five cultivars from this list and make a seed blend in equal proportions.					
Preakness Livingston Plush Eagleton SR2000					

[a] Special thanks and appreciation to Richard H. Hurley, Turfgrass Agronomist, for his time and insight in selecting the cultivars listed in Table 4.5.

It should be noted, however, that there is a good deal of variation in the turfgrasses that are best suited to the various overlap zones. For example, in the Northwest overlap zones (in Oregon and Washington), the cold hardy bermudagrass cultivars will survive as perennials, but their response to cold weather (slowed growth and loss of color when temperatures drop below 50° F) makes them unacceptable for fields that will be used during the fall, winter, and spring seasons. In this part of the country, these bermudagrass cultivars provide acceptable turf only during the summer. For these reasons, the predominant turfgrasses in the overlap zones of this region are the cool season grasses.

On the other hand, the overlap zones found in sections of the Upper South (Missouri, Illinois, Kentucky, Tennessee, North and South Carolina, Virginia, and Georgia) provide a different set of climatic circumstances. In these areas, the climate is more variable from year to year, making the choice of turfgrass more difficult than in the overlap zones in the

Northwest. In the Upper South, both cool season and bermudagrass species are commonly found on sports fields. Bermudagrass would be favored on unirrigated fields with high summertime use and low budgets; cool season species would be justified for irrigated fields with higher maintenance budgets.

In any of the overlap zones, the criteria for choosing between cool or warm season turf-grasses include (in addition to climate) the level of field activity, the time of year when use is greatest, the level of aesthetic appeal desired, and the available maintenance budget. All of these criteria are useful, but you will have to decide on the appropriate balance among them.

The variability in climate in overlap zones results in a corresponding variability in turf-grass performance. It is these factors that make managing a baseball or softball field in an overlap zone so difficult. Because of the complexity of the task, it is especially useful to seek help from an experienced field manager in your area or a state university cooperative extension specialist before making a final choice.

4.5   OVERSEEDING WITH PERENNIAL RYEGRASS

Throughout this chapter, we have focused on the attributes of a perennial turf. However, a common practice for optimizing the performance of athletic turfgrass is overseeding, which is seeding into a stand of existing turfgrass. (Because of its lower cost, a field manager may be tempted to choose annual ryegrass for overseeding. However, because of its faster growth, requiring more maintenance; its lower stress tolerance; and its wider blades, which can affect ball response, annual ryegrass is not recommended for overseeding.)

In the cool season zones, overseeding by slit-seeding of perennial ryegrass into an established cool season turf is a well-established practice. There are times when slit-seeding an existing stand helps to alleviate poor turf density and/or prepare for anticipated heavy field activity. In this situation, overseeding with perennial ryegrass is recommended in all of the cool season zones. In the cool season Primary Zone, overseeding with perennial ryegrass will add density and may make a permanent change to the species composition. In the cool season Secondary Zone, overseeding perennial ryegrass in the fall will increase turf density for the following spring and early summer. However, the ryegrass will typically die during the first summer hot spell.

In warm season zones, overseeding usually takes the form of slit-seeding or broadcasting perennial ryegrass into established bermudagrass in the fall to provide green and healthy turf until the bermudagrass fully greens up the following year. As in the cool season Secondary Zone, the overseeded perennial ryegrass will die when temperatures rise in the summer.

(For information on the mechanics of overseeding [by slit-seeding] perennial ryegrass into cool season turfgrass, see Chapter 6, Section 6.3b. For information on overseeding perennial ryegrass into bermudagrass, see Chapter 8, Section 8.5e.)

4.6   CONCLUSION

Each turf manager will have unique challenges in selecting a turfgrass species and/or cultivars for his or her fields. The maps included in this chapter provide a good starting point in your decision making, but it is important to learn as much as possible about each of the turfgrass species and their respective cultivars. If possible, always seek advice from experienced field managers in your area before selecting turfgrass, because you will have to live with the results of that choice for years to come.

Chapter 5

Construction and Reconstruction

5.1   INTRODUCTION

After surveying the field and developing a grading plan, it is time to start construction. In this chapter, we will consider some of the factors that may be taken into account in order to result in a field that performs well under varying circumstances related to weather and level of competition.

Of course, it must be noted that there are a number of successful approaches to this kind of construction. This chapter presents ideas and suggestions based on our experience in field construction. The reader may find it helpful to incorporate some of our thinking in developing his or her own way of building a field.

Whatever practices are used, it is essential for construction personnel to carefully follow the plans that have been developed for a project. The person supervising the project should not assume that these professionals, however experienced they may be, will always do their work exactly as the plans direct. This is especially true for crews who have little experience in sports field construction, because some of the practices used in building other facilities will not produce a consistently playable baseball or softball diamond.

5.2   CONSTRUCTION

The critical first step in the construction process is to transfer the grading plan to the field. Transferring the plan can be performed with the use of grade stakes or laser-guided grading equipment. Unless you are an experienced surveyor, it is wise to secure the services of a professional surveyor to ensure that the contour plan is correctly transferred to the site. The surveyor will also help to set the dimensions of the field, beginning with home plate and the foul poles and including critical points like the fence lines.

5.2a   Rough Grading
When the plan has been transferred to the field site, the next step is rough grading. This phase of the project includes three steps: stripping off the existing topsoil, excavating the subsoil to establish the subgrade (using specifications stated in section 2.3e), and installing the topsoil in an even layer as specified by the design. In many cases, the topsoil stripped from the site will be stockpiled so that it can be reinstalled later in the process.

It is important to avoid stripping, stockpiling, and reinstalling topsoil when it is wet. Soil stockpiled when wet will take years to fully dry in most areas, and soil installed when wet will be subject to excessive compaction. Always work with dry topsoil.

5.2b Final Grading of the Skinned Area and the Infield

Once the rough grading process has been completed, it is time to proceed with final grading. This is the process of making the final adjustments to the grade of the topsoil and installing and grading the skinned area soil to match the contour plan. In performing the final grading process, we begin with the skinned area and the infield, because these are the most critical areas of the field. These areas typically have two to three times as many grade changes as other portions of the field.

String Line Grading Techniques

As mentioned in Chapter 1, the skinned area of a baseball diamond typically has a percentage of slope ranging from 0.5% to 1.5%, whereas infields (either skinned or grass) should have a 0.5% downward slope from the base of the pitcher's mound to the base lines. Because these are such gradual slopes, it is necessary to use as many as 50 grade stakes for such areas, to avoid low spots that hold water on the finished field.

As an example, consider the grading plan shown in Figure 5.1, which is the preferred infield/skinned area design discussed in Chapter 1. The first step is to set grade stakes. The

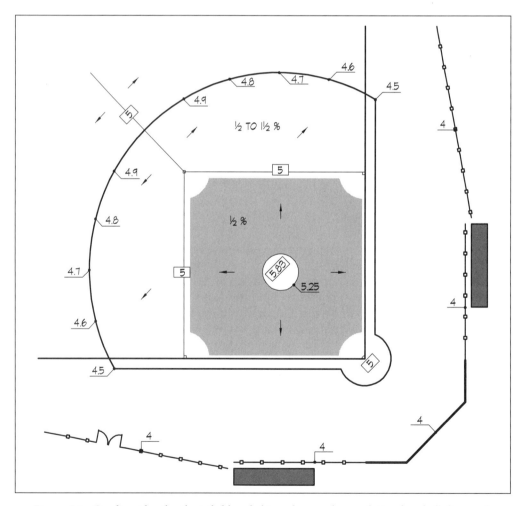

Figure 5.1. Grading plan for the infield and skinned area of a regulation baseball diamond.

stakes used by the surveyor in transferring the contour plan to the site may have been removed in the course of rough grading, but stakes marking the correct location of home plate and the foul poles should still be in place. If they have been removed or disturbed, the site needs to be resurveyed to establish these 3 points.

Begin by placing string lines between home plate and the foul poles. Measure off the required distances to first and third base and install a marker (often a 10 in. to 12 in. nail) at each base. The nails must be driven in securely enough to hold a string line. Using two tapes, measure from first and third to find the location of second base, and set another nail at that point. Then set a string line from home to second, measure out the appropriate distance to the pitcher's rubber, and install a nail there.

Measuring from the nail at the pitcher's rubber, establish the outfield arc. (For a regulation adult baseball field, the distance to the arc should be 95 ft.) Using a field striper, paint the outfield arc on the field. Measuring from the nails at the bases and home plate, paint the arcs around those areas. Paint the circle where the pitcher's mound will be located, with the center of the circle 18 in. in front of the pitcher's plate.

Now it's time to begin setting stakes, using sharpened 1 × 2 in. lumber at least 12 in. long. Begin by establishing the outline of the infield, measuring from the string lines and nails you have already placed. Set a stake where the arcs around the bases and home plate reach the required distances from the foul line and the base paths between first and third. Set one stake midway between each pair of bases, so the infield will end up being marked by 12 stakes.

Now establish the outside (foul side) of the first and third base paths, measuring outward from the foul lines. Start where the home plate arc meets the outside of the base path, and set a total of 4 stakes from there to the outfield arc in line starting at home plate circle. (Set the third stake next to first and third base, because the grade usually changes at this point.) Then set stakes as indicated along the outfield arc, typically using about 9 additional stakes to cover the distance. Finally, place stakes around the pitcher's mound and the arc in foul territory around home plate. It may seem like a lot, but we like to use 8 stakes around the mound and 5 additional stakes around home plate. We also install 1 additional grade stake in the middle of the arc around each base.

If you have been keeping count, you can see that the suggested process would include the placement of 46 stakes and five nails for the infield and skinned area. This total should allow very accurate string line grading.

Now set stakes to establish the location of the backstop and the fence around the infield and skinned area. Use at least 5 stakes for this purpose. The fence layout shown in Figure 5.1 would require at least 8.

A common mistake is to fail to set grade stakes in foul territory around the infield to allow for a continuous grade from the infield to the dugouts, backstop, and foul line fences. These are highly used areas of the field of play; players will be running through these areas, looking straight up for foul balls and grabbing throws from the outfield, with runners approaching the plate. Obviously, under these circumstances, good traction (and thus good drainage) is essential.

As the stakes are being placed, mark the location of each of them on a copy of the contour plan. If the plan does not include enough infield detail (as shown in Figure 5.2), you will have to calculate the correct elevation at each stake, using the elevations for the bases shown on the overall field plan. Mark the elevations for each stake on your copy of the plan, creating what is known as a "shop drawing."

(A useful practice is to make sure that the elevations on the outside—or foul side—of the base paths are ¾ in. to 1 in. lower than the elevations on the inside—or fair side—of the base path. This will allow the base paths to drain properly.)

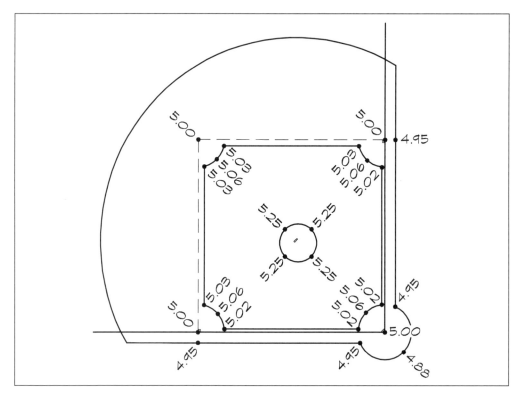

Figure 5.2. Shop drawing for the construction of an infield and skinned area.

With the grade stakes set and your shop drawing in hand, the next step is to mark the grade on the stakes, using a surveyor's level and elevation rod. The surveyor who performed the original transfer of the plan to the site will have established a benchmark on the site, installing a hub in the ground and marking the elevation on the hub (or using an existing point, such as a curb or catch basin). This benchmark is then used to set the grade at each stake. Place the level anywhere on the field, and take a reading at the benchmark. Add your reading to the elevation marked by the surveyor. The sum of these two values is known as the "height of instrument."

For the next step, you will need two helpers. Choose any of the stakes you have set, and subtract the number written on the shop drawing for that point from the height of instrument you have calculated. Have one helper hold the elevation rod next to the stake, while the other kneels next to the stake with a marker in hand. Have the holder of the rod move it up and down until you read the appropriate value through the level. The kneeling helper will then make a mark on the stake at the bottom of the rod. This mark represents the correct field elevation for that point. Continue this process around the entire area, marking each stake.

The next step is to tie string lines on all of the stakes that have been placed for straight lines, such as those along the base paths. The string should be attached to each stake right at the mark that has been made on it. These string lines serve two purposes: They separate the grass areas from the skinned areas, and they serve as a visible guideline for the crew's use in establishing the final grade of the field. (See Figure 5.3.)

Figure 5.3. String line grading. The infield turfgrass will be installed on the far side of the lines, and the near side will be filled with skinned soil to become the home plate area and third base path.

The same process can be used for the arcs and circles, although it will be necessary to let the painted arcs serve as the dividers between the skinned area soil and the topsoil. Obviously, the more stakes placed on each arc, the more accurate their guidance will be. (That is why we recommend 8 stakes around the pitcher's mound.) Because soil will be placed on the field, obscuring the paint, the arcs and circles are often painted two or three times at various stages of the project.

Once the stakes are set and the strings lines stretched, have the topsoil and skinned area soil brought onto the field and dumped in the appropriate areas. Be sure to take down strings to allow vehicles to pass onto the area without disturbing them, and watch to be sure that no stakes are run over. Replace the strings (and any damaged stakes), and begin grading.

First, grade along the straightaways and the arcs, then use string lines to hand grade the entire infield by attaching a string to a stake at the base of the pitcher's mound and pulling it to another stake at the base line. Grade the topsoil to the string line. Then, leaving the string line tied to the stake at the mound, move it to a point 5 ft to 6 ft down the base line from the original point. Install a temporary stake and tie the line so that it touches the string line along the base path. Now grade to the string. Continue around the infield until it is entirely graded. If the area will be seeded, grade right to the string lines. If sod will be installed, find out how thick the sod will be cut, and leave the grade that distance below the lines. Loosen the soil with a pulverizer to ensure good rooting, then smooth the surface with a power rake.

Now establish the grade of the skinned area, using a similar process. Tie a string from a stake between first and second base, and stretch it across the skinned area to a stake on the outfield arc. Use temporary stakes when necessary, as described earlier, and grade the skinned area soil to the level of the string lines.

The grading process itself is typically performed using a bulldozer or a tractor with a blade or bucket. This means that the equipment will be compacting the soil while the grading is going on. Because the stakes and string lines that outline the field are in place and the tractor is avoiding them, the soil along the lines will be less compacted than the soil on the rest of the area. To prevent these areas from oversettling and forming low spots, remove the strings, drive the equipment over the area they formerly occupied, then replace them and check the grade. Use foot pressure around the stakes until they are finally removed, then drive over those areas as well. (Leave the stakes around the pitcher's mound to help in building that structure.)

Laser Grading Techniques

If you have never constructed a field, the string line grading process may sound like a complicated and painstaking task. Even experienced professionals know that it is. An alternative way to construct a field is by contracting with a firm that uses laser-guided equipment to perform the process.

The laser grading process requires the placement of stakes and string lines to separate the turf areas and the skinned areas, just as described in the preceding section. Once the stakes and lines are in place, the laser-guided equipment follows them in establishing the correct grade of the field. (See Figure 5.4.)

Figure 5.4. Laser grading equipment in use. The sensor at the top of the pole permits precise adjustments of the grade. (Photo courtesy of Don Uber, Sportscape of Texas, Inc.)

The advantages and disadvantages of laser grading are probably obvious. The technology is more accurate than the human hand and eye, and it performs the work more quickly than human labor. However, the cost is higher because of the cost of the laser equipment itself.

In many areas, it is possible to rent laser grading equipment. However, because of the sophistication of the gear and the differences between the various brands, we do not recommend that inexperienced operators attempt to build a baseball diamond with laser-guided equipment. If a contractor hired for a job claims he or she can use this type of equipment, find out what experience the contractor has and check past jobs to make sure they came out well.

5.2c Building the Pitcher's Mound

With the final grade established for the infield and skinned areas, it is time to construct the pitcher's mound. (This, of course, applies to baseball; softball diamonds do not have a mound.)

Before addressing the construction sequence for the mound, the material to be used should be considered. Some designers specify that clay should be used in building the whole mound, but in our experience this is unnecessary and can cause additional complications. Clay must be kept wet during the entire installation process. Each 2 in. to 3 in. layer of clay must be moistened and tamped, making a repetitive job even more tedious. Instead, we recommend building the mound from the same soil used for the rest of the skinned areas, with special clay-based material installed in specific spots, as described in the following paragraphs.

Figure 5.5 shows the details of a correctly constructed pitcher's mound.

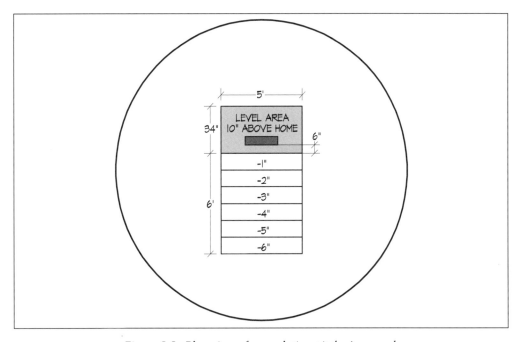

Figure 5.5. Plan view of a regulation pitcher's mound.

Begin by dumping about 5 to 6 tons of soil on the mound (about 3 to 4 cu yd). Then shovel and rake the soil into the rough shape of the mound. Once the rough contour has been established, use a tamping tool to compact the soil to the specified mound height. Then install the pitcher's plate at the proper distance from home plate and at the height specified by the appropriate governing body. With the pitcher's plate installed, contour the sloped area on the home side of the mound, where the pitcher's feet will fall as he steps forward to deliver the ball.

An easy way to set the correct slope in front of the pitcher's plate is to make a measuring tool from a piece of 2 × 4 × 10 lumber, as shown in Figure 5.6. Lay the 2 × 4 on top of the pitcher's plate, and stake it level on the home plate side. Mark the board 18 in. in front of the pitcher's plate, and then every foot until there are six marks. There should be 6 in. of level soil in front of the plate, and then the soil begins to slope downward. Adjust the slope until the first mark is 1 in. above the ground, the second mark is 2 in., and so on, out to 6 ft, 6 in. in front of the pitcher's plate. The rest of the mound can be sloped evenly to the bottom.

Using Clay-Based Pitcher's Mound Products for Stability

Having established the correct contours of the mound, we recommend installing the special clay-based material mentioned earlier. Several manufacturers now produce a treated clay material formulated to resist the displacement so often seen in front of the pitcher's plate. To install this material, remove a rectangle of soil 3 in. to 4 in. deep and replace it to ½ in. below the specified grade with the pitcher's mound material. Then cover to the surface with skinned area soil. (See Figure 5.7.)

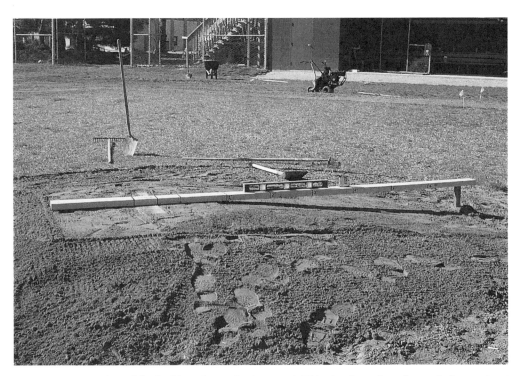

Figure 5.6. A simple tool for building the pitcher's mound. This simple tool can be made from a 2 × 4 and used to accurately set or reset the grade for a pitcher's mound.

Figure 5.7. To ensure optimal pitcher's mound or batter's box performance, a clay-based soil material can be installed. Some manufacturers are now producing a material specifically designed for this purpose. (Use of this material in batter's boxes is shown in Figure 3.4.)

Manufacturers typically recommend installing a rectangle of the material 5 ft wide and 6½ ft long in front of the pitcher's plate. However, in most cases, it is possible to economize by reducing the width of this rectangle, making it 2 to 3 ft. Nearly all pitchers will place their feet in this reduced rectangle, and you will cut your cost for the material by 40% to 60%.

(This clay-based material also works well in the batter's boxes and behind the plate where the catcher crouches. Just dig out the soil in those areas and replace it with the product, as described in the preceding discussion.)

Using this material reduces the "cupping out" that affects the mound and the batter's boxes, but does not eliminate the problem altogether. Some daily maintenance is still required, and manufacturers provide directions for this process.

5.2d Installing Skinned Area Conditioners

In Chapter 3, we discussed the benefits of skinned area conditioners. To make the best possible use of these materials, they should be installed in the skinned area soil during the construction process. Most skinned area conditioners are formulated with calcined clay or diatomaceous earth (DE). In this section, we illustrate the process using a DE conditioner; the procedure for installing calcined clay products is very similar.

(Some supply yards can mix a conditioner into the skinned area soil before delivering it to the site. Obviously, this saves time and labor during the construction process and improves the overall uniformity of the mix. If this service is available and the budget allows, we recommend taking advantage of it.)

Using the manufacturer's specifications for the amount of conditioner to be used on the field, place the bags of conditioner evenly across the skinned area. In the case of DE conditioners to be mixed into the top 3 in. of the soil, a regulation skinned area will require about 3½ tons of material. The 25 lb bags of conditioner will be placed about every 6½ ft over the surface. Break the bags and spread the material evenly across the skinned area (creating a layer about ⅜ in. deep) with standard aluminum rakes. Till the product into the soil to a depth of 3 in. Then go over the skinned area with a pulverizer, a leveling tool such as the Straight-Edge Field Leveler (Figure 5.8), and a roller.

Installing the prescribed 3½ tons of DE conditioner and tilling it in about 3 in. deep on an official-size baseball field with a grass infield takes about 40 man-hours from start to finish. Obviously, installation time is somewhat less for a smaller field, such as a Little League field.

Note: Once the conditioner has been installed, it will withstand normal foot and tractor traffic right away. However, the first time the field gets a soaking rain, it is important to keep all traffic off the skinned area until it has dried thoroughly. When the soil has been thoroughly soaked and dried one time, it is ready for normal use.

Figures 5.9 through 5.12 illustrate the described installation sequence for skinned area conditioners.

5.2e Constructing the Outfield

Constructing the outfield involves procedures very similar to those described for the infield and skinned area. However, because of the distance between stakes, string lines are impractical; it is almost impossible to apply enough tension to prevent sagging. Out-

Figure 5.8. The Straight-Edge Field Leveler is a tool designed by Sportscape International for use by its crews in leveling both skinned and turf areas of athletic fields. (This tool is available for sale through the company. For more information, call 1-888-784-5586.)

Figure 5.9. The first step in installing a conditioner is to spread the material evenly over the surface of the skinned area.

Figure 5.10. Once the conditioner has been distributed evenly over the surface, it is tilled into the soil to the depth indicated by the manufacturer's directions.

Figure 5.11. After tilling, a pulverizer helps to firm up the skinned area soil.

Figure 5.12. A tractor with field leveler helps to fill in any low spots and provides a uniform surface for the conditioned skinned area.

fields require fewer grade stakes because the turf areas have less complicated contours. However, the longer distances between stakes can be very challenging, because even a small variation from the contour plan can disturb runoff and create wet spots. It is important to have an even grade from contour line to contour line, so an adequate number of grade stakes and frequent spot elevation checks are necessary to ensure an outfield that drains well.

(For these reasons, laser-guided grading equipment is ideal for outfield construction. Just be certain to supervise the grading to make sure that the contractor really is using laser-guided equipment. Some will take a few elevations using laser surveying equipment and declare that they have performed "laser grading." Real laser-guided equipment has sensors on the grader to ensure strict conformance to the grade.)

Start by setting grade stakes. If the field is designed with even contours from the skinned areas to the outfield fences, set grade stakes 50 ft to 100 ft on center throughout the outfield. If the field is crowned, set stakes on the contour lines. Then grade to the contour plan. Remember that grading equipment tends to "glaze" the surface, causing a thin layer of heavy compaction at the surface. Before seeding or sodding, this layer must be broken up using a pulverizer, followed by a power rake. Otherwise, the turfgrass may not root properly.

5.2f   Finalizing the Surface over Drains and Irrigation

Once the final grade is established, the irrigation and drainage systems specified for the turf areas should be installed. An exception is the installation of drain and irrigation lines for a sand-based field, where the subsurface lines must be installed in the subsoil before the gravel layer and growing medium (amended sand) are applied.

It is important to remember that these installed systems can affect the uniformity of the field surface. Some of the soil dug out for an irrigation system, and nearly all of the soil removed for a drainage system, will have to be carried away from the field. Because of the volume of the installed drainpipe (or irrigation lines), gravel, and sand, not all of the topsoil will fit back into the trenches. Furthermore, the trenches will go through the topsoil and into the subsoil, and so the topsoil removed from the trenches will be contaminated with subsoil, which may contain rocks and clay and is not as well suited to supporting the growth of turfgrass. Any of this soil that is not needed to backfill the trenches should be hauled away—not spread over the surface of the field.

A common mistake is to backfill the trenches slightly higher than the level of the field, trying to guess how much settling will occur. This almost never works. Let the soil settle naturally, then use more topsoil to level the surface above a trench. If the field is to be used before a full natural settling can be counted on, a good practice is to "water soak" the trenches to speed up the settling process. When water soaking is used, the trenches are not backfilled all the way to the surface, leaving the soil 1 in. to 2 in. below the final grade. Then the trenches are filled with water using a hose; sometimes the end of the hose is shoved into the soil every foot or so to encourage the penetration of water throughout the backfilled material.

As soon as the water has soaked in completely, place more soil in the settled trenches, filling them all the way to the surface. Then water soak again (this time, soaking only the new soil you have applied) and fill to the surface one more time. It is important to check the surface over the trenches after the first heavy rainfall (of 2 in. to 3 in. or more), to make sure the surface is uniform. If necessary, make a final application of soil to level the surface.

When backfilling a sand-filled trench drain, tamp the sand as you are filling the trench; then, after the first heavy rain, refill to the surface and seed or sprig.

5.2g Installing Turfgrass

After the final grading of the playing surface and the installation of the irrigation and drainage systems, it's time to install the turfgrass. A variety of methods are used for this process, the most common of which are seeding, sprigging, and sodding.

Preparation for Planting

It is always wise to test soil fertility and pH prior to planting. Soil testing is an inexpensive procedure offered by universities and by private testing labs. (Soil testing is discussed in detail in Chapter 8, Section 8.3.) Of particular importance for turfgrass establishment is the data on soil pH and on the levels of phosphorus (P) and potassium (K) in the soil. Turfgrasses perform best when the soil pH is slightly acid (6.0 to 6.5), and new plantings need adequate levels of P and K to aid in initial root and shoot development. If the soil test reveals any limiting factors, particularly in soil pH, the best time to correct them is prior to planting the turfgrass.

For soils lacking in P and K, a good practice is to apply an agricultural-grade fertilizer such as 6-24-24 at 10 lb per 1000 sq ft, tilling the fertilizer into the soil to a depth of 4 in. to 6 in. The grade is then finalized with an implement such as a power rake or with a pulverizer and hand rakes. At the time of planting, apply a starter fertilizer such as 18-24-12 at 5 lb per 1000 sq ft, leaving the fertilizer on the surface while seeding, sprigging, and sodding are performed.

In preparing to install turfgrass, it is wise to keep all construction equipment off the field whenever it is wet or damp. Avoid the use of heavy road-building-type equipment that compacts the soil so much it can inhibit the growth of roots later and can also cause water to run off instead of penetrating to the roots of the turfgrass, where it needs to be. Moreover, this heavy equipment can reduce pore space, cutting off the flow of oxygen to the roots, promoting disease, and causing a very slow recuperative potential that requires extra aerating to correct.

One of the greatest concerns in any new establishment is weed control, particularly the control of very aggressive summer weeds such as crabgrass and goosegrass. When seeding cool season turfgrasses, be aware that there is currently only one herbicide labeled for application at the time of establishment: siduron (Tupersan). This product is a preemergent (PRE) herbicide for crabgrass control in spring establishments and has virtually no activity on winter annual weeds (particularly annual bluegrass). There are no labeled herbicides for similar use on seeded bermudagrasses.

For vegetative establishments of sprigging or sodding there are more choices in PRE herbicides, with some considerations. In sodding a turf, the sod itself will serve as a very effective weed control barrier by covering the soil, so the time and expense of using a PRE herbicide prior to sodding may be eliminated without a large loss in turf quality. However, when sprigging is performed (described in a following section), there is a significant opportunity for weeds to germinate, so a PRE herbicide such as oxadiazon may be recommended because it has no growth-suppressive activity on the sprigged bermudagrass. Other PRE herbicides such as pendimethalin, dithiopyr, prodiamine, and oryzalin have labeled uses for sprigging establishments, but they can adversely affect the rooting of the bermudagrass sprigs. Follow all label directions very closely when considering herbicides for this purpose. (For more discussion on weed control, see Chapter 8, Section 8.4f, in this book or the relevant material presented in the authors' *Sports Fields: Design, Construction, and Maintenance,* Ann Arbor Press, 1999.)

Seeding

Seeding a field can be performed either conventionally or by "hydro-seeding," which is a process of spraying a mixture of water, seed, fertilizer, and mulch over the surface.

Hydro-seeding should be performed by an experienced contractor, but conventional seeding can be done with commonly available equipment.

When performing conventional seeding, use a rotary (centrifugal) or drop spreader to apply the seed evenly at the rates listed in Table 5.1. A rotary spreader works well if there is little wind blowing, but a drop spreader can be used almost any time with little regard for wind. Drop spreaders are preferred for seeding along defined edges like those of the infield and foul territory and around the outfield arc, because they apply the seed with greater accuracy. To ensure the appropriate lines and arcs, be certain that string lines are in place and arcs are painted on the surface.

When seeding with rotary spreaders, be sure to overlap the area of spread at least 25% (e.g., a 12 ft spread means the operator should overlap 3 ft). With drop spreaders, the operator must be careful to overlap wheel tracks in order to avoid gaps in the turf. To ensure full coverage, it is a good idea to apply half the seed in one direction, then apply the other half in a perpendicular direction. Just calibrate the spreader for half the rate listed and go over the area twice.

Once the seed has been applied, gently rake or lightly drag the seed into the top of the soil, then roll lightly to improve seed-to-soil contact. Mulching with straw or a commercial turfgrass mulch allows faster germination. (Wetting the mulch helps prevent displacement by wind.)

On warm season fields, the ideal time to seed is from mid-spring to mid-summer, when soil temperatures at a 4 in. depth reach 65°F. Seeding can also be performed in mid-to-late summer if good irrigation is available. However, it is important to remember that the later the seeding is performed, the lower the chances of achieving the desired coverage and turf density, and the greater the risk of turf loss due to cold temperature injury.

Seeding in the cool season zone can be done just about any time the soil can be worked, because the northern grasses will germinate and become established in a wider range of temperatures. The best time, however, is from mid-August to mid-September, because the soil temperatures at that time of year are optimum for seed germination and there is a longer establishment period before the turf encounters its most serious winter stresses. In addition,

Table 5.1. Planting Times and Rates for Sports Turf Species

Seeding		
Type of Grass	Planting Time	lb/1000
Kentucky Bluegrass	Apr. 15–Sept. 15	2–3
Perennial Ryegrass	Apr. 15–Sept. 30	7–10
50% Ky Bluegrass 50% P Ryegrass	Apr. 15–Sept. 15	4–6
Creeping Bentgrass	Apr. 15–Sept. 15	1–1½
Tall Fescue	Mar. 15–Sept. 15	7–10
Bermudagrass (hulled seed)	Apr. 15–Aug. 15	1–1½
Bermudagrass (unhulled seed)	Apr. 15–Aug. 15	2–3
Sprigging		
Type of Grass	Planting Time	Sprigs/sq ft
Bermudagrass	Apr. 15–Aug. 15	20–25
Sodding		
Type of Grass	Planting Time	
All	Above Freezing Temperatures	

there is more competition from the very aggressive annual grassy weeds such as crabgrass in the spring, and summer planting requires more water. Although seeding is sometimes performed in October, this is a risky practice. To achieve good establishment before the onset of freezing temperatures, the plants should progress to the three-leaf stage of development. If October and November are unusually warm, this development can take place. If not, the plants will still be seedlings when cold weather hits, and the winterkill can be especially destructive.

In the Transitional Zone, seeding times should be determined according to the type of turfgrass being seeded. If warm season grasses like bermudagrass are being seeded, they should be seeded during the typical southern turfgrass planting season (although the seeding season can begin somewhat later and end a little sooner). If northern turfgrasses like Kentucky bluegrass or perennial ryegrass are chosen, they can be planted according to the cool season timetable. For turf-type tall fescue, sometimes used in the Transitional Zone, seeding can begin as early as March 15.

Sprigging

An alternative method of turfgrass installation, and one that is fairly common in the South, is sprigging. This is referred to as a form of "vegetative" planting, because it uses live plant material to establish the turfgrass. A sprig is a plant stem that includes multiple growing points that will establish roots, shoots, and leaves, and develop into a mature plant when properly planted. (See Figure 5.13.)

Sprigging rates are often specified in terms of "bushels" of sprigs per unit area, but there is some confusion about the actual number of sprigs in a bushel. It is better to specify the desired planting rate of sprigs per square foot. Most commercial sprig planters con-

Figure 5.13. Bermudagrass sprigs, such as this one, can be successfully planted in prepared soil.

sider 10 to 20 sprigs per square foot to be a "low" rate, 20 to 30 sprigs per square foot to be "medium," and more than 30 sprigs per square foot to be "high." When specifying rates in terms of bushels per acre, 200 to 400 bushels is considered a "low" rate, 400 to 600 bushels is described as "medium," and more than 600 bushels is considered "high." Of course, the main advantage of higher sprigging rates is quicker establishment.

The sprigs are distributed over the soil surface and pressed into the soil by a machine called a "sprigger." Some devices, called "row planters," actually create furrows into which the sprigs of grass are placed and then covered with soil by a roller. (See Figure 5.14.) In both cases, maximum sprig:soil contact results in the best establishment. If a sprigging machine or a row planter is unavailable, you can perform sprigging by simply spreading the sprigs over the prepared soil and then topdressing with ¼ in. to ½ in. of matching soil material. If you simply spread the sprigs and topdress, you should expect more loss of plant material because sprig:soil contact will be reduced. For this reason, planting rates are usually increased in using this method. However, spreading, topdressing, and irrigating to keep the sprigs and soil moist will generally result in an acceptable stand of turfgrass.

You should expect the sprigs to lose most of their green color following any of these planting techniques. It is normal for most of the existing leaves to die and be replaced by new ones during the establishment period. Experience shows that planted sprigs look their worst just before they begin their first growth surge.

Sprigging can be performed whenever soil temperatures reach 65°F. In the South, this typically occurs between April 15 and August 15, but the best results are obtained with plantings between May 15 and July 15. Planting later in the summer increases the risk of winterkill.

Figure 5.14. A sprigging machine, also called a "row planter," creates furrows, distributes sprigs, and covers them with soil to maximize sprig:soil contact.

Sodding

Sod is supplied in several forms: square-cut sod comes in rectangular pieces; rolled sod is delivered in 18 in. × 6 ft rolled sections. Both of these forms are meant to be installed by hand. Big roll sod is supplied in rolls 24 in. or more wide and up to 40 ft long and must be installed using a machine. (See Figure 5.15.)

An important practice in installing any form of sod is to keep the seams tight. A common mistake is to position the sod by pulling on it. That stretches the sod, which will eventually shrink back to its original size, causing gaps between the pieces. After laying the sod, be sure to water it liberally for the first two weeks, because letting the sod dry out too much contributes to shrinkage. A week or so after installation, inspect the sod for gaps (even with well-installed sod, there are usually a few). Fill the gaps with matching soil and hand seed or sprig with matching turfgrass. Rolling the new sod with a garden-type roller just after installation, and again after the plants are rooted, can also help to improve surface smoothness. (Avoid using heavy road-building-type rollers, which can overcompact the soil and separate the seams.)

Some sod installation is performed by a process called "dormant sodding"—the installation of turf when the plants are in a dormant phase. Although installing turf during the growing season is preferred, it is possible to achieve successful dormant sodding. If this method is used, it is important to avoid a common mistake: failing to water adequately. Even dormant sod needs water to root and establish; dormant sodding requires less water than sodding during the summer, but failure to water at all can desiccate the sod.

Sodding in warm season areas can be done almost any time of year, as long as temperatures are not expected to dip substantially below freezing for the first few days after the

Figure 5.15. Big roll sod must be installed using a machine to maneuver the heavy rolls as the sod is put in place. (Photo courtesy of Don Uber, Sportscape of Texas, Inc.)

sod is laid, and as long as adequate rainfall or irrigation is available. The window for successful sodding in the North extends from mid-April to mid-November.

5.2h Postplanting (Grow-in) Strategies

There are a number of important steps that can be used after planting to ensure the best possible establishment of a new turfgrass. These steps form a transition between the planting process and the routine maintenance practices that will be used once the turfgrass is fully established.

Irrigation

Careful attention to irrigation is required during the grow-in period, whether the new turf is being established by sodding, seeding, or sprigging. Water new sod liberally (soaked) immediately upon installation and make sure it is kept wet for two weeks. Then irrigate as you would any established turf. After either seeding or sprigging, irrigate "lightly and frequently" to minimize seed or sprig desiccation and to avoid washing the seed or plant material off the site. (Keep the top ¼ in. of soil moist, but do not irrigate to the point that water is standing on the surface.) As the turf establishes, reduce the frequency of irrigation and increase the amount of water that is being applied at one time.

Mowing

Avoid mowing new sod during the establishment period, when it is being kept wet at all times. (Mowing at this time will cause permanent ruts and gaps in the sod.) After the sod has firmed up and is rooted, begin mowing according to the "one-third rule," cutting off no more than one-third of the plant at a time until the desired height is reached. For seeded or sprigged turf, begin mowing whenever the plant reaches 150% of the height at which you intend to maintain it. (As with new sod, make sure the soil is firm enough to be mowed without rutting.) When mowing new grass, it is especially important to keep the mower blades sharp to avoid stressing the plants.

Fertilization

If preplanting fertilization has been performed as described in Section 5.2g, apply 1 lb nitrogen (N) per 1000 sq ft at one-month intervals for the first four months for cool season turfgrass. About twice that much can be applied to warm season turfgrasses for quicker establishment. If the preplanting regimen was not followed, you will have to supply both P and K at the same time.

Weed Control

If no PRE herbicide was used in preparation for planting (and in many cases it simply is not appropriate at that time), then weeds will appear in your stand. Postemergent applications should be delayed until the turf is well established (we recommend two to three months) to avoid damage to the turf.

5.2i Installing Bases

It is critically important to follow all manufacturers' instructions when installing bases. For a base designed to be anchored into a concrete square that remains in the ground when the base is removed, it is a good idea to make a wooden form and pour the concrete at a shop or other location, and then carry this square to the base location and install it so that the top of the anchor is slightly below the surface (about 1 in.) of the skinned area. Alternately, you can use half of a standard cement block, with the anchor cemented into the opening in the block. In making either kind of anchor block, allow the metal base anchor to project 2 in. above the anchor block, to ensure that the block will be buried safely under the surface.

We do not recommend pouring the concrete directly into a hole dug in the skinned area because of the difficulty in maintaining the correct dimensions and elevation. We recommend using a square, rather than a round form, because a round form may rotate in place, causing the bases to be misaligned. Another bad practice is using a coffee can as the form and placing the can filled with concrete into the soil; the rusting coffee can itself can become a safety hazard to players and maintenance personnel. (See Figures 5.16 and 5.17 for examples of the recommended types of concrete forms.)

When installing bases, it is necessary to have string lines in place along the foul lines. It is important to remember that the stated distances to first and third base are measured from the white point of home plate to the back (farthest) edge of the base itself. That means you need to have a base with you to measure correctly. Set the outside edge of the base on the foul line, and measure to the back edge. The distances from first and third to second are measured from the foul line to the center of second base. The edges of second base are to be set parallel to the edges of first and third.

5.2j Installing a Granular Warning Track

The section of Chapter 1 on the design of warning tracks mentioned that these portions of the field are usually of either granular material or all-weather construction, similar to running tracks. When all-weather construction is used, the process should be referred to professionals experienced in this kind of work. In this section, the discussion is limited to the installation of granular warning tracks.

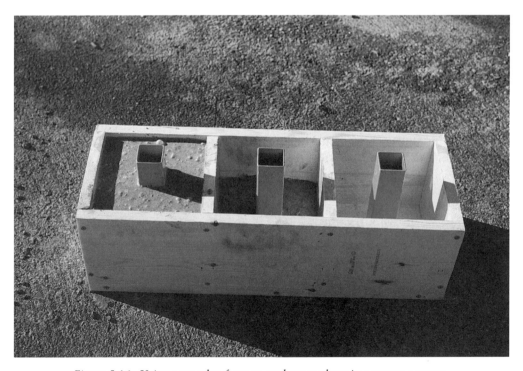

Figure 5.16. Using a wooden form to set base anchors in concrete squares.

Figure 5.17. Concrete block halves can also be used as "forms" for setting base anchors. This method uses less concrete.

To help establish the correct grade for the entire field, we recommend installing the warning track after construction of the rest of the field. Because topsoil should not be placed under the warning track material, remove all topsoil down to the subbase and replace it with subsoil up to the appropriate depth. Then install the warning track material and level it, with a leveling bar or a similar tractor attachment, to the same level as the turf. (Remember to allow for settling, about ½ in. for a 4 in. deep track.) Finally, roll the area with a standard garden roller to firm up the surface.

If a warning track is being installed on an existing field, lay out the area with paint lines and use a sod cutter to establish the edge of the warning track. Excavate the area to the desired depth. Then edge the grass area next to the warning track by hand, install the warning track material, level, and roll. (See Figures 5.18 and 5.19.)

5.3   RECONSTRUCTION

It is probably fair to say that at any given time, there is almost as much baseball or softball field reconstruction work as new construction going on. The principles to be observed in reconstructing an existing field are quite similar to those for new construction. However, because there are some considerations unique to reconstruction a discussion of this process can be of value to designers and installers of ball fields.

The reader may wonder how "reconstruction" differs from "renovation," which is discussed in Part II. For our purposes, *reconstruction* is defined as the process of destroying an existing facility and rebuilding it in a substantially improved fashion. In the case of a

Figure 5.18. After sod cutting the edge, remove the topsoil in the warning track area to the desired depth.

Figure 5.19. A dump truck tailgates the material in place. Finalize the warning track by leveling and rolling.

baseball or softball diamond, that includes such changes as improving the field contours, installed drain and irrigation systems, and even the topsoil or other growing media. *Renovation* simply means restoring a field to good condition after it has been damaged by use. Renovation employs minor remediation techniques that should be performed periodically on every field.

5.3a Planning for Reconstruction

It is worth taking some time to review the design principles presented in Chapter 1 (especially the design criteria discussed in Section 1.3) before undertaking any reconstruction project. As with new construction, it is almost impossible to wind up with a good field if sound design principles are not observed.

When approaching a reconstruction project, the sports field professional is well advised to consider the diamond as a whole, even when the observed problems are limited, for instance, to the infield. Trying to design a reconstruction project without a full understanding of the dynamics of the field will typically lead to "Band-Aid" fixes that are likely to fail. The entire field (including the outfield, foul territory, and the surrounding areas) should be carefully surveyed to get a complete picture of the contours affecting the movement of water through the site. Likewise, observing the behavior of water on the surface during a heavy rain can yield important insights about the field. Without this kind of understanding of the field as a drainage unit, planning an effective reconstruction project is next to impossible.

A survey can often instantly reveal the cause of the problems observed at the facility, and suggest solutions. Figure 5.20 is an example of a worksheet that can be used to conduct an effective survey of an existing field. By taking an elevation reading at each of the indicated marks and filling in the appropriate values, the planner will collect more than 65 different elevations of the field surface—enough to gain an accurate understanding of the existing grade of the field and how it will have to be adjusted to result in a sound diamond.

Before surveying, lay out the field using string lines for the straightaways and paint lines for the arcs. Then take an elevation reading at each point indicated on the layout sheet, and mark the reading on the line provided. The new (or proposed) spot elevation can then be marked beneath each line, giving the planner a snapshot of the changes needed at each point on the field. Notice that the points are very close together in the area where the skinned area meets the outfield grass. This is frequently a problem area, because soil from the skinned area accumulates at the grass edge, causing a lip or mounded ridge and restricting runoff.

In discussing the process of constructing a new field, we said that the surveying could be performed on a grid pattern to yield a good understanding of the contours of the site. However, in surveying an existing field before reconstructing it, we recommend taking the elevations as indicated on the worksheet in Figure 5.20. Using a grid pattern will almost always lead to missing some of the critical points, such as the bases and the arc of the outfield grass.

In redesigning a skinned area, it is worthwhile to try to get water to run off toward the foul lines, as shown in Figure 5.1.

Once the planner has a clear idea of the dynamics of the diamond, planning for the reconstruction should begin with adjusting the difference in elevation between the pitcher's mound and home plate (specified as 10 in. for a regulation field, 8 in. for Pony League, 6 in. for Little League, and level for softball). The next step is to adjust the height of the bases to make them as nearly level with home plate as possible. It is important to

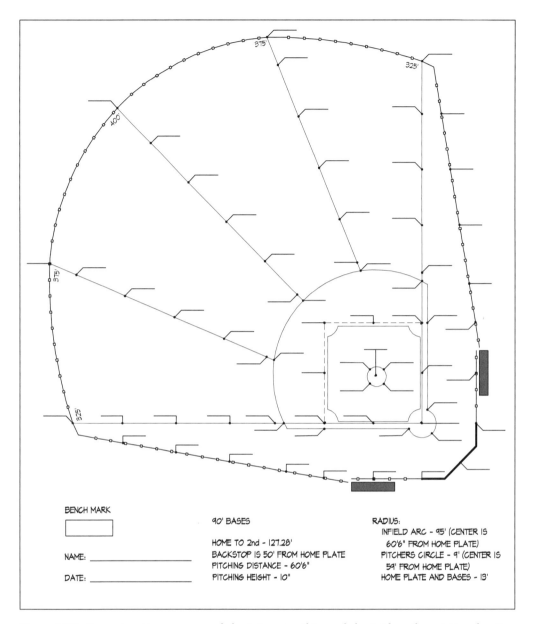

BENCH MARK

NAME: _____

DATE: _____

90' BASES

HOME TO 2nd - 127.28'
BACKSTOP IS 50' FROM HOME PLATE
PITCHING DISTANCE - 60'6"
PITCHING HEIGHT - 10"

RADIUS:
INFIELD ARC - 95' (CENTER IS
60'6" FROM HOME PLATE)
PITCHERS CIRCLE - 9' (CENTER IS
54' FROM HOME PLATE)
HOME PLATE AND BASES - 13'

Figure 5.20. Reconstruction survey worksheet. In using this worksheet, place the existing elevation on top of each line and the proposed elevation beneath.

adjust the base heights carefully, because any variation will affect the slope between the pitcher's mound and the base lines. Finally, refine and adjust the arc of the outfield grass, foul territory around the infield, and the outfield itself (when necessary).

There is a special challenge in planning for reconstruction of a field that was originally designed incorrectly, as when the entire infield is sloped to conduct surface water toward one foul line. In these circumstances, making the bases level will create a field with an uneven slope and may result in wet spots. When reconstructing a field with such irregular contours, try to make the base lines as flat as possible without restricting positive surface runoff.

Correcting field problems may require solutions that, at first blush, seem excessive, but it is important not to take shortcuts. We have completed reconstruction projects that began with the addition of 2 ft of soil on the infield to allow for the required positive surface drainage and to prevent outfield and sideline water from crossing into the skinned area and infield.

The planner will sometimes face questions about the need for such substantial reconstruction of a field, and about the wisdom of the associated expenditures. If you have a problem field that may need reconstruction at some point, it is wise to keep accurate maintenance records, as well as records of rainouts, makeup games, and the related inconvenience and expense. These records will help to bolster the case for a major reconstruction instead of a few small fixes.

Figures 5.21 and 5.22 show the dramatic difference in playability that can result from a well-planned reconstruction project.

5.3b Performing Reconstruction

For the most part, the processes involved in reconstructing a field are the same as those used in new construction, and we will not reiterate those processes here. Instead, we will look at the steps that are unique to reconstruction.

Figure 5.21. A high school field before reconstruction. This Eastern Ohio field drained so poorly that it had been all but abandoned within a few years after construction.

Figure 5.22. The same field (Figure 5.21) after reconstruction. After the field was reconstructed, raising the infield 2 ft to allow for positive surface drainage, the field won a national 1995 Baseball Field of the Year Award and has been consistently playable ever since. (Photo by David Grantonic.)

The first major difference between construction and reconstruction is that reconstruction projects usually include the removal of existing turf in the areas to be reconstructed. The existing sod is typically removed with the use of sod cutters and tillers. (For any substantial area, you'll want to use a tractor-driven tiller.) Haul away the old sod and loosen the soil. If you will be cutting (lowering the grade), loosen the soil down to the desired new grade. Then make the necessary cuts, remove the excess topsoil, and loosen the surface once again to a depth of 6 in. before seeding or installing sod.

A complication in making cuts is that they may leave an uneven layer of topsoil, which can affect rooting and drainage. It may be necessary to remove all the topsoil from the area being reconstructed, then cut some of the subsoil before replacing the topsoil on the site. To help in the planning process, use a shovel to check the relative depth of the topsoil at several points around the area.

If you will be filling (raising the grade), you should still loosen the soil before adding new material, to prevent the creation of a layering effect that may restrict rooting and drainage. It is a good idea to use matching soil when filling, which also helps to avoid the layering effect. Remember that any new soil added to the field will settle about 1 in. for every 6 in. added. (See Figures 5.23 and 5.24.)

When adding skinned area soil during the reconstruction process, it may be tempting to simply spread the new material on top of the old. However, it is important to loosen the existing soil (by tilling or scarifying) before installing the new material, because new skinned area soil will not adhere to the old soil. This is true even when cutting soil from one part of the skinned area and moving it to another part. Loosening the existing

Figure 5.23. Cutting for positive surface drainage. This field had such a pronounced mounded ridge that the skinned area would not drain. Soil had been added in an unsuccessful effort to improve drainage. To the right of the dozer is extra soil being removed to establish proper contours.

Figure 5.24. On the same field (Figure 5.23), sod had to be removed from the infield so topsoil could be added to establish positive surface drainage.

surface is the only way to ensure a dependable, uniform surface on the reconstructed skinned area.

(This is also a good opportunity to add conditioners to the skinned area soil. Just be careful to check the depth of the skinned area soil before tilling in the conditioners, because areas that have been cut may now have a shallower layer. It is important to avoid tilling past the skinned area soil and bringing up stones and subsoil from beneath.)

PART II

Renovation and Maintenance

Although the processes of designing, constructing, and reconstructing a field may be contracted to a firm that specializes in this kind of work, renovation and maintenance are usually performed by a local staff under the supervision of the person responsible for managing the field. Part II considers some of the important principles to be observed in managing this work.

At this point, a review of the definitions of renovation and reconstruction may be helpful. For purposes of this discussion, *reconstruction* is defined as tearing down (or tearing up) an existing facility and rebuilding it in a substantially improved fashion. That includes improving field contours, installing drain and irrigation systems, and even upgrading topsoil or other growing media. Reconstruction always includes either cutting some of the existing grade or filling with new material.

Renovation, on the other hand, is defined as restoring a facility to sound condition after it has been damaged by use. For our purposes, renovation includes using minor remediation techniques that should be performed annually, or at least every two to three years. Some fields never need reconstruction, but every field needs periodic renovation.

Chapter 6

Renovation

6.1   INTRODUCTION

As defined in the introduction to Part II, renovation is the process of restoring a field to its original condition. Although renovation typically does not require substantial removal of turf or major changes to the grade, it still should be deferred until after the playing season is over. The reason is that the renovation process requires a two- to four-week period after the work is completed to let the field settle back into playable condition. In planning for renovation, it is important to consider the delays that can be caused by weather. If a process is begun before the season and heavy rains delay completion, the field may not be playable when the season starts.

Because the steps required to renovate skinned areas differ from those used for a granular warning track or turfgrass areas, these areas are considered separately. We begin with skinned areas, which are the areas with the most frequent (and critical) need for renovation.

Over years of performing regular renovation on a variety of baseball and softball diamonds, we have developed a sequence of steps that provide a logical progression. In this chapter, we follow these steps for each of the three major portions of the field: the skinned area, the turfgrass areas, and the warning track. Obviously, the renovation process can follow a different sequence, but the steps described here constitute a workable process in most cases.

6.2   SKINNED AREA RENOVATION

In reviewing the processes involved in renovation of skinned areas, we address two similar but distinct situations. "Minor renovation," as used here, refers to the set of procedures that are followed for a skinned area that has been renovated within the last year or two. "Major renovation" refers to the more involved work that must be performed on a field that has not been renovated for three years or more. Figure 6.1 is an example of a field that needs major renovation. If the field had been renovated yearly, minor renovation techniques would have solved the problem of standing water on the skinned area, and this unplayable condition would have been avoided altogether.

In performing either a major or a minor renovation project, a good time to add skinned area soil conditioners is after the grade has been reestablished, as described in the following paragraphs. The sequence of steps for installing a conditioner is described in Chapter 5 (Section 5.2d and Figures 5.9 to 5.12).

6.2a   Minor Renovation

For a minor renovation of the skinned area, begin by installing string lines from the white point of home plate to the outside edge of each foul pole. Then measure the distances from home to first and third bases to verify that the bases are still in the correct places. (In some

Figure 6.1. The standing water on this field is caused by a failure to perform necessary renovation steps between seasons. In many cases, removing built-up mounded ridges will allow positive surface drainage and dry up problem areas like this one.

cases, competition and replacement of the bases will have moved the bases.) Mark the correct measurements on the foul lines with 8 in. to 10 in. nails. Then measure from first and third to second base to verify the correct location for second. If second is in the correct position, a nail should be placed in the center of the base, so you may need to improvise a way to anchor the string lines at second. For instance, you might place two nails a foot or so past second base, so that the lines from first and third actually cross at the center of second.

Figure 6.2. A tape is stretched from the white point of home plate to second base to make sure the two foul lines intersect at a 90° angle. The square of the distance from home to first base plus the square of the distance from first to second should equal the square of the distance from home to second (by the Pythagorean theorem, $A^2 + B^2 = C^2$).

Finally, stretch a measuring tape from the white point of home plate to second base, to verify that the diamond is square. (See Figure 6.2.) Use the Pythagorean theorem $(A^2 + B^2 = C^2)$ to perform this calculation. Square the distance from the white point of home to the nail at first base and the distance from the nail at first base to the correct location of second base, and add these two values. Then compare that sum with the square of the distance from home to second base. You should arrive at two numbers that are exactly the same (or at least within 2 to 3 in.). If you do not, recheck the measurements and recalculate. (If you don't want to do the math, see the correct values for standard field sizes included in Chapter 11 of this book.)

If the distance from home to second is not correct, then home plate is out of place. Remove the plate and move it along the axis to second base until the distances are correct. If the distance is too long, move home toward second; if the distance is too short, move home away from second. Then reinstall home and start over by resetting the string lines to the foul poles and repeating the sequence.

With the tape in place from the point of home to second base, check the distance from home plate to the pitcher's plate. Install a nail at the correct distance from home. (Again, see Chapter 11.) If the pitcher's plate is in the right place, the nail would be placed against the front edge of the plate. If necessary, remove and reinstall the pitcher's plate at the correct distance from home, and in such a position that the tape passes through the middle. Install a second nail 18 in. in front of the center of the pitcher's plate, to be used in measuring the circle around the mound itself.

Now put the "0" end of the measuring tape on the nail at the pitcher's plate (or at the specified point, as indicated in Chapter 11) and measure the correct distance to the arc of the outfield grass. Use a paint gun and turf marking paint to mark the correct arc.

It is helpful to wrap the tape around the marking gun and have one person maintain the tension on the tape while another person operates the gun. (See Figure 6.3.) Before painting the arc, walk the arc with the tape stretched, checking for any uneven footing that may reveal the presence of a mounded lip that has been created by the intrusion of skinned area soil into the edge of the turf. If you can feel the presence of a lip, measure past the lip and paint the arc where the surface is level.

Figure 6.3. Painting the outfield arc, with a tape stretched from the radius point. The tape has been wrapped around the marking gun, and a helper (foreground) *maintains tension while the arc is painted.*

If you are renovating a field with a grass infield, the next step is to mark the correct edges of the grass infield. If you are renovating a field without a grass infield, you can skip the next three paragraphs.

Start with the arcs at the bases by placing a measure tape on the nail at the base, stretching the tape to the recommended distance (See Chapter 11), plus a few inches to clear any mounded lips you discover. Paint the arcs a foot or two past the straightaways to make it easier to mark the straight edges later. Following the same procedure, paint circles at the pitcher's mound (on a baseball field) and home plate. The center of the circle at the pitcher's mound is usually 1½ ft in front of the plate. This nail should have been installed when you had the tape measure stretched to check the distance between home and second.

With the arcs painted, the next step is to set up string lines along the straight edges of the infield grass. Measure on either side of the foul lines, and install string lines to mark the desired edges of the base path. The rule books for a regulation baseball field call for the base path to be 6 ft wide, with the foul line running right down the middle, but many fields have the grass coming closer to the foul line on the infield side. A more common way to establish the base paths during renovation is to measure the greatest distance from the foul line to the infield grass edge, including lips, and to install the string line at this distance (from the foul line) all the way from the circle at home to the arcs at first and third. Then follow the same procedure to set up string lines between first and second and between second and third. With the string lines in place, use a marking gun to paint the straight edges of the infield grass (as shown in Figure 6.4) and the outside of the first and third base lines. (Remember to check for mounded lips all the way around the infield as you paint the lines on the field.)

Figure 6.4. Painting the straight edge on the infield side of third base line with string lines in place to straighten the grass line. (Note that on this field, the left field foul pole was found to be in the wrong place; the string line on the left shows that it needed to be moved about 3½ ft.)

Figure 6.5. Using a bed edger to remove small lips (2 in. to 3 in. wide).

You now have the entire infield and skinned area painted on the diamond.

The next step is to edge along all painted lines. Remove the mounded lip, using a standard landscaping bed edger (See Figure 6.5.) where the lips are 2 in. to 3 in. wide. If the lips or mounded ridges are more than 2 in. to 3 in. wide, use a sod cutter (See Figure 6.6.) or, for spot fixes, a shovel. If this requires you to remove a foot or more past the desired

Figure 6.6. Using a sod cutter to remove the mounded ridge and straighten the edge along the third base line.

distance, you will have to remove the mounded ridge and seed or sod. (This situation borders on major renovation, discussed in the next section.)

With the painted lines edged, it's time to regrade the skinned area. If grass and/or weeds have established themselves on the skinned area, use a sod cutter and hand rake to remove these plants. (See Figure 6.7.) Then break up the soil, using an implement that is more aggressive than a nail drag. The best implement for this purpose is a tractor-mounted pulverizer. (See Figure 6.8.) A Power take-off (PTO)-drive vibrating solid-tine aerator also works well and has the additional advantage that it is narrow enough to break up the soil at the base paths without tearing up the turf. (See Figure 6.9.) If you buy or rent a pulverizer (a good investment for field renovation), we recommend that you choose a model no more than 6 ft wide, to allow you to renovate standard-width 6 ft base paths without damaging the turf. Place a flag at each base and at the plates to avoid disturbing or destroying the base pegs and to avoid hitting home plate and the pitcher's plate.

With the soil broken up, relevel the large areas using a field leveler (such as the Straight-Edge Field Leveler shown in Figure 5.8). Use hand rakes to level the base paths, the areas around the bases, the edges next to any grass, and the circle around home plate. (For a softball field, also rake around the pitcher's plate.) Roll the leveled areas with a standard garden roller. (See Figure 6.10.)

The final step in a minor renovation of a baseball diamond is to reestablish the shape of the pitcher's mound, as described in Section 5.2c. Use a homemade tool such as the one

Figure 6.7. Removing weeds from the skinned area by sod cutting. The loose weeds at left will be hand raked for disposal.

Figure 6.8. A pulverizer breaks up the skinned area soil to get it ready for leveling.

Figure 6.9. A solid-tine aerator can be used on base paths to loosen the soil without disturbing the grass edge.

Figure 6.10. After leveling is complete, roll the skinned area with a standard garden roller to firm up the soil.

shown in Figure 5.6 to reset the slope from the pitcher's plate to the forward (home plate) side of the mound.

6.2b Major Renovation

A major renovation is usually performed on a field that has not been renovated in a number of years. However, sloppy maintenance practices can sometimes create the need for major renovation every year. For example, such renovation may be necessary when incorrect dragging procedures pull skinned area soil into the grass edge, where it prevents proper surface drainage. (See Figure 6.11.)

The primary difference between minor and major renovation is the width of the mounded ridges that must be removed. In some cases, these ridges may be 4 ft to 5 ft wide.

The human eye will be sufficient to determine how far into the grass these ridges extend. Use a marking gun to paint all the way around these areas, being sure to include the entire ridge. Then use a sod cutter to remove the entire marked area of turfgrass. If the soil is not loose enough for easy removal, use a tiller to go over the area where the turf has been removed, loosening the soil to the depth of the cut. With a front-loader, bulldozer, or box scraper, remove the excess soil and haul it away from the site. Then pulverize the area where the mounded ridge has been removed, along with the rest of the skinned area. Use a field leveler to reestablish the correct grade.

Now place all the string lines and paint the arcs and edges as described in the previous section on minor renovation. Resod the areas where the original sod has been removed, back to the correct edges that have been painted on the field. Figures 6.12 to 6.14 show the sequence for lip removal and sodding.

These areas may be seeded rather than sodded, using a different sequence of steps.

Figure 6.11. Standing water on the skinned area due to the buildup of skin soil in the grass edge. (Photo courtesy of Ron Nagy, Sportscape of Michigan.)

Once the presence of the mounded ridge has been established, use a power rake to remove the ridge and reestablish the proper contours. Hand rake all debris and dispose of it. Then paint the proper arc for the outfield grass and seed the area on the outside of the painted line. (Figures 6.15 to 6.17 demonstrate the steps needed to prepare for seeding.) It should be noted that seeding will have to be performed by mid-summer in the South and by late summer in the North if the turfgrass is to be ready for the next season.

Before performing a major renovation, it is a good idea to do a topographical survey (using the worksheet shown in Figure 5.20) to verify that the grade changes you are considering will really improve the surface drainage. In most cases, it will not be necessary to add soil; but where the skinned area is dished, you may have to add soil to bring it up to the proper grade. This is the best time to add skinned area soil, because there is plenty of time for settling.

A Final Note on Skinned Area Renovation: Forget Subsurface Drains

If a muddy skinned area has been a major headache, you may consider the installation of drains. Our advice: Forget it. Installed drain systems can work like a charm on turf areas, but they typically work poorly in a skinned area. Water percolates through most skinned area soils at just $\frac{1}{100}$ in. per hour, so it doesn't reach drain structures quickly enough to make a difference. Proper positive surface drainage is the only way to prevent standing water on a skinned area.

Figure 6.12. To remove the lip at the grass edge, use a standard sod cutter.

Figure 6.13. Once the sod has been removed, lower the grade to allow for positive surface drainage.

Figure 6.14. When the correct grade is established, the turf is replaced by sodding. (Photo courtesy of Ron Nagy, Sportscape of Michigan.)

Figure 6.15. The mounded ridge is easily seen by laying a rod across the edge of the outfield turf. Note that the rod does not lie flat.

Figure 6.16. Using a power rake, the lip is removed. Make one pass, check the area again with the rod, and make a second pass if necessary.

Figure 6.17. When the rod lies flat, paint the outfield arc, rake up any debris, and seed outside the paint line.

6.3   TURFGRASS RENOVATION

The purpose of renovating a stand of turfgrass is to achieve a thicker, smoother, and more uniform playing surface. The renovation of turfgrass includes a number of processes, with aerating, topdressing, and leveling the most commonly practiced. To fill in bare spots and thicken the turf, additional grass is often planted using a variety of methods that differ from one region of the country to another. In this discussion of turfgrass renovation, major and minor projects are not differentiated. There is, however, wide variation in the type and complexity of the work involved. A field that is renovated annually and maintained carefully may need relatively little renovation, whereas a problem field may require extensive work, including the addition of spot drainage solutions.

In any part of the country, turfgrass renovation on a baseball or softball field should be performed during the normal growing season of the grass. The turfgrass needs time to recover from the stresses of renovation, and any new grass seeded, sprigged, or sodded into the area must be able to establish itself before the onset of the winter. We first discuss aeration and topdressing and spot drainage improvements, then consider some of the specific turfgrass renovation steps performed on warm season and cool season turf.

Aeration and Topdressing

Aeration and topdressing are included in the sections of this book dealing with both turfgrass renovation and turfgrass maintenance, because these processes are widely used as a part of both disciplines.

The first step in turfgrass renovation is aeration (disturbing the soil to relieve compaction and allow air, water, and nutrients to reach the roots), which is widely practiced using several different types of equipment. Core (or "hollow-tine") aeration removes a core of turf and soil, leaving a vertical channel through the turfgrass canopy. Solid-tine aeration creates vertical channels without removing a core. Equipment used for solid-tine aeration often sends vibrations through the tines to fracture the soil without disturbing the existing turfgrass, as shown in Figure 6.18. (This feature is especially useful during a renovation process.) Generally, core aeration is preferred where the soil is fairly moist, whereas solid-tine aeration works best on dry soils.

A newer type of aerating equipment uses high-pressure jets of water to create vertical channels, and sometimes to inject solid materials like sand or other amendments that improve the soil texture. (See Figure 6.19.)

In the renovation of turfgrass, aeration is usually performed in combination with topdressing and/or slit-seeding. Topdressing is the process of adding a thin layer of soil or sand to the surface. It is typically performed to smooth the surface, because the topdressing material fills in holes and low spots. To effectively level the surface, a ⅜ in. layer of material should be spread over the surface, using one of a variety of types of equipment manufactured for the purpose. In planning for topdressing, have enough material on hand to spread 1.5 cu yd for each 1000 sq ft of turfgrass surface. After the topdressing material has been applied, a field leveler, such as that shown in Figure 6.20, is used to make sure that it fills the holes and low spots. The process also helps to control thatch by intermingling topdressing material (with its population of microbes) into the thatch layer.

Spot Drainage Improvements

Just as aeration and topdressing constitute an overlap of renovation and maintenance, drainage improvements represent a kind of "gray area" between reconstruction and renovation. However, to maintain consistency with the distinction between reconstruction

Figure 6.18. This solid-tine aerator works well in renovating turfgrass. It will loosen bare spots to prepare the soil for seeding without damaging the existing turf.

Figure 6.19. This machine is injecting a diatomaceous earth amendment into the soil through channels created by high-pressure water jets.

Figure 6.20. The Straight-Edge Field Leveler, shown in Chapter 5 as a tool for use on skinned areas, can also be used to level sports turf.

(which involves cutting and filling to change grade) and renovation (which does not), spot drainage improvement is included here. It should be noted that the term *spot drainage* may refer to a fairly large area of a field, as well as to a smaller wet section. For the purposes of this discussion of renovation, *spot drainage* refers to a defined area where problems have been observed, as opposed to the entire turfgrass area of a baseball or softball diamond. (If it is determined that the field needs a complete installed drainage system, see Chapter 2, Section 2.3 for information on the design of such a whole-field system.)

The most effective technique for solving the problem of wet areas on turfgrass is to install sand-filled trench drains. We do not recommend subsurface pipe drains for this kind of spot application, because they require trenches 8 in. to 12 in. wide—too wide to be filled with sand. Sand-filled trenches that wide would cause surface instability and result in a safety hazard. If the wider trenches are filled with soil, too little surface water reaches the pipe drain to correct the problem of a wet area on the field.

An effective type of sand-filled trench drain is based on "strip drains," which are fiber-wrapped structures, ideal for use in treating problem areas. Strip drains are about 6 in. high and 1 in. thick; you install them by digging a trench, 12 in. deep, from the problem area to a nearby catch basin. (Don't forget to check the trench to make sure it runs downhill toward a collector drain.) Place the strip drains in the middle of the trench and fill to the surface with sand. (See Figures 6.21 and 6.22.) To provide adequate drainage of wet areas, install these drains a maximum of 15 ft apart throughout the affected area.

When tying a collector drain into an existing catch basin, dig out the closest side of the catch basin to a depth of about 1 ft beneath the point at which the drain will reach the catch basin. Then score the side of the catch basin with an appropriate hammer and chisel, and break out the scored section with a sledgehammer. (Be sure to observe good safety practices in this operation, especially in regard to using eye protection.) Install the collector drainpipe into the opening, then cement around the opening at the outside of the catch

Figure 6.21. Installing strip drains in the middle of the trench. At top, a homemade tool made by nailing 1 × 4 or 1 × 6 boards on either side of a 2 × 4 helps to keep the strip drains centered in the trench so that they are completely surrounded by sand to prevent clogging with silt and clay.

Figure 6.22. Filling the trenches to the surface with sand. One member of the crew uses the homemade tool to keep the strip drain centered while the others backfill the trench with sand.

basin. (Failure to seal around the pipe with cement will allow soil to wash into the catch basin and may cause a dangerous sinkhole next to the catch basin itself.)

One 4 in. pipe can typically serve as the collector drain for about one-quarter of a regulation outfield. To drain a larger area, use multiple collector drains or a larger-diameter pipe. Remember that the trench for the collector drain will be wider than the trenches used for the sand drains, and so will cause greater surface disruption. Whenever possible, place the collector drains outside the fence.

6.3a   Renovation Steps Specific to Warm Season Turfgrass

Renovating warm season turfgrass that has been worn by competition can sometimes be accomplished simply by aerating and fertilizing the turf to allow the existing grass to fill in the thin areas. If the season's use of the field is completed by mid-August or earlier, and at least 50% coverage remains, aerate the turf and apply 1 lb nitrogen (N) per 1000 sq ft. Repeat the fertilizer application in September, and follow with ½ lb N and 1 lb to 2 lb potassium (K) in October. In most cases, this regimen will help the turf to thicken to full coverage by the next season.

If the schedule lasts beyond the middle of August, or if the turf has less than 50% coverage, additional planting will be required. The fertilization scheme described in the preceding paragraph cannot be counted on to achieve full coverage. Seeding, sprigging, and plugging can be performed until mid-August. After mid-August, only sodding can be relied upon to have the turf ready for the next season. Dormant sodding of bermudagrass can be performed, as long as the soil is not frozen when the sod is installed, and as long as irrigation is available to prevent desiccation. Whatever establishment process is used, choose bermudagrass to match the existing turf. If the existing turf is one of the dense, finer-bladed bermudagrasses that can only be vegetatively established, then you must sprig, plug, or sod the thin areas.

In establishing new turfgrass during the renovation process, follow the procedures described in Chapter 5, Section 5.2g, "Installing Turfgrass."

6.3b   Renovation Steps Specific to Cool Season Turfgrass

To renovate thin areas of sports turf in the cool season zone, seeding can be performed until mid-September. After that point in the year, only sodding can be relied upon to have the turf ready to support competition the next season. Dormant sodding of cool season turfgrass can be performed until mid-November, as long as the soil is not frozen when the sod is installed, and as long as irrigation is available to prevent desiccation. Be sure to choose seed or sod to match the existing turf, and follow the procedures described in Chapter 5, Section 5.2g, "Installing Turfgrass."

Slit-Seeding

A common process used in renovating northern turfgrasses is slit-seeding. This process opens narrow channels in the turf, into which seed can be planted. Some types of equipment make slits through the turf and into the soil, and seed is then broadcast over the surface. Other equipment includes a hopper for seed and directs it into the slits in the turfgrass canopy. Whichever type of equipment is used, it must make slits at least ¼ in. into the soil itself for effective germination to take place. (See Figures 6.23 and 6.24.)

Slit-seeding substantially improves the establishment rates of turfgrass, as the seeds are planted directly into slits in the soil. However, because the new grass can appear in visible rows, slit-seeding in two directions will result in quicker establishment. The two directions should be 45° apart; passes at 90° can be too aggressive and tear at the turf.

Figure 6.23. A walk-behind slit-seeder.

Figure 6.24. The slit-seeder creates narrow channels in the soil. Seed can fall into the channels,
improving seed:soil contact and enhancing germination.

On northern fields, if there is at least 75% turf cover and a good stand of grass, seed 100% Kentucky bluegrass at 2 lb per 1000 sq ft. If the coverage is less than 75%, it is necessary to use a mixture of 2 lb of Kentucky bluegrass to 5 lb of perennial ryegrass. (The perennial ryegrass establishes itself faster than Kentucky bluegrass, so the field is better prepared for the following season.) Completely bare areas should get an additional 5 lb of perennial ryegrass per 1000 sq ft.

6.3c   Renovation Steps Specific to the Transitional Zone

For the most part, renovation practices in the Transitional Zone are determined by the type of turfgrass on the field. Use appropriate cool season renovation techniques for fields using cool season species such as Kentucky bluegrass and perennial ryegrass, and use warm season practices for bermudagrass.

There is, however, a species of turfgrass commonly used for sports fields in the Transitional Zone, but hardly ever used in the cool season or warm season zones: turf-type tall fescue. The principles for renovating tall fescue are basically the same as those used for cool season Kentucky bluegrass and perennial ryegrass. In filling in thin areas, seed can be broadcast or slit-seeded into the turf. However, broadcasting provides a more uniform stand of turfgrass, because tall fescue does not spread laterally as readily as Kentucky bluegrass and so may maintain a striped appearance as it grows in the slits created by the slit-seeder. Timing for establishing tall fescue is the same as that described earlier for cool season turfgrasses.

6.4   RENOVATION OF A GRANULAR WARNING TRACK

With proper maintenance, the only renovation a granular warning track will need is the addition of more material after three to five years of use. The material may settle into the soil, or the soil may migrate up into the warning track. Filter cloths help to prevent this problem, but also add to the initial cost of the installation. One inch of new granular material is usually sufficient to make a warning track look like new.

Before applying the new material, measure out from the fence the specified width of the warning track, and mark with a paint gun. This may show that turfgrass has intruded into the warning track material, which will have to be removed using a sod cutter or bed edger. (At the same time, use the sod cutter or edger to remove any weeds growing in the warning track itself.) Once the track is edged, use a pulverizer to loosen the surface. If no new material is being added to the warning track, use hand rakes to spread the granular surface back to the edge of the turf. If new material is needed, place it on top of the pulverized old granular surface. There is no need to mix the new and old materials, especially because the new material will have a better color than the old.

Once the new material is in place, smooth the surface with a field leveler and roll it, to ensure firm and uniform footing on the finished warning track. It is also a good idea to mat drag the surface to achieve a finished look; however, if the field will not be used for several months, this dragging may be deferred until just before the playing season.

6.5   CONCLUSION

Regular renovation of a baseball or softball field is vital to maximizing its playability. Many small problems can be corrected easily during an annual renovation process, but left uncorrected, these small difficulties will grow into major problems that can seriously compromise the playability of the field.

Chapter 7

Skinned Area (and Warning Track) Maintenance and Management Procedures

7.1   INTRODUCTION

This chapter describes the basic steps required to maintain the skinned areas of a baseball or softball diamond. The reader will note that the final section of this chapter considers the maintenance procedures for a granular warning track. Warning tracks are not, strictly speaking, skinned areas. However, their maintenance is more like skinned area maintenance than the processes required to maintain turfgrass, so warning tracks are included in this chapter.

It is probably fair to say that no area of a baseball field has a greater impact on the playability of a facility than the skinned area. A smooth and uniform skinned area allows consistent footing and ball response, whereas a bad skinned area results in constant errors by players trying to field ground balls, and even player injury, not to mention chronic puddling in rainy weather. Most readers are probably familiar with the widely quoted "80/20 rule" (referring to the 20% of a project that requires 80% of the effort), and that rule applies to skinned areas as well. A skinned area may represent 20% or less of a baseball or softball field, but it probably requires 80% of the maintenance effort. (Furthermore, it is probably true that 80% of the errors in a game occur on the skinned area.)

The careful planning and performance of maintenance operations on the skinned area is a critical part of a field management program. If these operations are performed in a sloppy or haphazard fashion, they will not only fail to deliver a sound playing surface, they may also degrade the quality of the facility as time passes. For example, poor dragging processes can compromise the ability of the skinned area to drain. Another all-too-common practice, sweeping water out of puddles with a broom, temporarily dries the area, but leads to the formation of progressively larger puddles with each subsequent rain.

This chapter considers the best practices for maintaining the skinned area of a diamond. It begins with a discussion of the critical importance of regular field inspection and then considers the proper steps to be taken to keep the skinned area in top condition.

The processes described here list the steps that must be taken continuously during the season to maintain playability. Before the first game, however, it is important to loosen the skinned area soil with a pulverizer to relieve winter compaction. After pulverizing, drag with a nail drag, and then with a mat drag, and the skinned area is ready for the first game. (This assumes, of course, that renovation has been performed after the last season, as described in Chapter 6. If the skinned area has not been renovated, then renovation should be performed as soon as weather permits in the spring.)

7.2   INSPECTION

A cornerstone of any effective maintenance program is information about the condition of the facility. To get that kind of detailed information, the field manager should plan to perform regular inspections of the field. It is helpful to have a form or checklist to guide your inspections, so that no critical steps are overlooked. A sample chart is included for this purpose (Table 7.1). This chart can be used as a guide for maintenance practices and can also serve as a planning tool for field improvement projects as they are needed.

As listed on the sample chart, there are a number of the things you should look for in inspections of the skinned area.

Check to be sure that proper dragging methods are being used and that soil is not being dragged into the turfgrass (probably the single most common problem in skinned area maintenance). Examine the base paths to make sure they are not becoming "cupped," or worn down in the middle so that they will hold water when it rains. Check for holes or excessive wear at the pitcher's mound, the batter's box, and the spots where infielders typically stand during a game.

Table 7.1. Sample Field Inspection Report

Inspection Report						
Baseball or Softball Field:						
Skinned Area	Proper Dragging Methods[a]	Cupped Base Lines	Holes at Pitcher's Mound	Holes at Home Plate and Bases	Lip Buildup at Grass Edges	Other: Dugouts, Fences, Spectator Areas, Trash, etc.
Date:						
Date:						
Date:						
Date:						
Date:						
Date:						
Date:						
Date:						

[a]Dragging: Start 6 in. from the grass edge and work toward the middle of the skinned area.

Check the edges of the turfgrass, to look for the buildup of soil in the grass edge. Left untreated, this buildup can form a lip and will eventually prevent proper surface drainage.

For the most effective inspection program, it is smart to inspect the field from time to time during or just after a heavy rain, even if no game is scheduled for a few days.

(Obviously, fields get the most attention during the playing season, but it is a good idea to inspect the field once a month or so during the off-season. Problems can begin to appear during the off-season, and these problems will need attention before players take the field again.)

Performing these regular inspections will provide you with a regular flow of information on the overall condition of the skinned area and can help you make better decisions about the maintenance program.

In addition to guiding the ongoing maintenance process, these inspections can be important in developing short-term and long-term improvement plans for the diamond. A prudent manager will always have a list of improvements that should be made right away, and another list of improvements that can wait (or that the current budget will not permit). By developing these lists based on your inspections, you can be budgeting for the needed field improvements.

7.3   SKINNED AREA MAINTENANCE

The task of describing a maintenance regimen for skinned areas is complicated by the wide variety of factors that affect their performance. Obviously, local climate and the number of events held on the field play a major role in dictating the maintenance steps required to maximize the playability of the skinned areas of a field. The staff and budget resources available to the field manager also help to determine how much work can be invested in these critical areas. The range of maintenance possibilities begin with major league parks, where the skinned areas receive daily intensive care, to local park and school fields, where skinned areas get only the care that can be given in the time spared from the many other duties staff members must fulfill.

To help the manager design and implement a maintenance program that achieves the best combination of playability and affordability, we suggest a look at the best practices of professionals in the major league ranks.

Relative to the following description of effective maintenance procedures is a consideration of the way infield conditioners are used on the skinned areas of some high-profile fields. Professional groundskeepers regularly apply a ¼ in. layer of conditioner (typically calcined clay) to the top of the skinned area, so that the playing surface is really a conditioner, rather than skinned area soil. This practice not only helps to manage skinned area moisture, but also assists in maintaining surface uniformity by filling in imperfections caused by players' cleats.

Some professionals mix calcined clay conditioner with a second product, vitrified clay. Vitrified clay is fired to a higher temperature for a longer period and thus is less absorbent. Adding this product allows some of the water applied to the surface to pass into the skinned soil below, distributing it more evenly. On a day when rain is not forecast, the groundskeeper might apply 60% calcined clay and 40% vitrified clay to allow more of the water applied to pass into the skinned soil below the surface. If rain is expected, he or she may apply 80% calcined clay and 20% vitrified clay to soak up rainwater at the surface and prevent slippery footing.

(Some field managers occasionally use cat litter, from the grocery store, to soak up standing water and allow a game to go on. However, it is important to be aware that cat litter is a clay product that is fired at a lower temperature and for a shorter time than cal-cined clay conditioner. Thus, although it can be useful in a pinch, it will soak up more water and can give the soil a slippery quality. It should be removed after the game and replaced with skinned area soil or real conditioner. The same is true of organic drying agents, which are discussed in Section 7.3c.)

7.3a Watering

A key consideration in skinned area maintenance is watering of the surface. Unlike turf area watering, which provides the moisture needed for the health of the turfgrass plants, watering of skinned areas has two basic goals: preventing dusty conditions and minimizing glare. Well-moistened skinned area soil, having a darker color, cuts down on the reflection of sunlight and provides greater contrast with a white baseball or softball. (See Figure 7.1.)

On a high-profile field (especially where the playing surface is a layer of calcined clay conditioner) the skinned area is watered several times on the day of a game, with the first watering of the morning considered the most critical. This "base watering" is used to soak the soil thoroughly—right to the point of full saturation, but not to the point of creating slippery footing. The manager will need to learn by observation when this point is reached. Additional water should be applied during the day to keep the skinned soil moist, with the last watering applied shortly before game time to settle the dust and darken the surface.

On a day when the field will not be used, water the skinned area thoroughly until small puddles are observed. Then stand in one of these puddles and test the footing, which should still be fairly solid and not slippery. If slipperiness is noticeable, future base water-ings should be slightly reduced.

In planning the schedule of waterings, professional groundskeepers check the forecast temperature and humidity, as well as the amount of sunlight and shadow a skinned area will experience.

Figure 7.1. Watering the skinned area before a game helps to prevent blowing dust and reduces glare. Note the helper supporting the watering hose to keep it from dragging over the skinned area and causing unpredictable ball response. (Photo courtesy of Jeff Limburg, head groundskeeper, Fifth Third Field, Toledo.)

For the school or park field manager, the goal should be to provide a moist skinned area, with no slippery areas or standing water, by the scheduled game time.

7.3b Dragging

Another critical maintenance function is dragging. Most experienced field managers find a nail drag to be the most useful tool for this process. (Whereas mat drags and brooms just smooth the surface, a nail drag loosens the top ¼ in. to ½ in. of the skinned area, creating a slightly softer and more uniform surface.)

A nail drag is of greatest benefit when the skinned area is moist, but not soaked. Care should be used in selecting a vehicle for pulling the nail drag; a vehicle that is too heavy will cause ruts and may diminish the effectiveness of the whole dragging process. In performing regular dragging, the professionals recommend varying the direction, using at least three and as many as five different directions. Although this procedure makes the dragging process take a great deal more time, it also helps to keep the skinned surface uniform and without high or low spots.

It is also important to give attention to the nail drag itself. A properly designed nail drag has multiple rows of nails, with the rows staggered to prevent the creation of an obvious grooved "corduroy" appearance in the skinned soil. (Figure 7.2 shows a nail drag design that performs well.)

The nail points themselves should be sharpened from time to time; blunt nails may contribute to soil layering. Methodically sharpening the nails can be a tedious task, but it substantially improves the performance of the implement.

(It should also be noted that a nail drag may be used to help dry the skinned area after a rain. The drag helps expose the soil to air and sun, speeding the release of moisture and shortening the drying time. A little time spent experimenting with this method in a

Figure 7.2. This nail drag can be built from 2 × 4 lumber and 16 penny steel nails.

Figure 7.3. Grooming the surface of the skinned area with drag brooms prior to (or during) a game will help to smooth the surface, but will not improve the surface as much as a combination of nail dragging followed by broom dragging. (Photo courtesy of Jeff Limburg, head groundskeeper, Fifth Third Field, Toledo.)

low-pressure situation—such as before a practice, rather than a game—will show how much the nail drag can speed up the drying process.)

Going over the surface with a steel or cocoa mat or with a drag broom helps to groom the surface before or during a game, but does not provide the surface improvement afforded by nail dragging. (See Figure 7.3.) Using a combination of the two techniques, going over the skinned area with a nail drag and then following with a mat drag, is probably the ideal way to leave the playing surface smooth and uniform, especially for a typical field with a soil (rather than conditioner) playing surface.

To prevent the loss of skinned area soil into the grass, dragging should begin 6 in. from the grass edge and work toward the middle of the skinned area. (See Figure 7.4.) When using a mat drag, it is also important to lift the drag before leaving the skinned area so that you don't pull soil into the grass edge, where it may block a critical surface drainage point and eventually create a mounded ridge or lip. (See Figure 7.5.)

7.3c   Correcting Wet Spots

Obviously, any spots on the skinned area where standing water is present need daily attention. If there are puddles on the field after a rain, chances are good that low spots have caused them. To avoid the reappearance of these puddles in the future, fill in the low spots with matching soil as soon as the rain lets up. It is a good idea to remove the standing water before filling in the low spots. Avoid the common practice of sweeping out the water with a broom, which displaces soil and makes a bigger hole to fill. Instead, use a hand pump as shown in Figure 7.6, or a water-removal pillow sold for that purpose. (Digging out a small depression in the middle of the puddle will concentrate the water and make its removal easier with these devices, or will allow you to scoop out most of the water with a coffee can or other small container.) Once the water has been removed, loosen the soil with a steel rake or hand cultivator. Let the wet soil dry out as much as possible, then spread matching soil to fill in the depression and hand rake to smooth and level. Be careful to avoid overfilling the depression and thus creating a raised area.

Figure 7.4. Dragging should be conducted at low speeds, and should begin 6 in. from the grass edge to avoid slinging dirt into the grass.

Figure 7.5. A mat drag should be lifted before leaving the skinned area to prevent pulling soil into the grass.

Figure 7.6. A hand pump can be used to clear away puddles on the playing surface, especially if a small depression is dug to concentrate the water. This photo shows the use of this technique on a turf area, but it can also be used on a skinned area. Make sure to refill the depression and carefully groom the surface after removing the puddle. (Photo courtesy of B. Prather, Mississippi State University.)

Conditioners also can be used to soak up extra water after a heavy rain. (Most conditioner manufacturers make finer-textured versions of their products that work best for this purpose.) They can be spread directly over small puddles or soggy areas to firm up the surface quickly. Remember that the organic drying agents manufactured from corncobs or other materials can work very effectively, but will have to be removed after the practice or game. Left in place, they will give the skinned area soil a gummy, sticky consistency and can eventually *prevent* soil from drying properly after it rains.

7.3d Grooming High-Traffic Areas
Some high-profile facilities reinforce their highest-traffic areas with high-clay materials that resist stress better. These areas typically include pitcher's mounds, batter's boxes, and the skinned paths between home plate and first and third bases. Some groundskeepers also reinforce the areas where the infielders typically stand on the skinned area and where the base

runners lead off from the bases. There are commercially available processed clay products formulated for these spots, and these products are coming into fairly heavy use, especially for the mound and the batter's box. They generally help to minimize the symptoms of heavy wear in these areas, but under some circumstances they can expand and contract as they absorb water and dry out. This factor has limited their use in the highest-profile facilities such as major league parks. However, they are widely used in minor league baseball, and even in applications such as the bullpens of big league parks. For most school and park diamonds, installing this material at the beginning of the season and replacing kicked-out areas three or four times during the season will result in superior overall performance of a skinned area.

The holes at the batter's box, the pitcher's mound, and the bases should be filled, tamped, and hand raked before each game. (See Figure 7.7.) It is also a good idea to hand rake the base paths and along all the edges of the turf, in the 6 in. wide area that is left when dragging.

7.3e   Marking Foul Lines and Batter's Boxes

Major league parks repaint their foul lines (as well as batter's boxes) before every game, to provide maximum visibility for the umpires, who must call batted balls foul or fair. Some groundskeepers at high-profile facilities formulate their own marking material; David Mellor of the Boston Red Sox uses a mixture of chalk, water, and latex paint to apply lines that can be seen easily and that stand up well to weather conditions. If it rains during a game, or if dirt is kicked over these lines, they can be swept clean to restore clear visibility. Mellor warns against using chalk alone, because it can mix into the soil in a way that impedes surface drainage across the lines, and because it can become caked into players' spikes.

Figure 7.7. After each game, holes at the pitcher's mound and batter's box should be refilled, tamped, and hand raked. Note the new clay material being applied here, which appears darker than the existing mound surface. (Photo courtesy of B. Prather, Mississippi State University.)

(It should be noted that a formulation like this one is meant for use *only* in marking on skinned areas; the use of turf-marking paint is the recommended way to mark lines on turfgrass areas. Chalk applied to turfgrass will eventually build up into a mounded ridge that can affect drainage and ball response, and can even become a tripping hazard for players.)

In reapplying foul lines, it is important to stretch a line each time, and not to rely on previously painted lines. Old lines can become slightly distorted over time as a result of player traffic, and relying on them as a guide for repainting can produce visibly crooked lines. The time invested in stretching the string line pays real dividends in terms of field aesthetics and consistent fair/foul calls. (See Figure 7.8.)

7.3f   Grass Edge Maintenance

To prevent the buildup of skinned area material in the edges of the turfgrass (where it can impede drainage), it is important to groom these areas regularly. Several tools can be used for this purpose. A standard leaf blower can be used to remove loose particles around most of the skinned area, although along the first and third base lines it may simply blow the material from one grass edge to another. A broom or leaf rake can also perform this task, and the extra effort required yields the benefit of extra control. (See figure 7.9.)

Turfgrass edges require a little more work on fields that are sometimes covered with a tarp. The tarp tends to pick up some of the skinned area material and drop it in the grass edge when it is removed from the field. Managers regularly using a tarp should pay attention to this effect.

Three to four times each year, high-profile managers cut away 2 in. to 4 in. of the turfgrass edge to remove any buildup left after maintenance and to reestablish a sharp, straight edge. (See Figures 7.10 and 7.11.) At the end of the season new sod is laid along these edges to restore the original lines.

Figure 7.8. A string line should always be stretched when remarking foul lines, to keep the lines straight. Do not rely on existing lines as a guide. (Photo courtesy of Jeff Limburg, head groundskeeper, Fifth Third Field, Toledo.)

Figure 7.9. Grooming the grass edge with a leaf blower (shown here), broom, or leaf rake will prevent buildup of skinned area soil or warning track material, which can impede runoff and lead to puddles. (Photo courtesy of Jeff Limburg, head groundskeeper, Fifth Third Field, Toledo.)

Figure 7.10. Reestablishing a sharp, straight grass edge using a painted guide line and a standard sidewalk edger.

Figure 7.11. After edging, loose material is collected and removed by hand.

On lower-profile fields, such as those at schools and parks, edging the grass areas should still be performed at least twice a year. On fields such as these, where edging is performed less frequently than on professional fields, a high-pressure water hose can be used to remove any of the skinned area material that has accumulated at the grass edge. Stand on the turfgrass area and direct the stream of water at the first 2 in. to 4 in. of turfgrass so that the loose soil is pushed out into the skinned area. Avoid directing the stream at the sand/clay soil. (See Figure 7.12.)

When this method is used, note that the large amounts of water applied to the field usually makes it unplayable for days afterward. For this reason, a high-pressure hose should be used only when the field will have sufficient time to dry before the next scheduled use, such as at the end of the season.

7.3g The Importance of Safety

Although the most obvious single difference between high-profile baseball diamonds and those typically found at parks and schools is the superior aesthetics of the big-time fields, professional groundskeepers will confirm that their single greatest consideration in making maintenance decisions is player safety. Professional franchises regard their players as their most vital assets and insist on having their diamonds maintained in such a way that risk of injury is minimized. In thinking about the steps that should be taken to properly maintain the all-important skinned areas of a field, this consideration should also be foremost in the mind of every field manager, no matter what the skill level of the players using the facility.

Figure 7.12. A high-pressure water hose directed at the grass edge will blast out skinned area soil that has collected there during the season. (Photo by David Grantonic.)

7.4   WARNING TRACK MAINTENANCE

Warning tracks (whether granular or rubber) look best when they are edged regularly to provide a distinct contrast with the grass areas. Among the tools used to edge a track are powered sidewalk edgers, string trimmers, and hand edgers. Edging should be performed at least twice a year.

The appearance of weeds is one of the most common problems of granular warning tracks. The best approach to weeding such tracks is to use a combination of three methods: application of preemergent herbicides, application of postemergent herbicides, and mechanical weeding. In applying preemergents, use a product that is labeled for the particular weeds that have been observed during the growing season. Prior to the next growing season, make a blanket application of a preemergent labeled for those weeds. A nonselective postemergent herbicide, such as Roundup Pro (chemical name: glyphosate), can be used to control weeds that have already emerged. Mechanical weeding with a hoe or by hand takes care of any random weeds that escape chemical controls.

Dragging helps to keep the granular material looking like new and should be performed at least once a month during the season. Use a nail drag to loosen the surface, and then a mat drag for final grooming. Failing to perform these regular maintenance steps often allows the warning track surface to become so hard that a nail drag will not penetrate. When this happens, use a pulverizer to loosen the surface, and then use a field leveler to smooth the surface. Finish the process by rolling and dragging with a mat drag.

Chapter 8

Turfgrass Maintenance and Management Procedures

8.1 INTRODUCTION

Having reviewed the steps used in maintaining the skinned areas of the field, we now consider the maintenance of turfgrass areas. In this chapter, we will begin by discussing the topic in general and then address the practices used to take care of the types of turfgrass used on athletic fields in the various climatic zones of the country.

8.2 INSPECTION

As mentioned in Chapter 7, regular inspections are important in the maintenance of skinned areas. It is likewise important to conduct regular inspections of the turfgrass areas of baseball and softball diamonds. Table 8.1 is an example of a chart that can be used to guide turfgrass inspections. Using this chart will help the field manager to be sure he or she has looked for the various factors and conditions that will affect decisions made in maintaining the field.

Because the turfgrass areas of a field represent a living ecosystem, it is important to take time to go beyond the superficial in making your inspections. For instance, thorough inspections should include the use of a soil probe to take samples of the soil profile at various spots around the field. Take samples daily at three or four spots on the turf and inspect the root system, the thatch layer, and the ends of the grass blades. Look for the presence of new roots, which will be white in color. Check the thatch layer, which should be no more than ½ in. on a baseball field. Look for cleanly cut grass blades; tearing and shredding at the ends are characteristic effects of dull mower blades. Inspect the soil in the sample for moisture level and for compaction in the top 1 in. to 2 in. of soil under the turf.

The most effective inspections are conducted in a variety of conditions—at different times of day, during dry periods and after a rain, when the turf needs to be mowed and after mowing, and so on. Make a point to inspect the field sometimes during or just after a heavy rain, to see where water is standing on the field and where the turf has become waterlogged. (You can hear squishy footsteps as you walk.) The more you vary the conditions under which inspections are performed, the more useful information you will have on which to base maintenance decisions.

Table 8.1. Sample Turfgrass Area Inspection Report

Inspection Report						
Baseball or Softball Field						
Grass Area	Overall Appearance	Clippings	Height of Cut	Sharpen Mower Blade	Soil Moisture	Other: Color, Density, Thatch, Compaction, Weeds, Catch Basins, Sprinkler Heads, etc.
Date:						
Date:						
Date:						
Date:						
Date:						
Date:						
Date:						
Date:						

8.3   SOIL TESTING

One of the keys to an effective maintenance program is the use of annual soil testing (or leaf tissue analysis). Sandy soils should be tested more than once a year, because they don't hold nutrients very well; sand fields should be tested at least twice a year, and up to four times a year when there are signs of low fertility such as thin and/or yellowed turf.

Soil sampling is a simple process. With a soil probe (available from a turfgrass materials supplier) or a small spade, dig a sample 6 in. deep at random locations around the field. Place about a pint of the soil into a soil test package (available from a country agricultural agent or commercial soil testing lab), and mail the sample to the agent or the lab. Most testing labs will send back a report within two weeks. Soil can be sampled at any time of the year, but the data collected at certain times can be more meaningful for turfgrass management. The ideal time to sample is late winter, before the spring growing season begins.

A typical soil test reports levels of phosphorus, potassium, calcium, and magnesium, as well as soil pH. Nitrogen levels are not usually reported because they can change rapidly in a soil, but the lab's recommendations will include application rates for nitrogen along with those for other nutrients. Most reports also provide guidance on bringing the soil pH up to recommended levels. Maintaining sand fields requires more detailed information on the presence of micronutrients in the sample, and most testing labs can provide this information for an additional charge.

An alternative type of testing is tissue testing, which describes exactly what nutrients are present in the leaves of the turfgrass. This technique can be useful for the highest-profile fields, but soil testing is adequate for most sports turf facilities. A testing lab can provide guidance on taking tissue samples.

To enhance the usefulness of soil or tissue testing results, avoid sampling from noticeable problem areas on the field, except to diagnose specific problems. (For such diagnoses, submit those samples separately from the general soil sample.) Of course, you should also avoid taking samples right after fertilizing; newly applied fertilizer in the soil or residue on the leaves can affect test results so that they do not provide meaningful information about the nutrient status of the field.

8.4   BASIC MAINTENANCE AND MANAGEMENT PROCEDURES

8.4a   Adjusting Soil pH

One of the most important pieces of information gained from a soil test is the soil reaction, commonly referred to as the "pH." A slightly acidic pH (ideally, 6.5) is the target pH for turfgrass, because it maximizes nutrient availability. To raise soil pH, a liming agent is applied. Elemental sulfur (S), or fertilizer containing sulfur, is used to lower pH.

There are a number of commonly used liming materials, some of which act slowly and others of which rapidly change soil pH. For established turfgrasses, it is best to choose slower-acting materials, because they have limited potential for foliar burn. These materials act over weeks or months but have effects that are relatively long-lived. Examples of slower-acting liming agents are calcium carbonate, magnesium carbonate, and dolomitic limestone. Faster-acting liming materials work quickly, but their effects are shorter in duration and these materials have a very high potential for foliar burn. Examples of faster-acting liming agents include hydrated lime, calcium oxide, and quicklime. (It is worth noting that the rapid effect of the hydrated or oxide materials makes them good choices for modifying soil pH by incorporating them into the soil *before* planting turfgrass on a field.)

The ideal times to apply lime are when cooler temperatures (daily highs of 50°F or less) reduce the potential for foliar burn. This timing is appropriate also because standard lime sources need a few months to have their full effect on pH. It is important to avoid applying powdered forms of lime on hot, humid days when the potential for foliar burn is at its highest.

How much liming material is required for a typical field? Only a soil test can provide authoritative guidance. However, a couple of points about liming different types of soil should be considered. Sandy soils need less liming agents, and heavy clay soils need more. The reason is the higher cation exchange capacity (or CEC, which is reported in the results of a soil test) of clay soil. It should be noted that although it is easy to change the pH of sandy soil by adding a liming agent, this change will be relatively short-lived, and regular applications will be required to maintain the desired pH.

It is important to avoid applying too much liming agent at one time. Even when the soil test calls for a substantial increase in pH, it is not a good idea to apply more than 40 lb of liming agent per 1000 sq ft in a single application. Exceeding that rate increases the potential for foliar burn.

There is even more concern about the potential for foliar burn resulting from elemental sulfur applications than from liming agents, so it is even more important to apply sulfur when daily highs are less than 50°. Application rates should be kept to no more than 7 lb of sulfur per 1000 sq ft at a time. When greater amounts are needed, these applications should be split, with one application in the spring and another in the fall.

The field manager should be aware that many nitrogen fertilizers also have the effect of gradually lowering pH. These fertilizers (particularly water-soluble materials such as ammonium sulfate, urea, and ammonium nitrate) will slowly lower pH with repeated applications.

8.4b   Fertilization

Because of the unusual stresses placed on a baseball or softball diamond, including heavy foot and vehicular traffic, it is very important to develop and follow a clearly defined fertilization schedule. Later in this chapter, you will find sample fertilization programs specific to warm season and cool season diamonds. It is beyond the scope of this book to provide specific programs for every climatic region in this country. This fact should be kept in mind when considering the programs presented in this chapter; using the results of regular soil tests, the sample programs should be modified to fit the particular needs of a particular field and climate.

A key point to remember in planning a fertilization program is that plants take up nutrients only when they are actively growing. (However, cool season turfgrass grows roots during the late fall, when no leaf growth can be seen. During this period, fertilizer application can be particularly beneficial in promoting root development and increasing the production of storage of carbohydrates.) Applying water-soluble fertilizers is pointless when the turf is dormant. However, dormancy can occur in the heat of summer, just as it can during the dead of winter. For warm season grasses, the primary growing period is from late spring through early fall. For cool season turfgrasses, two growth periods occur: one from late winter through late spring, and the other from late summer to late fall. These are the times when fertilizer should be applied.

The three nutrients required in the highest amounts are nitrogen, phosphorus, and potassium. Typically, the first fertilizer applied in the spring is a complete source containing these nutrients. Sandy soils tend to be more deficient in phosphorus and potassium and may need a complete source all year round, whereas heavy clay soils often require mostly nitrogen after the first application of the spring. Plan the fertilization program for the rest of the growing season based on your annual soil or tissue tests.

Potassium is critical to enhancing stress tolerance, so many sports turf managers now apply nitrogen and potassium at 1:1 ratios, particularly on sand-based fields where potassium leaching can be a problem. Phosphorus, on the other hand, helps to promote root development, so it is important to ensure that adequate levels are present during the period when root development is taking place (that is, in mid-summer for bermudagrass, spring and fall for cool season turf).

It should be noted that there is a micronutrient of great importance to sports fields: iron (Fe). A liquid application of iron results in rapid green-up without a burst of shoot growth that would require additional mowing. This treatment will improve the appearance of a field for an important game or tournament, but the green-up is temporary. Iron is immobile within the plant, so as the turf is mowed, the effects of the iron are removed with the clippings. An iron application to most sports fields that are mowed once or twice a week will provide some greening response for about 10 to 14 days (less if the turf is mowed more often). Liquid iron sources also are commonly tank mixed with many pesticides or plant growth regulators to mask the yellowing these chemical might cause, but be sure the chemicals are compatible and will not negate their respectable responses.

8.4c   Aeration and Topdressing

Chapter 6 considered the use of aeration and topdressing in renovating a field after the completion of play. We now turn our attention to how these techniques are used in routine maintenance during the season itself.

When timing an aeration event, be sure that the grass is actively growing so that it will recuperate quickly. Different types of equipment require different amounts of moisture in the soil; it is a good idea to check with the equipment distributor to determine the ideal moisture levels at which the aerator should be used. Despite its long-term benefits, aeration causes some stress on the turf. If lime or fertilizer applications are needed, coordinate them with planned aeration events to help get the materials directly into the soil and encourage turfgrass regrowth.

Multiple passes (in different directions) are often required at each aeration event, depending on the spacing of tines and the severity of compaction.

Types of Aeration

A wide variety of aeration equipment is available for sports turf, each providing its own benefits to the turf, but also having associated drawbacks.

The most common type of aeration is *hollow-tine (core) aeration,* one of the most useful practices in sports field maintenance. (See Figure 8.1.) It may be that the beneficial effects on soil properties of hollow-tine aeration cannot be equaled by any other process. Core aeration reduces compaction and improves soil aeration and water infiltration and percolation rates. The ultimate result is healthier root systems.

Figure 8.1. A core (or "hollow-tine") aerator removes cores of soil, typically ¾ in. in diameter and 3 in. deep. This method improves the health of the turf, but may be too disruptive to the surface for use during the competition season.

However, two problems of core aeration must be addressed: surface disruption and the need to deal with the cores that are removed by the process. Core aeration (the most disruptive type) must be planned around games scheduled on the field, because core aeration holes (and the cores, if they are not removed) can create unsatisfactory playing conditions. Unbroken cores can affect footing and disrupt ball response, and the holes can catch players' cleats. After a heavy rain, they can also turn into mud on the surface. In most soils and conditions, full recovery from core aeration takes about 14 days for cool season turfgrasses and one week for bermudagrass.

For these reasons, core aeration is not an ideal maintenance technique during the playing season. However, if the schedule includes a break of a week or more when the field will not be used, core aeration can be conducted at the beginning of this period, as long as cores are removed or broken up. To reduce recovery time after core aeration, fertilize and irrigate in amounts sufficient to promote vigorous plant growth.

There are numerous depths and diameters of tines available for core aeration. For most sports field aeration needs, effective performance can be achieved by standard units (¾ in. in diameter by 3 in. deep). However, the field manager must match the needs of the particular field with the types of equipment available. Fields with standing surface water can benefit from deep-tine aeration, which temporarily improves field drainage because of the holes it creates. Deep-tine aeration can also help to relieve serious compaction problems. (See Figure 8.2.)

It is worth noting that no single form of aeration can provide all the benefits needed for healthy turfgrass culture. Because of the disruptive nature of core aeration, for instance,

Figure 8.2. A deep-tine aerator is designed to remove deeper cores than standard equipment—up to 10 in. to 12 in. below the surface. This type of equipment both fights compaction and temporarily improves drainage on many fields.

this type of equipment has limited usefulness during the season. Perhaps the best advice in regard to acquiring aeration equipment is to secure a core aerator for renovation and off-season use and choose a less aggressive type for maintenance applications during the season. The less aggressive types are discussed in the following paragraphs.

Solid-tine aeration differs from core aeration in that it creates holes in the turf but does not remove cores. Solid-tine aerating can have substantial benefits in reducing compaction. The equipment for solid-tine aeration varies widely in its aggressiveness. The least disruptive type, the best choice for in-season maintenance, has smaller tines (usually 3 in. to 4 in. long and no more than ⅜ in. in diameter). Larger-tine equipment, especially the type designed to fracture the soil with a vibrating or "quaking" action, can produce holes large enough to snag spikes or otherwise compromise players' footing. (See Figure 8.3.)

It is important to realize that the repeated use of solid-tine aeration can actually reduce the water infiltration and percolation rates of a soil. As a matter of fact, excessive use of any type of soil aeration device can *create* a compaction zone in the soil, particularly if tines of the same diameter and depth are repeatedly used. (This fact supports the recommendation that more than one type of aerator should be used in the care of every field.) A planned program of off-season core aeration and in-season solid-tine aeration will typically provide steady improvement in the physical properties of a soil as a growing medium for turfgrass.

A relatively new type of aeration equipment that provides many of the benefits of solid-tine aeration with virtually no surface disruption is the high-pressure, *water-injection aerator.* (See Figure 8.4.) This equipment uses self-contained pumps to generate microstreams

Figure 8.3. This solid-tine aerator with quaking action relieves compaction, but also causes substantial surface disruption, as can be seen behind the equipment. This effect should be avoided in aerators chosen for in-season maintenance.

Figure 8.4. Water-injection aerators use a thin jet of high-pressure water to loosen the soil without substantial surface disruption.

of water at very high pressure. These streams create holes so small that most people walking across the turf won't realize aeration has taken place. The limited surface disruption means that water-injection aeration can be performed right up until game day. This type of equipment is currently being used to inject soil amendments right along with the stream of water. The newest designs can also perform "air injection," opening holes with air instead of water. However, the point raised about other forms of aeration equipment also applies to air injection: It should not be relied upon as the only form of aeration, but should be used in combination with core and solid-tine equipment.

Spiking and slicing equipment uses solid metal blades to penetrate the soil, creating channels that allow water and air to reach the roots. (See Figure 8.5.) Spiking and slicing also severs the lateral stems of bermudagrass and Kentucky bluegrass, encouraging lateral growth that thickens the stand of turfgrass. The benefits of spiking or slicing are generally more short-term than the effects of core aeration, but because they are less disruptive, these processes can be performed frequently (as often as weekly) throughout the season.

Blades are available in a wide variety of sizes; not surprisingly, larger blades cause greater surface disruption.

(Slicing equipment is also helpful in overseeding existing turf. Slicers create grooves in the soil that give seeds a desirable environment in which to germinate. This practice is used in the planting technique called "slit-seeding.")

Topdressing

Topdressing is discussed in Chapter 6 in relation to renovation of a facility. However, there are some limited circumstances in which topdressing can be a useful maintenance practice

Figure 8.5. Spiking and slicing equipment allows water and air to reach the turfgrass roots and encourages lateral growth of some varieties. Because such equipment creates minimal surface disruption, it can be used during the season.

as well. For example, it can be helpful when a heavy thatch layer makes the turf feel spongy or when the surface has become bumpy or uneven as a result of foot or vehicular traffic. As with core aeration, topdressing material must settle through the turfgrass canopy before field use resumes, especially if ¼ in. or more of material is applied. Thoroughly watering the turf, or dragging it with a mat drag, will accelerate the rate at which the topdressing material is incorporated into the turfgrass canopy. However, it is important to be aware that some topdressing materials can be abrasive to the turfgrass leaves, and topdressing often creates an undesirable appearance on the field. Therefore, after the procedure is performed, the field should not be used again until the turfgrass shows evidence of active growth.

Topdressing material can take the form of soil that matches the existing growing medium, or of sand chosen to improve the performance of the field. If the field's growing medium is amended sand, the topdressing material should be matching sand. (Some sports field managers topdress amended sand fields with a mixture of sand and 10% conditioner such as calcined diatomaceous earth or calcined clay to increase water retention.) When topdressing is performed without aerating first, applying a ¼ in. layer will require about ¾ cu yd of material per 1000 sq ft.

Topdressing can be most effectively performed in combination with core aeration. (See Figure 8.6.) (And, because a field requires at least a week to recover from either procedure, you may as well schedule both at once.) However, it is important to account for the amount of topdressing material that will be required to fill all the holes created by the aeration process. For instance, topdressing with a ¼ in. layer of sand on a field that has been

Figure 8.6. This sample soil profile shows a sand channel through the soil created by aerating and topdressing. Note the presence of deep roots in the sand channel at the bottom of the sample.

aerated with standard ¾ × 3 in. hollow-tine aerating equipment (with 3 in. tine spacing) will typically require about 1½ cu yd of sand per 1000 sq ft.

If the condition of a field can be improved by topdressing with sand, aeration provides a logical time to do that. The most common example is a heavy-clay field, which is by nature subject to compaction and drainage problems. Under these circumstances, topdressing with coarse to very coarse sand (particles between 0.5 mm and 2.0 mm), then dragging to backfill the core holes, will gradually improve the overall quality of the field if these procedures are performed two or three times a year. (Obviously, most of these topdressing treatments will have to be conducted off-season.) Sand also works better than soil to help firm up a thatch layer on the field.

In performing the topdressing operation, begin by mowing the turf to allow the material to easily reach the surface of the soil. Then apply the topdressing material at a uniform depth, using equipment designed for the purpose. Once the material has been spread evenly over the surface of the field, drag or brush the field to settle the material onto the surface (or, when topdressing is performed in combination with aeration, to push the sand into the aeration holes). Water thoroughly to wash the material off the leaf blades.

Topdressing also provides a good opportunity to level the field if a bumpy or uneven surface has been observed. When planning to perform this leveling operation, it is necessary to apply slightly more material, about an additional ½ yd of material per 1000 sq ft. Apply the material as described earlier, then use a tractor with a field leveler attachment to level the surface before dragging or brushing, and finish by watering.

8.4d Mowing

Like Rodney Dangerfield, mowing gets no respect. But a case can be made that mowing is the most important of all turf management processes. If you do it right, mowing helps thicken the turf, regulate moisture in the soil, control pests, and recycle nutrients. Unfortunately, if you do it wrong, this operation alone can result in thin, yellowed, unattractive turf.

(This section does not deal with the process of mowing for decorative striping and patterning. For information on that subject, see Chapter 9.)

The following four rules for sound mowing are probably the most important rules for doing this job in such a way that the turfgrass culture is enhanced:

- *Rule 1: Always mow with a sharp blade.* Sharp blades cut each plant cleanly, which minimizes the impact of mowing on the health of the turf. A dull blade pulls and shreds the plants. That exposes more of the surface area of each plant and increases turf vulnerability to disease-causing microorganisms. Mowing with a dull blade results in a visible whitish sheen on the new-mown turf. (See Figure 8.7.)

  Keeping the blades sharp enough to achieve a quality cut may require sharpening rotary blades frequently—even every day. If staff and budget allow, you can also have two or three

Figure 8.7. Mowing with dull blades shreds the turfgrass plants, increasing vulnerability to disease.

sets of blades available and sharpened for installation as often as feasible. An alternative is to sharpen blades after a specified number of mowing hours—for example, after every 15 to 20 hours of operation. (Reel mowers require blade sharpening less frequently, perhaps only a few times a year. But these mowers also need regular adjustment of the reel to the bed knife to ensure a clean cut.)

- *Rule 2: The one-third rule.* Cut off no more than one-third of the grass blade at any single mowing. Cutting off more than one-third compromises plant health and leaves an excessive layer of clippings on the turf. Of course, the difficulty in following this rule is obvious: A field that is being maintained at lower heights requires more frequent mowing. Turf kept at 2 in. will have to be mowed when it reaches 3 in., perhaps every three or four days. But for turf kept at 1 in., following the one-third rule means mowing when it reaches 1½ in. That could mean mowing every day—or at least every two to three days.
- *Rule 3: Keep blade speed up.* When using a rotary mower, always use the highest possible blade speed. High blade speed cuts the plants more cleanly and evenly and distributes the clippings more uniformly.
- *Rule 4: Keep ground speed down.* Speeding across the field gets the job done faster, but it tears the grass blades and results in uneven mowing. From a safety standpoint, it is also unwise to exceed the manufacturer's recommended ground speed with any type of mower. This underscores the importance of making sure the operator is adequately trained in the operation of the equipment and understands the importance of observing all appropriate safety precautions.

A final general principle is to avoid mowing when the soil is saturated; the mower wheels will produce ruts that can cause problems with footing and ball response.

Types of Mowers

Classified by cutting action, the three types of mowers used on sports turf are rotary, reel, and flail.

Rotary mowers (the most affordable type) vary from 3-horsepower 21 in. models, commonly used for residential mowing, to gang units that cut a swath up to 15 ft wide. (See Figure 8.8.) Rotary mowers cut by the impact of a spinning blade on the grass leaf; strictly speaking, the action is not a true cut, but rather more a tearing action. Sharp blades and high blade speed make for cleaner, higher-quality mowing. The operation of rotaries around people, animals, buildings, or cars requires great care, because debris can be discharged at high speed along with turf clippings and can cause serious injury. It is essential to follow all manufacturer's directions in regard to the use of shields for directing and controlling discharge. Consider purchasing either a self-contained mulching mower or a rear-discharge mower.

Reel units provide the best-quality cut, especially in mowing heights of less than 2 in. These mowers shear the grass between the blades on a spinning reel and a "bed knife" at the base of the cutting unit. This shearing action allows them to cut more cleanly than any other type of mower. (See Figure 8.9.)

For turf that will be mowed at a lower height, a reel with more blades is preferred. Manufacturers recommend that for turf maintained above 1 in., a five-blade reel is sufficient. For mowing heights between ½ in. and 1 in., six-blade reels should be used, and for heights of less than ½ in., seven or eight blades are recommended.[1]

Properly adjusted, reel mowers provide the closest cutting heights possible, making them the mowers of choice for the highest-quality fields. However, special equipment is

---

[1] Nolan Meggers, "The Cutting Edge on Reel Mowers Versus Rotary Mowers," *SportsTURF* (February 1998): 14.

Figure 8.8. This type of front-end rotary mower is one of the most common machines used for mowing sports fields in North America. This type of mower is appropriate where cutting heights will be above 2 in.

Figure 8.9. This view of a reel mower shows the blades, roller, and bed knife. (Photo courtesy of D. Nagel, Mississippi State University.)

needed to maintain the reels and bed knives, and adjusting the mower properly takes both patience and experience.

Flail mowers have pivoting blades or "flails" that spin at high speed around a horizontal axle, cutting the grass with a tearing action similar to that of rotary mowers. The flails have the flexibility to bounce over debris or raised spots in the turf, reducing the chances of impact damage to the mower. The discharge of debris is less problematic with flail mowers than with rotary models, making flail mowers a popular choice when mowing must be done around people or animals.

Height and Frequency

There is no single "ideal" mowing height; factors that must be considered include the type of grass, local climate, time of year, even the speed and style of play of the home team. Table 8.2 shows recommended mowing heights for optimum turf quality with various turfgrasses. Turf can be cut shorter than recommended, but will require more frequent mowing to observe the one-third rule. Closer-cut fields need more water, more fertilization, and more weed and disease control.

Many field managers raise mowing heights to 3 in. and above during the off-season. The greatest risk in this strategy is that the process of cutting the grass back to playing height (unless it is done very gradually) can compromise the quality of the turf. Reducing mowing heights to game-competition levels must begin at least four to six weeks in advance of the first game.

Like all processes involved in maintaining turfgrass, proper mowing requires planning. The recommended frequency is based not on the number of days since the last mowing, but rather on the one-third rule. For each field, specific circumstances determine the cutting height. For example, a heavily used practice field would be mowed at the high end of the cutting height range as a buffer in order to reduce wear and tear on the turf. On the other hand, a game field may be mowed at a cutting height based on the desires of coaches and players. If a baseball team lacks foot speed on defense, the coach may want the grass to be cut higher to slow ball movement—a very important and entirely legal "home field advantage."

Clipping Removal

With regular mowing, clipping removal is not usually necessary, except where the closeness of the cut and the turf's playability can be affected by the clippings. Contrary to popular belief, clippings actually don't contribute significantly to the formation of thatch. (Rather, they act as slow-release fertilizer for the turf.) So it makes sense to leave clippings on the turf whenever possible. However, if mowing results in excess clippings, collectors are available for most mowers. There are also sweepers, ranging from affordable models

Table 8.2. Recommended Seasonal Mowing Heights

Type of Grass	Lowest to Highest	Spring	Summer	Fall	Winter[a]
Kentucky Bluegrass	1½–3 in.	1½–2 in.	3 in.	1½–2 in.	
Perennial Ryegrass	1½–3 in.	1½–2 in.	3 in.	1½–2 in.	
Tall Fescue	1½–3 in.	1½–2 in.	3 in.	1½–3 in.	
Bermudagrass	¾–2 in.	¾–1 in.	¾–1 in.	1–2 in.	1–2 in.

[a] Overseeded bermudagrass

Note: A reel mower should be used for cutting heights less than 2 in.

with ground-driven brushes to more expensive power take-off (PTO)-driven units that can pick up clippings from several acres in a short period of time.

Safety

As mentioned earlier, there are precautions that must be taken in mowing around people or animals. Insist that employees keep all shields and guards in place—they must not yield to the temptation to remove them to ease clipping discharge. Also, ensure that employees review the manufacturer's safety information before operating any mower. Insist that operators use proper eye and ear protection and footwear, and that all safety procedures are followed to the letter.

8.4e Irrigation

The average person, if he or she thinks about irrigation at all, probably thinks of it as a process designed to keep turfgrass attractively green (and, in some circumstances, to keep it alive). However, on a baseball or softball field, adequate irrigation has positive effects that go far beyond appearances. Proper irrigation is critical to promoting the healthy turfgrass culture that allows a field to withstand the stresses created by sporting events. Well-irrigated turfgrass has deep and healthy roots, which allow it to recover quickly from the damage inflicted by competition. On the other hand, a poorly irrigated field may be unable to recover from this kind of damage and may be largely unplayable by the end of a season.

Furthermore, properly irrigated turf usually has fewer weeds and insects. As a result, the field may need less fertilizer and fewer pesticide applications, all of which can slash maintenance costs.

Even more important, well-irrigated turf promotes player safety, because it is softer and because it promotes more uniform ball response.

General Principles of Turfgrass Irrigation

Many sports turf managers observe the principle of "deep and infrequent" watering of established fields. This practice is generally effective for providing adequate irrigation while allowing air to move into the soil. It also prevents some of the problems associated with frequent light watering—especially shallow roots and the diseases that can strike turf that is constantly wet.

However, in planning a watering program, the physical characteristics of the soil should be considered. Clay soil will not accept as much water as a sandy soil; 20 to 30 minutes of watering with the average system will cause substantial puddling on the field. On the other hand, a sand-based field can sometimes be watered for an hour without much puddling, and may need that much water.

Automatic systems are becoming increasingly more popular in turfgrass management, but an important point should be noted about their use: Overreliance on the system's controller can lead to excessive or inadequate watering. The manager still needs to physically walk out onto the turf daily to make sure it is getting enough water (but not too much).

Most turfgrass needs as much as 1 in. to 1½ in. of water per week during the growing season, either from rainfall or from supplemental irrigation. (Of course, the amount of water varies, based on the location, soil type, and grass species on the field.) Inadequately watered turf will send its own signals to tell an attentive manager that it needs additional irrigation. Leaves will roll up and wilt. Sustained footprinting will be observed. (The turf will not spring back quickly after foot or vehicular traffic.) Turf color will take on a blue-green hue. All of these are symptoms of desiccation—excessive dryness.

Consideration must also be given to events that are scheduled on the field; heavy watering shortly before a game can produce slippery (and even dangerous) playing conditions.

The best time to irrigate turf is early in the morning, just before or just after sunrise. Early morning watering usually does not interfere with practices or games, and it has the additional advantage of minimizing the length of time the turf remains wet. (Leaving the turf wet for extended periods can lead to outbreaks of disease.) Furthermore, because evaporation rates at that time of day are at their lowest, early morning irrigation tends to get more water into the soil where the plants can use it. Moreover, there is less wind disruption of the irrigation pattern in the early morning hours, so watering is more uniform. Finally, early morning irrigation usually allows the field to dry adequately before competition or practice, thus preventing slippery surfaces.

8.4f   Weeds, Insects, and Disease (Pests)

Although common usage applies the term *pests* to insects that can infest a stand of turfgrass, this discussion uses a definition that is broader and more inclusive. In this section, the term *pest* is used to mean any living organism that competes with turfgrass plants for nutrients, light, water, air, and even space. This broader definition includes pest-incited diseases, weeds and nematodes, as well as insects. (Infestations of nematodes are customarily categorized as diseases, and the control of these organisms is discussed in a following section.)

Some pests, especially aggressive insects like bees and fire ants, cannot be allowed to remain in sports turf because of the danger to players. But for the most part, the objective is to control, rather than totally eradicate, the pest in question. As long as pests are sufficiently controlled to prevent their diminishing the quality and playability of the turf, wiping them out completely usually is not worth the trouble and expense. It is also more environmentally responsible to avoid the kind of chemical applications necessary for total eradication.

It should be noted that good cultural management practices (irrigation, fertilization, mowing, and so on) can make a big difference in reducing problems related to pests in turf areas of a baseball or softball field. Taking good care of the field also reduces the need for pesticide applications, because it helps to maintain a dense, healthy turf that resists weeds, insects, and diseases. Of course, as any field manager knows, it is almost impossible to maintain dense turf cover on a heavily used athletic field all year long. This means that, eventually, just about every field will be infested by some sort of pest.

Weeds

It is important to keep in mind that the definition of a weed is "any unwanted plant." Every baseball field manager recognizes common turfgrass weeds like dandelions, clover, and crabgrass, but some of the toughest weeds to manage are turfgrasses other than those planted on the field. For example, the hardest weed to manage on a Tifway bermudagrass baseball field is another type of bermudagrass. Tall fescue and creeping bentgrass can present weed problems in a Kentucky bluegrass or perennial ryegrass field. For this kind of weed problem, there are very limited chemical control solutions. Short of replacing the turf entirely, the most practical course is to plan maintenance strategies such as mowing, fertility, irrigation, and the like, to favor the desired turfgrass. Remember that maintaining a dense turfgrass canopy is *always* the most effective means of weed control.

It is also worth keeping in mind that many weeds are "indicator plants" that help to identify underlying problems that contribute to weed infestations. For instance, goosegrass and knotweed are indicators of compacted soil, sedges suggest poorly drained soil, and large amounts of clover usually indicate low fertility. Correcting the underlying problem indicated by these plants will often improve the turfgrass and reduce the infestation.

Another common strategy for controlling weeds is the application of herbicides, which are classified by many different methods. *Preemergent* (PRE) herbicides are applied before the target weed emerges from the soil; *postemergent* (POST) herbicides are used to control weeds that have already appeared.

Preemergent herbicides are preventive treatments. They are typically applied in areas that cannot tolerate any weeds at all (like a granular warning track) or when the turf has a history of serious weed problems. Preemergent herbicides are watered-in following application, to get them into the upper soil profile where weeds are germinating. When used according to label instructions, PRE herbicides cause little or no turfgrass discoloration. However, PRE herbicides can have a negative effect on seeding operations for several months following their application. So if overseeding is in your plans, choose a PRE herbicide labeled as suitable for use in newly seeded areas.

Postemergent herbicides are applied to existing weeds and are most effective in controlling weeds that are young and actively growing. Postemergent herbicides are often mixed with a *surfactant,* which is a chemical additive designed to improve herbicide effectiveness. If you are planning to apply a postemergent herbicide, check with your supplier about available surfactants to increase its effectiveness.

Postemergent herbicides are further classified as those with *selective* and *nonselective* action. Selective herbicides control one specific weed or a group of weeds and have little effect on the turfgrass. Most herbicides used in weed control programs on baseball and softball fields are of the selective type.

Nonselective herbicides kill (or at least damage) all plant tissues they contact. These herbicides are usually used for renovation (to kill all vegetation in a specific area) or in situations where any vegetation at all is undesirable (such as skinned areas of baseball fields, along fences, and on warning tracks).

Before applying any herbicide, it is important to know as much as possible about the weed you are targeting, including its life cycle (annual, biennial, or perennial) and when it is likely to appear in the turf. Of course, it is also critical to understand the chemical agent being applied and to carefully follow label directions for safe and effective use. Remember that factors like air temperature, irrigation and rainfall, spray volume and pressure can all affect the safety and effectiveness of the product.

Insects

A wide variety of insects can be found in the turf of almost any field. This discussion of insects includes only those that actually cause damage to turf. When sports turf problems appear, it is often hard to distinguish between insect problems and those caused by disease. The symptoms of insect damage include chlorotic (yellow) spots on turfgrass leaves, as well as missing or dead plant tissues. However, these symptoms can also be observed when disease has struck the turf. Thus, for the field manager, the first step is to determine what problem is present. Because insect problems are easier to identify than disease, it is advisable to start by checking for the presence of large numbers of insects.

Identification and Sampling. To accurately determine what and how many insects are present, we recommend the use of one of the following sampling methods:

1. *A floater can.* Remove both ends of a large can, like a large coffee can. Then press or drive the can about 1 in. into the soil, and fill the can with soapy water about halfway to the top. Most of the insects in the circular section of the turfgrass canopy will float to the top of the water. Check the surface of the water for the type and number of insects present. (See Figures 8.10 and 8.11.)

Figure 8.10. A good method of checking for insect infestation is to remove the ends of a can, drive it into the soil about 1 in., and fill with soapy water.

Figure 8.11. Insects will float to the surface, where a count can be taken to determine the severity of the infestation.

2. *The soapy flush.* Apply a soapy water solution (1 oz liquid detergent per 2 gal water) on an area of approximately 1 sq yd. This soap solution is an irritant to the insects and partially obstructs their breathing apparatus. In less than a minute, insects will emerge from the soil, where they can be identified and counted. This is a good way to detect surface-feeding insects in the canopy.

3. *Soil sampling.* Use a shovel, a golf course cup cutter, or a sod harvester to remove a sample of soil. Check the soil for the presence of subsurface root feeders like grubworms; if they are actively feeding, they will be very close to the surface, where they can eat plant roots. This is the only reliable way to verify the presence of grubworms in the soil. A standard threshold for treatment with a pesticide is accepted to be five grubs per square foot. However, because grubs vary widely in size, some species may have a much higher threshold; consult your area extension specialist to determine whether treatment is necessary.

4. *Natural observation.* In some cases, observing the ecosystem can provide clues to insect infestation. For example, the presence of a flock of birds on the field in midsummer is often a good indicator of armyworms. Burrowing damage caused by insect-eating mammals like skunks, armadillos, and moles indicates the presence of grubworms. (The burrowing animals cause more damage than the insects; getting rid of the insects usually causes the mammals to depart as well.)

Some insects also leave visible signs of their presence. Sod webworms spin a web over the hole in which they live, and this web can be seen easily on mornings when dew is present. However, the fungal mycelia for the disease "dollar spot" look almost identical to webworm webs, and so do spider webs. To be sure the problem is sod webworms, look for a hole in the ground or use the soapy flush method described earlier. This is an example of the importance of correct diagnosis; misidentifying the pest can lead to useless applications of an insecticide to control a disease or of a fungicide to deal with insects.

Insect Control Strategies. When observation and sampling methods have confirmed that the problem of a stand of turfgrass really is insect infestation, a method of control must be chosen and implemented. Here, we consider three general strategies: the use of insecticides (chemical control), biological methods, and cultural practices.

Chemical Control. The most widely used strategy for the control of insects is the application of chemical insecticides. Once the insect has been correctly identified and it has been determined that it is necessary to apply an insecticide, there are many products to choose from. These products, when used according to manufacturers' instructions, are highly effective in controlling most common insects. However, because of the nature of chemical agents, a number of factors must be considered in the selection, handling, and use of the products.

1. In the use of chemical agents, safety must always be a predominant concern. There is very little risk to humans or animals when pesticides are properly applied. However, failure to follow manufacturers' instructions can result in serious problems for people, animals, and the environment in general. Always keep in mind the potential effects of an insecticide on the surrounding environment, which are called "nontarget effects." An example of a nontarget effect is the contamination of nearby water sources by off-site movement of an insecticide.

    Remember that problem insects are not the only creatures that can be killed or harmed by an insecticide application. Small mammals and fish can be sensitive to insecticides, and their poisoning, even if unintentional, is no longer tolerated. Do not risk a public relations nightmare by being careless about following label instructions.

    Many insecticides are also particularly toxic to earthworms, a creature that has a positive value in cultural management. Earthworms help to decompose thatch, as well as improve soil porosity and aeration.

    It is also critical to remember that some athletes may suffer reactions to certain pesticides. Every product's label instructions provide for a specified period after application before use of the field is safe (usually indicated on the label as the "product reentry period"). A wise manager will insist that the field not be used until that specified period has passed, and that signs are posted to inform the public that a pesticide has been applied.

2. To get the maximum benefit from an insecticide, it is important to give careful attention to the timing of the application. Insecticides are formulated to control each insect at a specified stage in its development. To work effectively, the products must be applied at the time indicated by the label. Apply an insecticide at the wrong time, and it may not work. For example, insecticides meant to control sod webworms should not be applied when adult moths can be seen flying out of the turf; application should be made when the number of adult moths has diminished substantially.

3. It is also important to consider whether watering will be necessary following an insecticide application. Some insects (like armyworms and chinch bugs) feed on aboveground parts of plants; controlling these insects requires leaving the insecticide on the leaf surface so that the pest will consume it. Other insects (grubworms and mole crickets) feed on underground plant parts like roots and stems; controlling these insects requires irrigation or rainfall after an application to carry the product into the soil. Be careful of making insecticide applications when rainfall in excess of ½ in. is forecast, because the material may be washed through the zone of effectiveness in the soil.

Armyworms, webworms, and grubs commonly infest turfgrass in both warm and cool season zones. A number of insecticides are widely available for controlling these insects. Mow the turf before application to ensure better coverage and improve control. Armyworm and webworm larvae feed at any time of the day but are most active late in the afternoon, so target applications for that time of day to maximize effectiveness. Do not irrigate or water-in the pesticide, because both are aboveground insects.

In treating for grubs, which feed on the belowground parts of plants, irrigate to move the pesticide into the soil where the grubs are feeding, unless rainfall is expected. Applications are more effective when made in summer to control newly hatched grubs than in spring or fall to control older, larger grubs.

Biological Control Alternatives. Nearly every insect has its own naturally occurring enemies. Serious infestations usually develop when a particular insect has no naturally occurring enemies or when there are so few of those enemies that they have little impact. For example, the mature and immature stages of ladybugs and ground beetles help to control other insects, many of which are turfgrass pests. However, it is important to note that chemical control programs can effectively remove natural biological controls—ladybugs and ground beetles are particularly sensitive to insecticides.

In situations where certain insects present a persistent problem on a field, another type of biological control now being used is the application of *Bacillus* species of bacteria (Bt). These bacteria produce toxins that are lethal to certain insects. Many strains of *Bacillus* are available, each attacking specific insects. It should be noted that although *Bacillus* species can be effective in controlling certain insects, they are usually not as effective as chemical controls. Successful use of *Bacillus* bacteria requires frequent applications, which lead to steady reductions in targeted insect populations but do not immediately control an infestation observed in the turf.

Cultural Strategies. Careful maintenance practices typically have the greatest effect in discouraging insect infestations. Taken together, these practices constitute "cultural control strategies" and minimize the need for chemical or biological controls. Keeping thatch at manageable levels (½ in. or less) will deprive many insects of the environment in which they thrive. Careful fertilization and irrigation will improve the recuperative potential of the turfgrass and help it to withstand insect infestation. Managing compaction through aggressive aeration and frequent mowing (observing the "one-third rule") can have similar effects.

Diseases

In turfgrass management, disease is commonly understood as a condition creating symptoms such as leaf spots, circular discolored patches, and the like. Diseases are caused by microscopic organisms like bacteria and fungi, but vulnerability of the turfgrass to disease is affected by the cultural management practices performed on the field.

For an outbreak of turfgrass disease, three elements must be present: a suitable *environment,* the ecosystem in which the turf is growing; a virulent *pathogen,* the disease-causing organism; and a susceptible *host,* the turfgrass plants. (Figure 8.12 shows how these elements interact in a "turf disease triangle.") Many of the disease-causing organisms are present in the turf canopy or in the soil all the time. Others are brought into the turf by maintenance equipment, foot traffic, water movement, wind, and so forth. In most situations, these organisms do not cause an outbreak of disease, because one of the parts of the triangle is missing. It is only when all three factors are present that a disease outbreak occurs.

The manager has plenty of opportunity to manipulate the turfgrass environment. This is especially true when it comes to the timing and amounts of irrigation. For instance, many disease-causing fungi require significant periods of leaf moisture to gain a foothold in the turf. So keeping the turf wet for extended periods increases the chance that these fungi will become a problem.

Another practice that can increase the likelihood of disease outbreaks is the use of covers to protect the turf or keep playing surfaces dry. Fungi are already present in the soil, and covers create very warm, moist environments beneath, often completing the disease triangle. The result can be an outbreak of a particularly devastating disease such as *Pythium* blight.

Disease-causing factors are designated as either "biotic" (living) or "abiotic" (nonliving). Some common disease-causing factors are categorized as biotic or abiotic in Table 8.3.

We usually think of the biotic factors as the causes of turfgrass diseases, but the abiotic factors also play an important role in causing disease outbreaks.

Among biotic factors, fungi are by far the most important (and most damaging) factor for initiating disease. There are thousands of species of fungi, some of which cause such common turfgrass diseases as snow mold, seedling damping-off, dollar spot, gray leaf spot, and red thread, in addition to the *Pythium* blight mentioned earlier. Bacterial and viral diseases are of minimal concern for sports turf.

Figure 8.12. Turf disease triangle.

Table 8.3. Biotic and Abiotic Disease-Causing Factors

Biotic	Abiotic
Fungi	Excessive thatch development
Nematodes	Mowing
Bacteria	Environmental conditions:
Viruses	temperature, moisture, wind
	Cultural management practices:
	fertility, cultivation, irrigation,
	pesticide applications
	Excessive vehicular or foot traffic

The role of abiotic factors in causing disease is not widely understood. Many experienced field managers, however, have learned by painful experience that even recommended cultural practices, if they are ill-timed or improperly performed, can weaken the plants, making them vulnerable to disease.

Excessive thatch contributes to disease by providing a favorable environment for fungi and by exposing the turfgrass roots and causing desiccation during drought-like conditions.

Mowing can also promote disease by creating a wound that weakens the plant and serves as an entry point for fungi. The amount of damage is increased when the mower blades are dull. Mowing too close also weakens the turf, because the turfgrass will have to expend all of its energy regenerating shoots and leaves.

Other maintenance practices, like core cultivation, fertilization, and irrigation practices, as well as foot or vehicular traffic, also have a role in causing disease. When performed correctly, these practices contribute to the health of the turf and its ability to resist disease. When they are done carelessly, however, they can weaken the turfgrass and lead to outbreaks of disease.

Disease Control Strategies. Obviously, it is important to know what disease you are trying to cure before deciding on a control strategy. Many diseases have characteristic signs (like the appearance of mushrooms in a fairy ring or reddish-brown spores on a leaf infected with rust) or symptoms (such as circular patches of blighted turf, striping or spots on the foliage). Consult a turf disease handbook to help with this identification (full-color books are the easiest to use), or send a sample of the affected turf to a testing lab for expert diagnosis.

Following proper identification of the disease and the disease-causing agent, appropriate decisions can be made to combat the disease. There are two primary strategies for dealing with disease outbreaks: cultural and chemical. Chemical applications should generally be the second choice. However, as any field manager knows, sometimes it is unacceptable to have any visible signs of disease on a baseball or softball field. In such cases, consider applying a broad-spectrum fungicide that will control as many kinds of fungus as possible. But be aware that certain diseases, such as *Pythium* blight, can kill broad areas of turf in a matter of hours, and this fungus can be controlled only by fungicides that target this particular organism.

Where disease outbreaks are limited and are not progressing rapidly, it is usually worthwhile to try cultural controls before spraying fungicides. These strategies fortify the turfgrass culture and encourage natural disease resistance. Improving soil drainage using short-term solutions (like deep-tine aerating), raising the height at which the turf is being mowed, modifying irrigation practices to reduce the time the turf remains wet, and improving air circulation are some of the cultural practices that can be used to control disease outbreaks. Many diseases are also sensitive to changes in fertilization practices. However, before making these changes, it is important to know what disease has broken out. When in doubt, send live plant material from areas where the pathogen is visibly active to a testing lab, which will diagnose the disease and make appropriate recommendations about changes in the fertility program. Do not send dead material from the center of a blighted area. Instead, send material from the edge of the area, where the pathogen is active but the plants are still alive.

When time does not permit the use of cultural controls, chemical controls provide the fastest and most effective relief.

Two strategies are used for disease control with chemicals: preventive and curative.

Preventive chemical disease control is practiced by applying chemical agents in advance of anticipated outbreaks of disease. This strategy is usually employed only on fields that have previously experienced disease problems, and when the field is a high-visibility facility where even small outbreaks would create unacceptable playability and aesthetic concerns.

On a field that does not have a history of disease outbreaks, preventive applications are usually judged to be wasteful and excessive. However, for fields that have been plagued by disease, preventive application will generally *reduce* the amount of chemical agents required. The reason is that an effective preventive application requires only one-third to one-half the amount of product that would be needed to control an outbreak that has already begun.

Curative applications are those used to control outbreaks that have already appeared in the turf. On fields with no history of disease problems, the curative approach saves time, money, and unnecessary applications. However, it is important for the field manager to keep a watchful eye on the turf so that he or she can respond quickly when an outbreak occurs. For example, many leaf spot diseases commonly afflict turfgrass, and most do not indicate the need for an immediate curative application. However, if the disease begins to progress, reaching the crown or base of the plant, "melting out" occurs, turning the entire plant yellow and sometimes leading to its death. At the first sign of melting out, a curative application should be made within a day or two to prevent the further progression of the disease. (Upon identification of other diseases, such as *Pythium* blight, drop everything and make an application as soon as possible.) Once a disease outbreak has progressed beyond a certain point, chemical applications will no longer effectively control it. When substantial areas have progressed to melting out, a curative application will prevent the spreading of the disease, but will not bring back the dead plants in the melted-out areas.

An isolated outbreak of disease does not necessarily indicate the need to switch from curative to preventive applications of fungicide (especially if the outbreak occurs during a season with unusual temperature or rainfall conditions). However, if an outbreak occurs during fairly normal conditions, and especially on a high-visibility field, the manager may want to consider preventive application. In any case, careful record keeping can help the manager know when to look for outbreaks, and help in dealing with them before they become hard to control.

Nematodes. Nematodes are microscopic worm-like creatures, some of which attack the root systems of turfgrasses. Nematodes can be a particular problem in high-sand-content soils, both native and those making use of an amended sand growing medium. Although most nematodes are actually beneficial, some species attack root systems with their piercing, sucking mouthparts. (See Figure 8.13.)

It is hard to diagnose nematode infestation by visual examination. Nematode-infested turf is patchy and moisture-stressed, with galling (swelling) of the root system, which can be detected upon close examination. If nematode infestation is suspected, sample the affected areas to a depth of 4 in. in late spring to early summer and again in late summer to early fall. Place the soil samples in a tightly sealed plastic bag and send them immediately by overnight courier to a disease diagnostic laboratory. (Nematodes can be killed by extreme temperatures, and unless the samples are sent at once, the laboratory examination

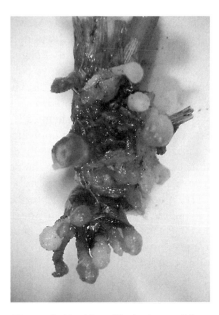

Figure 8.13. Magnified view of ber-mudagrass roots damaged by nema-tode infestation. (Photo courtesy of M. Tomaso-Peterson, Mississippi State University.)

may provide erroneous information.) In addition to diagnosing nematode infestation, lab-oratories can also recommend appropriate treatment.

Diagnostic laboratories have established threshold levels for the nematodes of their own regions, based on experience with the local ecosystem. These thresholds indicate how many nematodes must be present in the soil to cause significant damage. Many nematodes have very high threshold values (several hundred per pint of sampled soil), but others such as the sting nematode (*Belonoliamus* spp.) may have a threshold value of 1—if just one specimen is found, chemical controls are recommended.

It is important to be aware that nematicides—the chemicals used to control nema-todes—are among the most toxic pesticides applied to turfgrass. For this reason, they should be used only when a laboratory can confirm that the threshold value for the infest-ing species has been reached. Nematicides should be applied only as a last resort.

8.5   MAINTENANCE PRACTICES FOR WARM SEASON TURFGRASS

Having reviewed the general principles of turfgrass maintenance, the discussion turns to the specific practices used for warm and cool season turfgrasses, beginning with warm sea-son turf. The most effective maintenance programs operate according to a formal plan, and there should be a separate plan for each individual field. Although a manager may choose to vary from the plan if weather, usage, or other conditions are unusual, failing to have a plan to work from may result in vital steps being overlooked.

Table 8.4 is an example of a maintenance program for a warm season baseball or softball field. This is not the only effective type of program that can be used for warm season turf;

Table 8.4. A Sample Warm Season Maintenance Program

Maintenance Schedule
(Warm Season)

Field Name:	Sean Rochelle Field	Address:	P.O. Box 4929
Type of Field:	Baseball Field		Elkins, AK
Condition:	good	Compaction:	moderate
Type of Grass:	Tifway bermudagrass	Drainage:	surface
Type of Mower:	3 gang reel	Irrigation:	installed automatic system
Type of Soil:	native sandy loam	Thatch:	¼ in. to ½ in.

Soil Test: Notes: Mow 3 times a week during
Year: 2002   Phosphorus: 20   active growth.
pH: 6.2   Potassium: 110

Time of Year	Fertilization	Aeration	Topdress	Overseed	⅓ Rule Mowing Ht	1 in. Week Watering	Weed Control
May	13-13-13 ½ lb N 13-13-13 ½ lb N	vertical mow late			¾ in.	as needed	
June	34-0-0 ½ lb N 13-13-13 ½ lb N	core aeration	⅛ in. sand		¾ in.	½ in. two times a week	POE grass and sedge
July	34-0-0 ½ lb N 13-13-13 ½ lb N	solid-tine aeration	⅛ in. sand		¾ in.	½ in. two times a week	POE grass and sedge
August	34-0-0 ½ lb N 13-13-13 ½ lb N	light vertical mow before overseed			¾ in.	½ in. two times a week	
September	13-13-13 ½ lb N		⅛ in. sand	12 lb perennial rye	¾ in.	light frequent for overseed	
October	21-2-20 1 lb N 0-0-60 1 lb K			3 lb perennial rye	1¼ in.	as needed	
November					1¼ in.	as needed	
December					1¼ in.		
January					1¼ in.		
February	21-2-20 ½ lb N 50% SRN[a]				1¼ in.		
March	21-2-20 ½ lb N 50% SRN				1¼ in.	as needed	
April	10-24-18 1 lb N 50% SRN				1 in.	as needed	

[a] Slow-release nitrogen

the local manager should adapt this model based on his or her own experience. However, it can serve as a starting point for planning a comprehensive set of maintenance practices.

(This sample maintenance program was developed for a baseball field used for fall practice, a spring season from mid-February through mid-May, and a summer season from mid-June to August.)

Warm season turfgrass experiences its strongest growth during the hottest part of the year—typically when daily afternoon temperatures are exceeding 85°F. This annual cycle influences every maintenance practice performed on the turf, inasmuch as the most intensive maintenance period coincides with the time of greatest growth.

8.5a Fertilization

Most of the fertilization needs for bermudagrass, which is by far the most common warm season sports field turfgrass, should be applied when the plants are experiencing their greatest growth—during the hottest months of the year. The typical field needs 5 lb to 6 lb of nitrogen (N) per 1000 sq ft each year, with the first application made about 14 days after spring green-up is complete (or when the threat of recurring frost has passed). Apply ½ lb to 1 lb at this point in the season, followed by 1 lb in each of four applications 30 days apart during the summer. Finally, in mid-September to early October, make another application of ½ lb to 1 lb to complete the program for the year. The October application should also include 1 lb to 2 lb of potassium (K) to help winterize the turf.

The sample program indicates rates of application of water-soluble (or "readily available") nitrogen sources, with slow-release nitrogen (SRN) material applied only during the overseeding transition periods of October and February to March. The 21-2-20 product listed in the sample program is 50% SRN and is used to give the newly emerging grass (which may be perennial ryegrass in the fall or dormant bermudagrass in the spring) a small dose of N without an accompanying flush of growth by the competing grass. It should be noted that there are many SRN materials that can be used throughout the primary growing season as well. These materials are normally applied at rates of up to 2 lb of N per 1000 sq ft and can reduce the number and frequency of applications.

In the warm season zone, bermudagrass is often overseeded with perennial ryegrass (typically in September in the Upper South and in mid-October in the Deep South). In this case, an additional application of ½ lb to 1 lb should be performed in November, followed by ½ lb each in December, February, and March and ½ lb to 1 lb in April. These applications are designed to supply the overseeded ryegrass with just enough nutrients to maintain active growth during cooler months. Exclusive use of SRN sources during the colder months is not recommended, because these materials may require warmer temperatures to supply the desired levels of N.

8.5b Aeration and Topdressing

Ideally, a heavily used warm season field should have at least two core aeration events during the year, along with one solid-tine aeration and one (or more) vertical mowing.

The best times for core aeration are in mid-to-late spring (when the turf has resumed active growth) through midsummer. However, it is important to remember that turf can take as long as 7 to 14 days to recover fully from core aeration, so performing this process during the playing season is usually impractical. On fields that will be in use throughout the summer without a break of at least 7 to 14 days, solid-tine aeration should be utilized and core aeration should be delayed until competition ends. Solid tines (no more than ⅜ in. diameter, 4 in. deep) can be used occasionally during the playing season over the entire field to provide temporary compaction relief without disrupting the playing surface.

But remember that solid-tine aeration does not replace the need for hollow-tine core aeration on compacted soil. At some point in the field maintenance schedule, it will be necessary to perform core aeration. Whenever core aeration is performed, it is necessary to deal with the cores, which can greatly alter field playability, either by removing them or by mat dragging to break them up.

Vertical mowing is performed to control thatch, stimulate new growth, and to help transition bermudagrass on fields overseeded with ryegrass. Vertical mowing should be done in late May to mid-June if a significant thatch layer (greater than ½ in.) is present. This mowing can be performed again in early August in preparation for overseeding in early September. The vertical mowing in August should include only one pass over the field, instead of the two or three passes performed when serious dethatching is the goal, because this practice has been shown to increase the winterkill potential for bermudagrass.

Topdressing with sand or with a selected soil is typically performed to make the playing surface more uniform (smoother) and to reduce thatch. This process is often performed in conjunction with core aeration, inasmuch as the soil channel can then be backfilled with a material that will improve drainage and root growth, such as medium-to-coarse sand for a heavy clay soil. Over time, this application of sand will modify the soil surface and improve drainage rates by creating sand-filled channels that allow water to pass readily through the soil. It is also very common to topdress with soil that is similar to the existing soil, to prevent the development of layering, which can reduce water infiltration and percolation rates.

Begin by aerating the turf. Then apply the matching soil or sand over the entire field to a depth of ⅛ in.; mat-drag the field to smooth the surface and to drag the sand (and broken-up cores, if hollow-tine aeration is used) into the aeration holes in the field.

Topdressing is also performed after overseeding to promote seed:soil contact. An application of ⅛ in. depth is sufficient to enhance seed germination and establishment.

8.5c Mowing

The ideal mowing height for bermudagrass fields is ¾ in. to 1 in. from May through September. Such heights encourage lateral spread and promote recuperation. Note that cutting this short requires mowing at least three times per week during periods of active growth. The cutting height should be raised to 1 in. to 2 in. from October through March to promote winter hardiness. The cutting height can then be gradually reduced toward ¾ in. to 1 in. by May.

8.5d Irrigation

The general principle of ensuring that turfgrass gets 1 in. of water per week whenever it is actively growing should be observed on native soil bermudagrass fields. In the absence of sufficient rainfall to provide the water needed, an effective irrigation strategy for typical sandy loam soil is to provide two irrigation events per week, each irrigation delivering approximately ½ in. of water. Where the soil has a higher clay content, more frequent applications (four per week, of ¼ in.) will help to prevent puddling and runoff.

If the field is overseeded with ryegrass for winter, water lightly but frequently, keeping the top ¼ in. of soil moist at all times to improve germination. After the seed has germinated, water on an as-needed basis to maintain the perennial ryegrass through the rest of the year—typically ½ in. per week.

Because bermudagrass requires some irrigation during the winter months, even when it is not overseeded with ryegrass, monitor rainfall and provide enough water to keep the soil from drying out completely throughout its dormant period. (For more information on off-season maintenance, see the later section entitled "Winter Care.")

8.5e   Overseeding Warm Season Fields

Bermudagrass fields are often overseeded with perennial ryegrass to support late winter and early spring use during the dormant season of the bermudagrass. However, it is important to consider both the benefits and the disadvantages of overseeding. The competition from the overseeded ryegrass is a major detriment to the overall health of the bermudagrass. On the other hand, if it is done properly, overseeding will help to provide a lush, green, actively growing playing surface during the winter dormancy period of bermudagrass and may make the difference between playing on grass and playing on mud for a field receiving heavy traffic. Fields receiving heavy use throughout the fall and winter months, which must be attractive and playable early in the spring, should be overseeded. But remember that bermudagrass turf will always be adversely affected by the perennial ryegrass with which it is overseeded.

Selecting Turfgrass for Overseeding

Warm season fields are usually overseeded with either annual ryegrass or perennial ryegrass. Each has its own strengths and weaknesses, as shown in Table 8.5

As shown in Table 8.5, perennial ryegrass is clearly superior to annual ryegrass for overseeding athletic fields. Annual ryegrass has a lower initial cost per pound of seed, but it is always important to distinguish between "price" and "cost." Although the *price* of seed for annual cultivars is lower, their rapid growth rate requires more frequent mowing, so some of the initial savings are quickly lost. Over the long term, the *cost* of annual ryegrass may actually be higher.

A new third option for overseeding bermudagrass is *intermediate* ryegrass, a hybrid between perennial and annual ryegrass. This type of turfgrass is meant to combine the best qualities of perennial ryegrass (including strong tolerance for extreme temperatures, resistance to pests, and excellent wear resistance) with the strengths of annual ryegrass (most notably, rapid spring transition). The goal of the development efforts currently under way is to offer intermediate ryegrasses that can be overseeded into existing bermudagrass turf, germinate rapidly to support early-season use, then transition quickly without competing

Table 8.5. Comparison of Perennial Ryegrass and Annual Ryegrass

Strengths	Weaknesses
Annual Ryegrass	
• Economical cost.	• Poor wear tolerance.
• Rapid germination.	• Poor tolerance to extreme temperatures.
• Excellent seedling vigor.	• Disease vulnerability.
• Rapid spring transition.	• May transition too quickly.
	• Rapid growth requires frequent mowing.
	• Stains sports uniforms.
	• No sports-turf-specific cultivars.
Perennial Ryegrass	
• Rapid germination.	• Seed is more expensive than
• Very good seedling vigor.	annual ryegrass.
• Improved pest resistance.	• Spring transition to bermudagrass
• Good tolerance to extreme temperatures.	can be difficult.
• Excellent wear resistance.	
• Slow spring transition.	

for nutrients with the existing bermudagrass when temperatures become warm enough to favor the bermudagrass.

The first intermediate ryegrass cultivars have been brought to market, but have not captured a significant share of the market for overseeding. This is largely due to the fact that the initial products have too many of the undesirable qualities of annual ryegrass, especially poor wear tolerance and rapid growth, which requires frequent mowing. However, the potential advantages of a successful intermediate ryegrass are so great that research and development efforts can probably be expected to continue until suitable cultivars are produced.

When to Overseed

Overseeding bermudagrass with ryegrass should be performed in late summer to early fall. However, it is a good idea to order the seed in the spring of the year to ensure an adequate supply for the fall overseeding. For recommended overseeding dates, see Table 8.6.

These recommended dates are based on times when soil temperatures are most favorable for the germination of ryegrass—65°F to 70°F at a 4 in. depth. Overseeding can be performed earlier or later as conditions permit, but may result in poor establishment. Overseeding too early risks too much competition from the bermudagrass, and overseeding too late can result in reduced seed germination.

The Mechanics of Overseeding

Begin the overseeding process by conducting a soil test, unless one has been performed within the last year. Apply the recommended fertilizer, being careful not to overapply nitrogen; too much N will promote competition from the bermudagrass. In the absence of laboratory recommendations, a rule of thumb for overseeding is to apply ½ lb N per 1000 sq ft. A supplemental phosphorus application (1 lb) will promote root establishment in the ryegrass. Most starter fertilizers have the correct ratios to satisfy these requirements.

A key consideration in successful overseeding is good soil:seed contact. Make a single pass with a vertical mower or slit-seeder to open up the turfgrass canopy so the seeds can drop into the soil. Mowing the turf to its lowest recommended level—typically ¾ in.— allows the vertical knives to penetrate more easily into the soil. If vertical mowing is not performed, cutting the turfgrass short is especially important to promote seed:soil contact.

With the turfgrass mowed short, it is time to spread the seed. Most of the field can be seeded with the use of a rotary spreader, but a drop seeder should be used along the edges of skinned areas and warnings tracks to maintain the shape and definition of these areas. After spreading the seed, mat drag it into the turf. A light topdressing (⅛ in. to ¼ in. depth) with sand or matching soil will further improve seed:soil contact.

Typical perennial ryegrass overseeding rates range from 10 lb to 20 lb of pure live seed per 1000 sq ft.

Table 8.6. Overseeding Dates

Overseeding Bermudagrass with Ryegrass	
Zone	Time of Year
Upper South	Sept. 1–Sept. 22
Mid-South	Sept. 15–Oct. 8
Deep South	Oct. 1–Oct. 21

For optimal germination, water lightly and frequently—a few minutes every couple of hours or so. Be sure that the seed does not dry out, but avoid keeping the area saturated (saturation can deprive roots of needed oxygen and can lead to seedlings damping-off, which will kill the new plants). Keep watering lightly until the seed germinates, then gradually reduce the irrigation frequency. When germination is complete, begin applying moisture deeply and infrequently to encourage the development of a deep root system and a mature, well-established turf.

Begin mowing when the ryegrass reaches the winter mowing height (typically 1½ in. to 2 in.). For the first couple of mowings, leave clippings on the field to avoid picking up the seed that has not yet germinated.

Winter Care

As long as the temperature remains above freezing, the overseeded perennial ryegrass will be growing, and when the temperatures rise above 50°F the growth will accelerate. Continue mowing and performing other maintenance functions throughout the winter to ensure that the turf will be in good condition when the next competition season arrives.

Fertilization rates also depend on field use and environmental conditions. If the turf continues to grow actively, it needs regularly scheduled fertilizer applications, usually about ½ lb of water-soluble nitrogen per 1000 sq ft a month. Avoid unnecessary fertilization, which creates extra mowing requirements and makes the turf susceptible to winterkill and disease. If soil tests indicate that phosphorus, potassium, or other nutrients are needed, they can also be applied in the winter. However, both bermudagrass and overseeded ryegrass get more benefit from these nutrients if they are applied at the time of overseeding, before the onset of winter weather.

Most of the country gets enough winter rainfall to make supplemental irrigation unnecessary. But winter desiccation of warm season turfgrasses is a vastly underappreciated contributor to winterkill, because dormant bermudagrass may not show the effects of dryness. Overseeded ryegrass will show wilt symptoms as a clear indicator of moisture stress. Be sure to monitor precipitation levels and provide irrigation to sustain active growth of the ryegrass—½ in. of water per week is usually sufficient.

Spring Transition

At some point in the spring, rising temperatures and lack of moisture will result in significant loss of the overseeded ryegrass and a transition back to a bermudagrass field. The ideal transition is hardly noticeable; the greening bermudagrass simply replaces the dying ryegrass. Of course, accomplishing such a seamless transition is easier said than done; the turf usually passes through a phase of brown or yellowed appearance.

Cutting back on irrigation usually makes this transition quicker. Increasing nitrogen fertility levels, reducing irrigation, and lowering mowing heights will all favor the emerging bermudagrass. However, if the fields are being used during this period, sustaining the ryegrass by watering frequently will slow the transition and keep the turf relatively thick until later in the spring when the bermudagrass can fully support competitive play by itself.

In addition, there are chemical products that can be used to assist in ryegrass removal during spring transition, including pronamide, metsulfuron, rimsulfuron, and imazaquin. All of these products have been shown to selectively remove ryegrass from bermudagrass. Although these products work similarly, it is important to be aware that their application directions differ substantially. Before applying these chemical controls, it is critically important to be fully aware of the restrictions and limitations on their use.

8.5f   Weeds, Insects, and Disease

Weed Control

The best way to prevent weed problems on any field is to maintain such a thick and healthy stand of turfgrass that weeds will have a hard time competing. A key element in this process is an aggressive fertility program that encourages a thick turfgrass canopy. Such a program reduces the need for applying preemergent herbicides and postemergent blanket programs. When weeds appear in this kind of healthy canopy, spot-applications of postemergents will usually control the problem at a modest cost.

On a bermudagrass field, the most common problem weeds are the summer annuals crabgrass and goosegrass. Scattered clumps of the perennial weed dallisgrass may have to be treated during June and July with arsonate herbicides such as MSMA or DSMA. Nutsedge can appear any time of year and can also be spot-treated. Both nutsedge and perennial (green) kyllinga can be treated during the summer months with halosulfuron, and imazaquin can be effective on certain sedges as well.

If a field has suffered from chronic and serious weed infestation, preemergents can be applied in early spring, after the bermudagrass has greened-up. For the most effective crabgrass control, apply the herbicide when soil temperatures at a 4 in. depth reach the 50°F to 55°F level for five consecutive days. If the field is not to be overseeded in the fall, this treatment can be repeated at that time of year to control winter annual weeds such as annual bluegrass.

Insect Control

Most turfgrass insect problems in the warm season zone are the same as those appearing in cool season fields. However, there are a few insects that are specific to warm season turfgrass.

Although their effect on the turfgrass itself is not extreme, *fire ants* are a particularly pressing insect problem throughout the entire South. This is because of their well-established danger to players and their habit of building mounds that disturb footing and ball response.

Killing the queen ants is the key to controlling fire ants, but their location deep in the soil makes this a difficult task, requiring repeated chemical applications. Minimize disturbance of the colony when applying a chemical; significant disturbance will cause the queen to move to a new location.

Effective chemical treatment of fire ants begins with broadcasting granular pesticide baits over observed mounds in the spring, when soil temperatures are between 70°F and 90°F and there is no chance of rain. Follow label directions on timing of applications. If there are only a few mounds to treat, you can drench the mound with an insecticide labeled for fire ants in midmorning as the sun warms the colony. Additional applications are usually required, because total eradication is next to impossible.

Fire ants are also being controlled with high-pressure steam injection of their mounds. Initial use of this method has shown good success.

Perhaps the best news for fire ant control is that close mowing of the turf is an effective cultural control for fire ant mounds, because the constant disruption of their mounds causes them to move to another location away from the field. However, these pests have been known to show up from time to time even in closely mowed turf.

Another warm season turfgrass insect problem of major importance is *mole crickets*, which infest fields in the Southeast, especially along the Gulf and Atlantic coasts. These insects become active in the spring when soil temperatures rise. Damage becomes evident as the male mole crickets construct tunnels located right at the soil surface; the visible tunneling in the spring is the first sign of activity. Such tunneling causes damage to the turf.

As with fire ants, controlling mole crickets usually requires a good deal of persistence, and complete eradication (especially in Florida) is seldom possible. When signs of an infestation are observed (usually in March or April), use a soapy water flush in problem areas to determine the number of mole crickets present. Once the soapy flush has confirmed mole cricket infestation, the rule of thumb is wait three to four weeks, then chemically treat the target areas. This delay allows effective control of mid-to-late nymphal-stage mole crickets and recently hatched crickets. (Younger crickets are most vulnerable to chemical control.)

In controlling mole crickets, it is important to select an insecticide with good soil residual properties so as to effectively control nymphs in various stages of development. When applying chemical controls, be careful to follow the label's instructions regarding irrigation and rainfall. Most insecticides perform better if the soil is moistened first, whereas others can be washed away completely if a significant irrigation or rainfall event follows application.

About three weeks after making an application, perform another soapy flush to check for evidence of further mole cricket activity. If necessary, make follow-up insecticide applications.

Commercially available biological control methods (including the use of nematodes, parasitic wasps, and tachinid flies) have shown promise for control of mole crickets. These biological controls typically do not control mole crickets by themselves, but they can significantly reduce mole cricket populations in a program that also includes chemical controls.

Disease Control

The bermudagrass fields of the warm season zone tend to be less affected by disease than the Kentucky bluegrass/ryegrass fields of the cool season zone. Field managers in the warm season zone are most likely to encounter disease problems in the ryegrass used to overseed their bermudagrass turf. (*Pythium* is typically the most damaging example.) Outbreaks of dollar spot, brown patch, and melting out on bermudagrass are not uncommon, but they are not usually a major problem because of the aggressive growth habit of the bermudagrass. Two diseases specific to bermudagrass that can be serious concerns are spring dead spot and Gaummanomyces decline. Many turf pathologists believe these two diseases to be closely related and likely generated by the same group of fungi. Spring dead spot has been shown to be effectively controlled with fall applications of the appropriate fungicide; the best time to treat is approximately 30 days before the first anticipated killing frost. Chemical control of Gaummanomyces decline, a disease that attacks the root system of the turf, has not been nearly so successful, and indications are that the best way to try to manage it is to simply raise the cutting height.

On most bermudagrass fields, disease outbreaks are usually not serious enough to justify blanket applications. When a serious outbreak occurs, blanket curative applications are usually required. (Some diseases can be spread by mowing equipment, so once a serious outbreak is diagnosed, spot applications usually will not control them.)

It should also be noted that most disease problems are aggravated by cultural mistakes, such as overcompaction of the turf and overwatering, which leaves the turf wet for long periods. It is also important to watch for outbreaks of *Pythium* when the field has been left covered for an extended period. The label directions of most fungicides also suggest other maintenance practices that can help to prevent disease outbreaks.

8.6   MAINTENANCE PRACTICES FOR COOL SEASON TURFGRASS

As mentioned earlier in regard to maintenance practices specific to warm season sports turf, it is important to operate according to a formal plan, which can be adapted according to the manager's experience with a particular field.

In considering the specific maintenance practices for cool season turfgrass, an important principle should be kept in mind: Intensive maintenance practices, including fertilization, aeration, and the closest mowing of the year, should all be performed when the turf is most actively growing. Cool season turfgrasses have their own annual cycle, with active growth in the spring and early summer, dormancy in the hottest part of the year, and another growing season in the late summer and fall. This cycle presents the field manager with a special maintenance challenge, inasmuch as the baseball season usually extends into the hottest part of the summer. Table 8.7 is a sample maintenance program that can be tailored for any baseball or softball field using cool season turfgrass.

8.6a   Fertilization

Because of the two active growth periods of cool season turfgrass, these fields need to receive about 30% of their annual nitrogen (N) fertilization in the spring, with very light summer fertilization and the rest applied during the late summer and fall. Restricting N application in the spring helps to prevent excessive shoot growth at that time of year and encourages root growth. (Deeper roots help the turfgrass withstand summer stresses.) Restricting N application in the spring also helps to reduce disease pressure that can result from excessive early-season fertilization.

A good choice for the first fertilization of the spring is a starter fertilizer like 18-24-12; the actively growing plants will benefit from the additional phosphorus (P) and potassium (K) at this time of year. One early summer application of a fertilizer light in nitrogen but heavy in potassium (½ lb N and 1 full lb K) enhances plant health during the heat of the summer and helps the turf resist disease.

Making the heaviest applications of N in the fall contributes to strong root growth and assists turf recovery from the stresses of the competition season. The ideal time to apply N is immediately after the final mowing of the season. At this point, the grass is still green; shoot growth has slowed dramatically, but root growth continues. (Once the turf has gone brown and dormant, there is little reason to apply fertilizer.) The fall application of nitrogen supports active root growth and helps the plants accumulate carbohydrates (stored food reserves) in the roots and stems. Good carbohydrate reserves will provide energy to the plants during the winter, encourage an early spring green-up, and prepare the turf to withstand summer stresses the following season.

8.6b   Aeration

Turf performance is improved by aerating frequently and by using differing types of equipment. On a baseball field, solid-tine aeration should be used instead of core aeration during the season unless the cores can be removed; leaving cores on the field causes erratic and potentially dangerous ball response. After the season ends (from late summer through fall), it is good practice to core aerate as frequently as once a month, dragging to break up the cores. Cores left unbroken (even after the season) may result in a bumpy surface the following year. Remember that any process as disruptive as core aeration should be performed when the cool season turf can most quickly recover—ideally, in late summer to early fall. (The process could be performed in the spring, but would adversely affect playability of the field.)

Table 8.7. Sample Maintenance Schedule for Cool Season Turfgrass

Maintenance Schedule
(Cool Season)

| Field Name: | Canfield High School | Address: | 100 Cardinal Drive |
| Type of Field: | Baseball Field | | Canfield, OH |

Condition:	good	Compaction:	yes—dugout, home plate, pitcher's mound
Type of Grass:	blue/rye	Drainage:	installed pipe drain system
Type of Mower:	60" rotary	Irrigation:	installed automatic system
Type of Soil:	clay/loam	Thatch:	½" infield, ¼" outfield

Soil Test: Notes: Chickweed near outfield fence.
Year: 2002 Phosphorus: 95 Some clover, crabgrass.
pH: 6.8 Potassium: 395 Check sprinkler head elevations.

Time of Year	Fertilization	Aeration	Topdress	Sod or Slit-seed	⅓ Rule Mowing Ht	1 in. Week Watering	Weed Control
April	18-24-12 ½ lb N 50% SRN[a]				2"		
May	24-5-11 ¾ lb N 50% SRN	12" solid-tine aeration			2"	as needed	spot-treatment
June		slice entire field			2¼"	deeper, less frequent	
July	16-0-31 ½ lb N 25% SRN				2½"	deeply	spot-treatment
August				blue/rye touchup spots	2½"	deeply	
September	32-5-7 1 lb N 50% SRN	core and drag	for surface leveling	sod worn areas	2¼"	water new sod	spot or blanket
October	20-5-10 ¾ lb N 50% SRN	core and drag			2"	as needed	
November	1 lb N after last mowing	core and drag			2"		

[a] Slow-release nitrogen

8.6c Topdressing and Slit-Seeding

Topdressing and slit-seeding are discussed earlier in Chapter 6, describing renovation. These are also important parts of an effective yearlong maintenance schedule for cool season fields.

Topdressing helps to control thatch and provides the additional benefit of leveling the surface. On fields with heavy thatch buildup or uneven surfaces, it is a good idea to topdress after the season ends and during the late summer–early fall growing season.

Begin the process by core aerating the field. Then apply the topdressing material, which should be matching soil or sand. Finally, use a drag mat or field leveler to break up the cores and leave the surface as uniform as possible.

If the turf is not as thick as you would like it to be, the late summer–early fall period is also a good time to slit-seed. This process can be used to plant additional turfgrass matching the existing grass or to introduce new varieties with improved performance characteristics into the turf.

8.6d Mowing

Cool season baseball and softball fields are typically planted with perennial ryegrass, Kentucky bluegrass, or a combination of the two. In the spring, the ryegrass starts growing first. On combination fields, the most common type, keep the mowing height at 2 in. or less. (Managers who are responsible for maintaining fields for other sports, especially football, may choose to begin mowing at 2 in. and slowly increase the height to 3 in. during the heat of the summer, but baseball and softball fields are typically kept at 2 in. or less.) If the mowing height is maintained at 2 in., the growing perennial ryegrass will be kept short enough that sunlight will reach the bluegrass when it is just starting to grow. If the season ends in midsummer, raise the height ¼ in. at each mowing to help the turf withstand the summer's heat.

Begin lowering the mowing height ¼ in. at a time when temperatures drop in September. The actively growing turf will easily accommodate the shorter cutting, and the lower height will make topdressing and leveling easier—a field leveler or drag moves much more smoothly over shorter grass.

It is important to keep mowing as long as the grass is actively growing, remembering not to remove more than one-third of the grass at each cutting. If the grass is left too long over the winter, the risk of snow mold increases. However; cutting off too much of the plants in late fall can expose their crowns to cold winter temperatures, thus weakening the grass.

8.6e Irrigation

Cool season turfgrass needs approximately 1 in. of water per week during the growing season. If rainfall amounts to less than 1 in., it may be necessary to irrigate to make up the difference. If spot-seeding or slit-seeding is performed in the fall, keep the soil moist until germination occurs, then make sure that it gets 1 in. per week for the rest of the growing season. If areas have been sodded around the base lines or the outfield arc as part of a renovation project, water the newly sodded areas enough to prevent them from drying out completely for the first two weeks or so after the sod is installed.

8.6f Weeds, Insects, and Disease

Weed Control

On most cool season turfgrass fields, spot-applications of postemergent weed control agents should take care of any weed outbreaks that occur. Make the application when the weeds and the turf are actively growing, and when there will be no activity on the field for at least 24 hours. (Federal law, and the laws in some states, require at least a 24-hour reentry period after an application.) If a blanket treatment is needed, it is better to perform this application in the fall when the field is no longer in use, but while the turf is still actively growing.

Insect Control

Grubs are probably the most damaging insect pests on cool season turfgrass. If grub damage is observed during the season, it usually appears in late July or early August. Make a curative application of a grub-specific insecticide the first time there is an opportunity to keep players off the turf for 24 hours after the treatment. It is a good idea to make an application of an appropriate preventive product the next spring, following manufacturer's instructions for correct timing.

For infestations of nearly every other insect pest, such as chinch bug and sod webworm, curative spot-applications of specific insecticides are usually sufficient, and preventive blanket applications are hardly ever necessary.

Disease Control

Although disease-causing fungi are present in nearly every stand of cool season turfgrass, disease outbreaks are seldom serious enough to justify the cost of blanket applications of fungicides. However, on the highest-profile fields (such as professional fields or major university facilities), preventive applications of broad-spectrum fungicides will enhance the appearance of the field throughout the playing season.

When a serious outbreak of disease is observed, blanket curative applications are typically required. (As mentioned earlier in regard to warm season fields, some diseases are spread by mowing, and once a serious outbreak is diagnosed, spot-applications are usually inadequate to control them.) Unlike insect infestations, outbreaks of disease during a season usually do not require preventive applications the following spring. Each year's conditions create different environmental conditions, which may or may not increase the likelihood of disease outbreaks. However, if you observe a consistent pattern of disease in a stand of turf, it may be necessary to take more preventive measures. For instance, this has been true of *Rhizoctonia* blight on some cool season sports fields.

The most common cool season turf diseases are dollar spot (which appears in the summer), red thread (in the fall, typically after the season), and *Pythium* blight (in the summer, and often caused by overwatering). The summer disease gray leaf spot (or blast) has also become a major problem in perennial ryegrass and tall fescue since the mid-1990s. Leaf spot, also known as *Helminthosporium* leaf spot, appears in the spring, and although the turf will usually recover without chemical controls, managers of high-profile fields may choose to treat this condition to improve the appearance of the turf. The disease referred to as "rust," which gives the turf a characteristic hue that discolors shoes and players uniforms, is more an annoyance than a threat to the turf. However, for the sake of aesthetics, the manager can prescribe a curative application of chemical controls. Cultural controls, including removal of clippings and scheduling irrigation to minimize the amount of time the turf is kept wet, will help to minimize problems with rust.

It should also be noted that most disease problems are aggravated by cultural mistakes, such as overcompaction of the soil, misapplication of fertilizers, and poorly planned irrigation. The label directions of most fungicides also provide guidance for the kind of maintenance practices that can help turf resist these diseases.

8.7   TRANSITIONAL ZONE TURFGRASS MAINTENANCE

A substantial portion of the fields in North America are in the Transitional Zone, where neither warm season or cool season turfgrasses are ideally suited. In planning a maintenance program for Transitional Zone fields, the manager should use the practices appropriate for the type of turfgrass on the field. Maintain warm season varieties according to the warm season program, and cool season varieties according to the typical northern program. Of course, maintaining healthy turfgrass in the Transitional Zone depends largely on selecting appropriate cultivars. Bermudagrasses with improved cold tolerance and Kentucky bluegrasses and perennial ryegrasses with improved heat and drought tolerance are the logical choices.

The primary difference is that the active growing period will vary slightly from that which would be typical in the warm season or cool season zones. By carefully observing the behavior of the turf on his or her own fields, a manager will be able to make slight adjustments to maximize its health and strength.

An exception to this principle is tall fescue, which is sometimes used for Transitional Zone fields, particularly in the northern sections of this region. The primary limitations of tall fescue are its bunch-type growth habit and fact that it must be mowed to a height of at least 2 in.—higher than most baseball players and coaches prefer. Tall fescue has a deep root system that allows it to withstand periods of moisture stress during the summer months, but it requires supplemental irrigation to achieve its highest quality.

Fertility programs for tall fescue typically call for the application of 1 lb of nitrogen in early May, followed by 1 lb to 1½ lb in early September and in early November. Heavy spring fertilization of tall fescue can trigger serious outbreaks of *Rhizoctonia* blight.

8.8   APPLICATION OF PESTICIDES

Because of the combination of safety and regulatory issues relating to the application of chemical controls, the manager should be aware of the principles involved in their use. First, a point of clarification: Although common usage sometimes employs the term *pesticides* to indicate only those products used to control insects, the true meaning of the term is any chemical control used for insects, weeds, or disease. Because the principles of safe use are typically the same, the information in this section applies to all products within this category.

8.8a   Label Instructions

It is important to remember that in the use of any particular pesticide, "the label is the law." Any use of a pesticide that violates label instructions is considered a violation of the law and is subject to legal action by the regulatory authorities. It is a good idea to read the label a minimum of three times before applying any pesticide, especially if it is one you haven't used before. There is no substitute for a complete understanding of the product and its safe use.

Manufacturers' labels provide specific direction on mixing, application, and disposal of a product to maximize its effectiveness and minimize any hazard related to its use. Labels also indicate other products, like fertilizers and other pesticides, that can be safely mixed with sprayable formulations. Failing to follow these directions can lead to turf damage as well as safety hazards.

Labels always contain a signal word to indicate the *toxicity*, the potential hazard represented by the product. The toxicity classifications are Caution, Warning, and Danger.

"Caution" appearing on a label designates the least toxic chemical agents, and "Danger" indicates the most toxic.

8.8b   Material Safety Data Sheets

Next to product labels, Material Safety Data Sheets (MSDSs) are the most critical documents for the use and handling of chemicals. An MSDS includes a written description of the chemical action of a product, detailed instructions for cleaning up spills, and directions on treating accidental exposure. The law requires that an MSDS be physically present whenever a chemical agent is being used or transported. The potential cost of failing to have an MSDS on hand can be staggering. When using a product for which you don't have an MSDS, contact the chemical distributor or the manufacturer to get this important document before handling or using the product.

These documents must be kept in an easily accessed location, and workers using chemical agents must understand (and be able to apply) the information they contain. Occupational Safety and Health Administration (OSHA) or Environmental Protection Agency (EPA) inspectors can ask crew members to produce the MSDSs for all chemicals in use at the job site and will usually ask them to explain the information on the sheet. If an inspector determines that the crew does not understand the information, the employer will be considered in violation of the law and may be subject to fines and other punishments.

(Pesticides are not the only materials considered "hazardous chemicals." Gasoline, solvents, and many other products typically used around a shop are also classified as hazardous. Be sure MSDSs are on hand for all of them.)

In addition to the Caution/Warning/Danger designation on the label of a product, its MSDS will also include Toxicity Classifications, expressed as LD_{50} and LC_{50} values. These values represent lethal dosages (LD) or lethal concentrations (LC) of a substance—the amount required to kill half of the test organisms (typically mice or rats) in a scientific study. The lower the LD_{50} and LC_{50} values, the more toxic the substance (that is, it takes relatively little to kill 50% of the test population). Table 8.8 illustrates the toxicity classification used on an MSDS. Note that the Caution/Warning/Danger designations correspond to levels of toxicity expressed as LD_{50} and LC_{50} values.

8.8c   Application Equipment

There is a wide variety of equipment on the market for applying pesticides and other chemical agents. Each type provides the manager a specific set of options for selecting and applying these products.

A critical factor in using any type of application equipment is calibration. Each piece of equipment should be carefully calibrated according to manufacturer's instructions before

Table 8.8.   Toxicity Classification

Toxicity Classification	Label Signal Word	Oral LD_{50} (mg/kg body weight)	Dermal LD_{50} (mg/kg body weight)	Inhalation LC_{50} (mg/l of volume)
I	Danger	<50	<200	<0.05
II	Warning	>50–500	>200–2000	>0.05–0.5
III	Caution	>500–5000	>2000–5000	>0.5–2.0
IV	Caution	>5000	>5000	>2.0

it is used, and the calibration should be checked regularly—even daily during large applications—to ensure uniform application. Be sure to clean your equipment before calibrating it. A dirty spreader or sprayer may deliver the product in amounts much different than the initial calibration would indicate. If a piece of equipment is calibrated at the beginning of a large job and then used for five days without cleaning or recalibrating, by the end of the application it is hard to tell what the actual application rate may be.

Whichever type of equipment is used, determining the amount of material to be applied requires an accurate knowledge of the square footage of the area to be treated. Experience with the equipment will help the operator know whether further adjustment is needed to maintain the desired rate of application. Monitoring the rate of application is an every-day process—a spreader is never calibrated "once and for all time." Be sure to record all settings and information in an application logbook to use as a reference for future calibrations and chemical applications. Although the settings can't be written in stone, because equipment and applicator performance vary over time, having this information handy will allow more efficient calibration in the future.

The most common types of application equipment are broadcast spreaders for granular materials and spray equipment for liquid products. To allow for a full range of options in applying chemical agents, it is a good idea to have access to one of each.

Broadcast spreaders include both walk-behind and tractor-driven models. Walk-behind spreaders are usually sufficient for a single field, but facilities with multiple fields should consider tractor-driven spreaders—they pay for themselves in reduced labor costs.

Granular broadcast, or "rotary," spreaders drop the material out of a hopper onto a spinning wheel that distributes the pellets over the turf. The advantages of rotary spreaders include the speed with which they can deliver material over large areas, the reduced chance of skips, and the fact that they can be used for virtually any grade (size) of fertilizer or pesticide. The disadvantages are that they sacrifice some uniformity in delivery and cannot accurately apply materials under windy conditions.

Spacing between spreader paths (equipment tracks) is probably the greatest variable. Common practice is to maintain a 40% overlap of the broadcast pattern; if the spreader is throwing a band 12 ft wide, overlap about 5 ft on the next pass to ensure uniform coverage. With walk-behind equipment, it is important to maintain a constant walking speed in order to achieve uniform application.

In selecting a sprayer, the key consideration is gallons per minute delivered. Most sprayers deliver between ½ gal and 4 gal per minute. Models applying 2 gal or less per minute, called "low-volume" sprayers, are adequate for most sports field applications. Weed control products typically can be applied at rates as low as ½ gal per minute, but insecticides and fungicides usually require a sprayer that can put out a minimum of 2 gal per minute.

For spray equipment, several components of the system play a critical part in maximizing performance. One crucial sprayer part is the nozzle, and for most sports fields applications, the best choice is a "flat fan" nozzle. Other types of nozzles (cone, hollow-cone, even-fan, etc.) are designed for applications that require specific spray pressures and for various chemical formulations. A type of nozzle coming into wide use is the large droplet or "low-drift" nozzle, which does not create the kind of mist that is likely to drift on the breeze, a common problem with spray applications. When in doubt, consult your equipment supplier for advice on which nozzle is best suited to your particular need.

As anyone experienced with spray equipment will tell you, proper maintenance is required to achieve optimum performance. Clogged, mismatched or damaged nozzles will not apply the material uniformly and at the desired rates. Sprayers also have filters to remove impurities and large particles. These filters should be cleaned and/or replaced periodically to prevent clogs.

Drop spreaders for granular materials are commonly sold to the public for treatment of lawns. However, their small size and the difficulty in controlling application rates make these devices unsuitable for most sports field uses. (They *are* useful for applying seed along base paths and other skinned areas, but not for application of pesticides.)

Whatever type of equipment is used, stress to staff members the importance of maintaining a consistent speed and overlap. Failure to observe these guidelines is probably the most common mistake in applying chemical agents and can substantially reduce the effectiveness of the materials applied.

8.8d Equipment Calibration

Effective application of pesticides or fertilizers requires the correct calibration of the equipment to be used. Here are suggested calibration procedures for the three commonly used types of equipment: boom sprayers, rotary (centrifugal) spreaders, and drop spreaders.

Boom Sprayer Calibration
1. Begin by inspecting your equipment to see that all parts are in working condition. Be sure to determine your pump drive setup.
2. Refer to the manufacturer's product label to determine the amount of water needed to properly apply the chemical.
3. Make nozzle and tip selections according to the specific use and/or boom configuration of your sprayer.
4. Determine the boom width. Measure the spacing between two nozzles and multiply by the number of nozzles on the entire boom. Express this value in feet.
5. Define a linear test course with terrain similar to the area to be sprayed. In preparing to apply the material to a baseball or softball field, use a grassy, level terrain rather than a paved parking lot or street. The test course should be at least 100 ft long.
6. Calculate the time it takes to travel the linear test course at the recommended (or desired) transport speed. If the pump for the system is powered by the vehicle's power take-off (PTO), be sure the PTO is engaged while calculating the speed. Machine speed should be measured with a running start.
7. Determine the area to be treated by multiplying the boom width (calculated in item 4) by the test course length.

The size of the area to be treated having been calculated, the next step is to determine the total nozzle output. (You will need a stopwatch to do this accurately.) Set the spray system to deliver the desired working pressure and fill the tank with water. Then measure the nozzle output for each nozzle for the amount of time it took to cover the test course. For instance, if it took 30 sec to travel the test course, place a graduated cylinder under the nozzle and spray for 30 sec. Check each nozzle on the boom. There should be no more than a 10% variation (plus or minus 5%) in nozzle output. If the volume collected from any nozzle exceeds this variation, check to see if it is damaged or clogged and then clean or replace it.

Divide the total output by 128 (the number of ounces in a gallon) to determine the application volume in gallons. Then divide the volume in gallons by the area of the test course. You will now have a volume/unit area expression. For example, if your calibration resulted in the delivery of 1 gal of water with a 15 ft boom sprayer to a test course 100 ft long, you would be treating a 1,500 sq ft area. You would be delivering approximately 29 gal per acre:

$$\frac{1 \text{ gal}}{1,500 \text{ sq ft}} :: \frac{x \text{ gal}}{43,560 \text{ sq ft}} = 29.04 \text{ gal per acre.}$$

(This is calculated by cross multiplying the numerators and denominators and solving for x.)

If your application rate has to be stated in gallons per thousand square feet, divide the number of gallons per acre (29.04) by 43,560 ÷ 1,000, or 43.56. The rate would then be stated as 0.67 gal per 1,000 sq ft.

Now you have calibrated the sprayer, and you are ready to calculate how much chemical is needed.

Add the appropriate amount of chemical and water to the tank to treat the desired area at the label rate. For example, suppose you are using a 50 gal sprayer that is calibrated to deliver 0.67 gal per 1,000 sq ft, as shown in the preceding calculation. You will be able to treat 50 gal @ 0.67 gal/1,000 sq ft = 74,627 sq ft of area.

If your pesticide were to be delivered at a recommended rate of 5.88 oz of product per 1,000 sq ft, you would apply

$$\frac{5.88 \text{ oz product}}{1,000 \text{ sq ft}} :: \frac{x \text{ gal product}}{74,627 \text{ sq ft}} = 3.4 \text{ gal}$$

Cross multiply, divide, solve for x, and you get 3.4 gal of product added to the tank, and then apply it to 74,627 sq ft (1.72 acres).[2]

After performing these calculations, record your calibration data for future reference.

(We recommend that you read the product label three times prior to any chemical application. This greatly reduces the chances of making a mistake.)

Rotary (Centrifugal) Spreader Calibration

1. Measure a test course (for the purposes of this exercise, 100 ft).
2. Place a known weight of granular product in the spreader.
3. If the product label has recommended spreader settings for the type of spreader to be used, select the recommended spreader setting. The recommended settings do not eliminate the need to calibrate, but they can speed the process because they are likely to be very close to the correct setting. If no recommended spreader setting is available, choose a low-medium setting as your starting point.
4. Distribute the product over the test course and determine the overall width of spread. Be sure to choose a calibration area similar in slope and terrain to your application area and establish a comfortable and repeatable walking speed. Drastic changes in terrain or walking speed from those used in the calibration run can substantially alter the accuracy of your product application.

   The "effective width of spread" for most rotary units is approximately 75% of the overall width of spread. (Spreaders cannot accurately deliver the product in an exactly uniform manner over the entire area because of the pattern of distribution created by a rotary spreader.)

   For example, if the material is being spread in a pattern a total of 12 ft in width, your effective width of spread will be 12 ft × 0.75 = 9 ft. Remember that some of the material has been spread beyond the effective width of spread, so you will have to overlap each pass by 25% to 33% of the overall width of spread to ensure uniform distribution of the material.

---

[2] Thanks to Pat Sneed, CGCS, Mississippi State University, for his help in developing these procedures for boom sprayer calibration.

5. After delivering the material over the test area, subtract the remaining weight of product in the spreader from the initial weight to determine how much has been spread. For example, if you began with 10 lb of product and you now have 7 lb of product remaining in the hopper, you have applied 3 lb of product. Now calculate the area over which this product has been spread by multiplying the effective width of spread (9 ft) by the length of the test course (in this example, 100 ft). This will give you an application area of 900 sq ft. Using the previous area calculation, you will have applied 3 lb of product per 450 sq ft. Next, transform this value to the target application rate from the label directions. For instance, the label directions may call for 4 lb per 1000 sq ft.

$$\frac{3 \text{ lb}}{900 \text{ sq ft}} :: \frac{x \text{ lb}}{1000 \text{ sq ft}} = 3.33 \text{ lb product/1000 sq ft}$$

In this case, you would slightly increase the spreader settings and repeat the preceding steps until the spreader is applying the material at the rate recommended on the label. (Many spreader companies now offer a "spreader skirt" that is attached to the spreader itself to directly collect the chemical being applied. After the effective width of spread over a short area is determined, the skirt is attached to the spreader and it is pushed across the test length. With this device, the material does not have to be actually distributed over the area, preventing the application of excessive product during calibration runs. If available, a spreader skirt will be a wise investment.)

Remember to record your calibration settings for this particular material and spreader, to make the process quicker in the future.

There are a number of other factors to consider in using rotary spreaders. These spreaders are ideal for rapid distribution of granular products over relatively large areas, but remember that there may be special situations that warrant more precise delivery than can be achieved with a rotary spreader. For instance, if you are applying seed with a rotary spreader in an outfield turf, you will want to avoid applying the seed to the warning track area; this would waste seed and create a potential weed problem. In this case, you should use a drop (gravity) spreader (described in the next section) to maintain a precise delineation of the turf and warning track.

Many spreaders have deflector plates or attachments that will direct the product application in a particular direction. These attachments can be beneficial, for instance, to prevent spreading the product onto an adjacent area. However, it is important to remember that they can cause the material to be applied at a greater than recommended rate if you fail to follow the manufacturer's instructions for operating the spreader with the attachments in place. This may lead to a disastrous overapplication and damage to the turf. As always, it is critical to familiarize yourself completely with the spreader's capabilities and to carefully follow the instructions for its use.

A final consideration is wind. Obviously, the accuracy of distribution is significantly altered when wind speeds exceed 10 mph. Larger and heavier granules will not be affected as much, but light particles such as seed can be blown in many directions before hitting the ground. Thus, before applying any product, consider the possible effects of wind on your application.

Drop (Gravity) Spreader Calibration

1. Determine the width of your spreader.
2. Measure a test course of at least 10 ft. The granular product will be applied across this test course, then collected and weighed.

Before beginning, you will have to consider how you will collect the product being applied.

If the manufacturer offers a "catch pan" that attaches to the spreader and collects the product as it falls, it is highly recommended that you purchase one; this simple device can really speed up the calibration process. If no such pan is available, you can accurately calibrate a drop spreader by dropping the material onto a known area of a smooth, clean surface (like a paved area) and sweeping the material up. Better still, you can drop the product on a known length of plastic sheeting that is wider than your spreader width. Then you can simply collect the product off the plastic and pour it into a measuring cup for weighing. (Remember to account for the weight of the measuring cup or any other container.)

3. Place enough material in the hopper to completely cover the bottom of the spreader.
4. Check the spreader handbook (or the manufacturer's label directions for the product to be applied) for recommendations regarding spreader settings. If none are available, select a low-to-medium spreader setting as a starting point.
5. Spread the material over the test course, maintaining a constant speed.
6. Collect the product that has been dropped and determine its weight. This will likely be a very small amount; an accurate set of scales capable of measuring in ounces or grams is needed unless your calibration area is quite large.
7. Determine the area of the test course by multiplying its length by the width of the spreader. Compare the weight of the product applied to the test course with the manufacturer's directions for the correct rate of application.

For example, if the label directions call for 1 lb of nitrogen per 1000 sq ft, and your source is a 20-5-10 fertilizer, you would need 1 lb/0.20 = 5 lb of fertilizer per 1000 sq ft. If your spreader is 3 ft wide and you have cut and placed a 20 ft length of plastic, your calibration area is 60 sq ft. Your goal would be to collect an amount of fertilizer corresponding to 5 lb of product per 1000 sq ft.

$$\frac{5 \text{ lb}}{1000 \text{ sq ft}} :: \frac{x \text{ lb}}{60 \text{ sq ft}} = 0.3 \text{ lb of fertilizer per 60 sq ft}$$

Because there are 16 oz in a pound, 16 oz × 0.3 lb = 4.8 oz of fertilizer.

If you have not collected 4.8 ounces of material, readjust the setting and repeat the preceding steps until the desired amount is being collected. Record the setting for future reference.

One of the major advantages in the use of drop spreaders is that they apply material very precisely. Therefore, it is common for drop spreaders to be used around the skinned areas of infields and warning tracks to avoid applying materials where they are not wanted. However, this precision in application also means that it is extremely difficult to deliver the material with a drop spreader without having "skips" in application, because there is no overlap. To avoid misses, it is necessary to apply materials in the morning when wheel tracks in dew can be seen, or to mark off the area repeatedly with string or a tape measure. (Remember that the material is spread only *inside* the wheels; overlap the width of the wheels to account for this characteristic.) Applicators often unintentionally stripe their turf when they apply materials in only one direction, so it is common for drop spreaders to be calibrated to deliver one-half the desired amount in one direction, and the other half in making a second application perpendicular to the first.

Care must be used in selecting materials for drop spreader applications because most coarser-grade products will not flow through the relatively small openings in the spreader. Many agricultural-grade fertilizers are not suited for drop spreader applications. Finer-grade, uniform particles are necessary for accurate delivery, because the sizes of the opening at the base of the spreader are limited.

Finally, as compared with rotary spreader applications, drop spreader applications are not affected as much by wind, unless seed is being applied.

8.8e   Safe Handling and Application

In preparing to apply any chemical agent, it is extremely important to carefully follow the manufacturer's instructions for mixing and handling the product. Remind staff members that it is during the mixing stage that chemicals are exposed in their most concentrated form, and that accidents at this stage can have tragic consequences.

Insist that your staff wear the clothes and protective equipment called for by the label. Many products require the use of goggles to prevent permanent eye damage. Some chemical agents can be handled safely only when the user is wearing rubber gloves. Watch out for employees who want to demonstrate their courage by neglecting to wear appropriate protective gear; they may not hesitate to file suit if a chemical injury occurs.

After a material has been mixed or otherwise prepared, it is still important to follow the label instructions on clothing and protective gear required to ensure safe application. This is especially true for spray applications, because of the possibility of drift. If the crew is found to be in violation of these safety requirements, regulators may impose fines and other penalties.

Obviously, the wisest course is to avoid spraying any chemical agent when it is windy or when the temperature is above the recommended maximum stated on the label. If, for some reason, it is absolutely necessary to spray during windy conditions, use a "skirt" or shield on the sprayer to cut down on drift.

In many states, anyone who operates spraying equipment must be formally trained and licensed by the state itself. Before permitting any staff member to perform these applications, it is important to be fully aware of the requirements in your state.

8.8f   Postapplication Instructions

An important part of the label instructions for any pesticide—and one that has a direct bearing on the use of these products in the sports turf industry—is the minimum reentry period following a chemical application. This information indicates how soon after an application humans and domestic animals can safely reenter the area, and is a critical tool in preventing unnecessary exposure. Be sure to prominently post a notice at every entrance to a field where a chemical application has been made, including a statement of when the field can be safely used.

When a chemical application is made, it is essential to make sure you can keep players off the field until the minimum reentry period has expired. Otherwise, the application may have to wait until after the season. If a particular problem demands immediate applications (when damage from a particular pest is severe and on the increase), the best course usually is to treat the problem immediately. That probably means accepting criticism from coaches who don't understand why practices must be moved or postponed. Do not yield to pressure to authorize premature use of a chemically treated facility; a chemical injury or severe allergic reaction will often result in legal claims.

8.8g   Record Keeping

It is important to keep careful records of all applications of chemical agents. Since the enactment of the 1990 U.S. Farm Bill, record keeping procedures have been federally mandated for all certified pesticide applicators. Within 30 days of the application of a restricted-use pesticide, a written record of the following information must be made:

- The brand and product name and EPA registration number
- The total amount of the product applied

- The specific location of the application
- The size of the area treated
- The crop (for our purposes, usually "turfgrass"), commodity, stored product, and site (specific field or fields) to which the pesticide was applied
- The month, day, and year of the application
- The name and certification number of the applicator or of the applicator's certified supervisor

Under federal law, all records must be maintained for a minimum of two years from the date of pesticide application.

(Be sure to check your state's requirements for maintaining pesticide records, which may include additional requirements not mandated under federal law.)

Chapter 9

Field Aesthetics

9.1 INTRODUCTION

In turning to a chapter entitled "Field Aesthetics," many readers would think first of the most obvious aspects of this topic—the striping and other advanced manicuring techniques that set major league and other high-profile fields apart from those encountered at most schools and parks. Although this chapter indeed focuses largely on these matters, it is important to note from the outset that the aesthetics of a field are determined largely by the day-to-day maintenance and management processes that govern the health of the turfgrass culture. As a general rule, the healthiest fields are also the most aesthetically pleasing. Proper mowing, fertilization, irrigation, aeration, and pest control play a greater role in producing an attractive field than any amount of striping and grooming. (See Figure 9.1.)

The importance of overall turfgrass culture has been stressed; however, there are a number of techniques that can be used to supply the finishing touches on a competition field. This chapter attends mainly to three of them: mowing and rolling patterns, lining and marking the field, using cosmetic fixes to hide turf damage.

9.2 MOWING AND ROLLING PATTERNS

The distinctive and attractive patterns in the turfgrass areas of a baseball or softball diamond would most likely be regarded by the untrained observer as "mowing" patterns. But, as the title of this section suggests, these patterns are created as much by the use of rollers as by the mowing equipment itself. (Of course, some mowers have integral rollers, combining both operations in a single step.)

As a general principle of striping, turfgrass that has been rolled *away from* the viewer's vantage point appears lighter, because more light is reflected from the leaf blades' surfaces to the eye. This is also true when mowing patterns. (See Figure 9.2.) Turfgrass that has been rolled *toward* the viewer appears darker, because less light is reflected to the eye and more shadows are visible under the leaf blades.

Cool season turfgrass varieties lend themselves much more readily to the creation of attractive striping patterns. This is due to the "growth habit" of bermudagrass, the primary turfgrass species used on sports turf in the warm season zone. Bermudagrass is characterized by a growth habit known scientifically as an "indeterminate rhizomatous" type—the elongated stems of the bermudagrass plants grow along the ground, rather than perpendicular to the ground as is the case with ryegrass and bluegrass turf (and, in the case of more northern portions of the United States and Canada, fescue). Because striping is

Figure 9.1. Carefully planned mowing can add substantially to the beauty of a field. However, it takes a healthy turfgrass to achieve this attractive mowing pattern. (Photo courtesy of David R. Mellor.)

Figure 9.2. To reinforce a previously established mowing pattern, mow in the direction of the light stripe and not the dark. (Photo courtesy of David R. Mellor.)

generally accomplished by bending the plants in a uniform pattern, the effects of rolling bermudagrass are substantially less noticeable than they are with cool season species.

9.2a   Mowing and Striping Equipment

The choice of mowing equipment is one of the first decisions to be made in applying a striping pattern to a field. Although any mower will create at least a faint striping pattern, rotary mowers typically leave a pattern that is barely perceptible a few hours after mowing, and one that is dominated by the wheel marks left by the equipment. Reel mowers, because they typically have a roller behind the blades, create a much more pronounced pattern. (See Figure 9.3.)

If the primary mower is a rotary model, application of a distinctive striping pattern will require either the attachment of a roller to the mower or the rolling of the field in a separate operation after mowing. The roller should be long enough to cover the full width of the mower (and wheels), in order to prevent the wheel marks from detracting from the aesthetics of the striping pattern, and should be positioned behind the mower deck or reel.

9.2b   Creating a Pattern

The first step in applying a pattern is to establish a straight line on which the rest of the pattern will be based. On a baseball or softball field, the obvious choice is one foul line. The most common alternative is to start at a point directly behind second base and mow directly to the center point of the outfield fence. To keep the line straight, establish a focal point in the fence and keep your eyes on that point; looking immediately in front of the mower or behind it will produce crooked lines. Glance down only as much as needed to ensure proper overlap.

Figure 9.3. Striping the infield using a walk-behind reel-type mower. The roller at the back of a reel mower is the secret to a distinct striping pattern. (Photo courtesy of B. Prather, Mississippi State University.)

When making turns, care must be taken to prevent turf damage that can be caused by mower wheels when sharp turns are made. The deck or reels may also tilt during sharp turns, gouging the turf. At the end of each stripe, stop the mower and back up far enough to allow you to make a slow, wide turn. Position the mower parallel to the last stripe, and begin mowing back in the other direction. If your equipment allows, lift the blades while making turns. (Don't worry if this method causes a little grass to be missed at the beginning/end of each stripe; "cleanup passes" around the perimeter at the end of the mowing process will cut any remaining unmowed grass.)

Mowing the entire field in this fashion will create a simple but attractive striped pattern.

To apply a more ornate checkerboard pattern, mow the entire field as previously described. (The checkerboard pattern is much easier using a foul line as a starting guide than beginning with a straight line from second base to the middle of the outfield fence.) Then mow the entire field a second time, perpendicular to the first mowing, using the other foul line as a guide.

If time and staff resources permit, you can make the checkerboard pattern stand out by going over the field a third time, disengaging the blades when possible, and using only the rollers. Go back to the first foul line, and roll only the stripes that were mowed outward, none coming back. Travel all the way around the field to avoid the return-direction stripes.

Obviously, the options for mowing and rolling-in a striping pattern are limited only by the planner's imagination and the amount of staff time available to execute the design. Professional groundskeepers have developed techniques for applying such designs as team logos and star players' numbers. For instructions on advanced designs, consult *Picture Perfect; Mowing Techniques for Lawns, Landscapes, and Sports* (Chelsea, MI: Ann Arbor Press, 2001) by Boston Red Sox director of grounds David R. Mellor, who has contributed a good deal of the information included in this chapter. (See Figure 9.4.)

Figure 9.4. Decorative mowing patterns are limited only by the creativity and patience of the maintenance staff. This one, created by Boston Red Sox head groundskeeper David Mellor, shows the American flag in the outfield. (Photo courtesy of David R. Mellor.)

In creating a pattern, it should be noted that driving the equipment back and forth over the foul lines would cause the lines to take on a zigzag appearance. This happens even when the blades and rollers are lifted, because the wheels themselves bend the blades of grass to one side or the other, creating a distortion of the foul lines. To prevent this problem, stop the equipment before it reaches the line and make the turn. Mow and roll cleanup passes along the foul line to erase these turnaround areas. If the lines are to be repainted after striping, this effect is reduced, but may still be present as the remaining traces of the original line create a bulging appearance when the wheels have passed.

To assist the umpires in making fair/foul calls, expert groundskeepers recommend mowing the foul lines outward from the umpire's vantage point. This bends the blades away from the umpire, so that when lines are painted, the maximum amount of paint will be visible. Mowing toward home plate will require the lines to be repainted more frequently to provide the umpires with the same visibility.

A final note on pattern creation: Excess clippings left on the surface will compromise the contrast, and thus the aesthetic appeal, of the pattern. For purposes of this discussion, excess clippings can be defined as those that are still visible on the surface 24 hours after mowing. When such clippings are apparent, remowing can break up and disperse them. When circumstances create the possibility of excess clippings, the wisest course is to collect the clippings at the time the turf is mowed. In nearly all cases, mowing according to the one-third rule when the turf is dry and leaving the clippings is the recommended practice for enhancing the health of the turfgrass culture.

9.3   LINING AND MARKING

On a baseball or softball field, marking the foul lines, batter's boxes, on-deck circles, and coaches' boxes is a critical process, because each of these areas can affect the outcome of a game. To maximize the aesthetic appeal of the field, and to prevent confusion in an umpire's rulings, care must be taken in the selection and application of materials used for these markings.

For skinned areas, the most common marking materials are powdered products such as chalk. Various manufacturers also produce dry line materials formulated for maximum visibility. Fabricated templates are available for marking batter's boxes. These templates allow precise sizing and positioning of the boxes in reference to home plate. It is possible to make your own template using lumber or metal, but a manufactured product is probably worth the modest investment for any field where aesthetics are important and will help to ensure accurate marking. (See Figure 9.5.) Avoid using any caustic product such as lime, which can cause skin and eye irritation in players. Another material used for marking the skinned area is a mixture of chalk, water, and latex paint as described in Section 7.3e, "Marking Foul Lines and Batter's Boxes."

For the foul lines, install a string line from the white point of home plate to the outside edge of the foul pole. Install the dry line material down the base lines to the edge of the turfgrass, keeping the line on the inside of the string. Because of the potential for mowing equipment and maintenance processes to slightly distort the portion of the foul lines on the turf, it is wise to use the string line each time you mark foul lines; don't just follow the old line on the field.

Dry material can be used to mark the entire length of the foul line, but marking paint provides a more visible foul line on turf. Moreover, using dry materials on the turf will gradually create a raised line, which can affect drainage, turfgrass health, and ball response. For all these reasons, paint is preferred for the foul lines on turfgrass.

Figure 9.5. A prefabricated template allows the precise marking of batter's boxes. (Photo courtesy of Jeff Limburg, head groundskeeper, Fifth Third Field, Toledo.)

To prevent the line material from gradually mixing into the skinned area soil and degrading visibility of the foul lines, professional groundskeepers remove these lines after each game and reapply them before the next use of the field. Use a flat shovel to remove the lines, taking as little skinned area soil as possible, then place clean soil to maintain uniformity.

9.4   COSMETIC FIXES FOR DAMAGED TURF

Sometimes, despite the best efforts of the field manager and his or her crew, the baseball or softball field will suffer unsightly damage at a time when it will be seen by the public. This may be wear damage in areas such as the front of the pitcher's mound, the coaches' boxes at first and third base, or around home plate. It may be created by underirrigation in dry weather. Improper turning (see Section 9.2b) may cause the mower to gouge the turf. Fields used for nonathletic functions, such as concerts, can also suffer damage that will compromise their visual appeal.

If such damage is observed before a big game, don't panic—there are a number of techniques that can be used to provide short-term cosmetic fixes.

One of the easiest ways to hide turf damage is to use a mowing pattern that conceals the area in which the damage has taken place. Experts recommend the use of patterns with narrow stripes; avoid double-width stripes that allow the damage to be seen. More ornate patterns such as the checkerboard will also help to conceal damage. (See Figure 9.6.)

Another technique for hiding turf damage is the use of colorants—green dye or paint that can make discolored turf look more lush and natural. These products are sold as powders and concentrates that can be mixed with water for application. Care should be taken to choose a product specifically manufactured for the purpose. Oil-based paints, for instance, should not be used because they will kill the grass to which they are applied.

When using colorants, a few factors must be kept in mind. First of all, test the colorant to make sure its color matches the turf on the field; some colorants are more blue and may not match the emerald green on the rest of a healthy field. Before making a large-scale

Figure 9.6. Wide mowing patterns like this look best when the turf is in good condition but can draw attention to unhealthy turf. Narrow striping does a better job of hiding damaged turf. (Photo courtesy of David R. Mellor.)

application, select an area that is less visible to spectators and try the colorant there. (This suggests the wisdom of having a supply of colorant on hand in case of emergency; ask your vendor for a small test quantity of the color or colors you are considering, then order the closest tint for general use.) When testing a colorant, check the test area from several angles and view it from a distance to make sure it looks as natural as possible. Nearly all colorants are designed for spray application; when using colorants near skinned areas (or warning tracks), mask the skinned soil with cardboard to avoid unsightly overspray.

Some professional groundskeepers who have used colorants suggest mixing the product at a slightly lower rate than label directions call for, to permit greater control over the amount of color applied; it is easier to put a little more down than to remove excess color. Treat small areas at a time, blending the colorant slightly into the surrounding grass.

Colorants are also used in some cases when drought or the end of the growing season has made large areas of the field look brown. Under these circumstances, consider raising the mowing height slightly and very lightly moistening the turf before applying the colorant.

Another technique for hiding worn or damaged areas is to spread grass clippings collected during mowing. These clippings will retain their color only for a day or so and should be handled with care if this technique is to be used. Groundskeepers who use this method suggest storing the clippings in the shade with a wet towel over them to prevent drying. Steve Wightman, turf manager at Qualcomm Stadium in San Diego, suggests storing the clippings on ice until just before they are applied. The clippings should be spread

Figure 9.7. Fresh grass clippings can be used to temporarily improve the appearance of damaged turf areas. This photo shows a damaged area before fresh grass clippings were spread over the bare soil. (Photo courtesy of Jeff Limburg, head groundskeeper, Fifth Third Field, Toledo.)

in a layer of ¼ in. to ½ in. to provide coverage without affecting ball response on the treated area. At the end of the day's play, remove the clippings to prevent discoloration and damage to the existing turfgrass. (See Figures 9.7, 9.8.)

There are also commercially available painted sand products, which can be applied to divots or thin areas to hide the damage. Topdressing equipment can be used to spread

Figure 9.8. After fresh grass clippings are spread over the damage, the turf appearance is substantially improved. Fresh clippings provide a good temporary fix, because they are the same color as the growing grass. (Photo courtesy of Jeff Limburg, head groundskeeper, Fifth Third Field, Toledo.)

Figure 9.9. Painted sand is also used to hide damaged turf areas, but it can be more difficult to match the color of the existing grass with painted sand than with fresh clippings. (Photo courtesy of B. Prather, Mississippi State University.)

these products over larger areas. As with colorants, carefully compare the color before treating the affected portions of the field. (See Figure 9.9.)

Note that these temporary fixes are meant only to improve the aesthetic appeal of the field and will not correct turf so badly damaged that it presents a safety hazard to players. Such conditions must be corrected to prevent injuries and associated liability risks, even if such permanent corrections are less aesthetically pleasing than the rest of the turf. Safety must always be the primary concern.

PART III

Ancillary Information

The focus of discussion in Part I was the design and construction of the field and its surrounding areas, such as the areas used for spectators, parking, swales, and access to the field. In Part II, we considered the renovation and maintenance of the field itself. Part III consists of two chapters focusing on topics that are just as important as any other in the book: fences, backstops, and other structures; and rules relating to the layout and dimensions of fields as published by various leading sanctioning bodies. Describing Part III as ancillary is not meant to suggest that these topics are less significant than other topics in this book; in fact, setting them apart allows their importance to be emphasized.

Chapter 10 considers design, construction, and maintenance of such structures as fences, backstops, dugouts, and bullpens, which are critical components of almost every baseball or softball field. These are placed in a chapter of their own so that we can consider their design, construction, and maintenance in depth and without interruption.

Chapter 11 presents rules regarding the correct layout and dimensions of baseball and softball fields, along with information on common points of confusion about these topics. This chapter is meant to be a useful resource that may be referred to at any time during the process of design, construction, renovation, and maintenance. Names and addresses of leading sanctioning bodies are included so that the reader can request copies of their respective rulebooks.

Chapter 10

Fences, Backstops, Dugouts, and Bullpens

10.1 INTRODUCTION

In addition to the playing surface itself, there are a variety of structures that play important roles in the function and safety of a baseball or softball diamond. In this chapter, we will consider the design and construction of these structures and review some of the options that affect their impact on player safety.

In a brief review of this type, only some general guidelines can be provided in regard to the installation and maintenance of fences, backstops, dugouts, and the like. Before making any final decisions about these structures, the sports field manager is advised to consult manufacturers' literature and standards for each, and to review the needs of the facility with the specialized contractors who have experience in their installation.

10.2 FENCES

On a baseball or softball field, fences have several specific functions, and the design of a fence (including the choice of materials) must include a consideration of which function is involved.

10.2a Fence Types by Function

The first thought of most players and fans, upon hearing the phrase "the fence," is of the outfield structure over which a ball is hit to record a home run. The outfield fence can be of almost any desired height, with higher fences sometimes used to enhance competition where the field has size limitations (e.g., the famed "Green Monster" at the old Fenway Park in Boston). As a general rule, it is probably true that a fence that is too short may present a substantial safety hazard for players who run into it. A player may suffer neck injuries of a whiplash type or may fall over the fence, suffering serious injuries in landing on the other side. For adult players, a fence at least 8 ft high will prevent many such injuries. Younger players can probably be safe with a shorter fence, but it is generally true that the higher the fence, the greater the safety achieved.

Foul line fences have the dual function of designating where batted balls are out of play and protecting spectators. For the safety of players, these fences should be the same height as outfield fences. Of course, it is impossible to give general guidance on how high a foul line fence must be to protect spectators. As any fan of major league baseball knows, batted balls are simply one of the hazards of watching a baseball game. Obviously, the higher the fence, the better for safety.

In designing foul line fences, it is generally preferred to angle the fences so that foul territory is narrowest at the outfield fence. This tends to direct batted balls back toward fair territory, minimizing the number of situations in which an outfielder must approach the foul line fence at a dead run to field a ball deep in the corner.

Foul line fences must provide access for players and maintenance equipment onto the field. For information on this subject, see Chapter 1, Section 1.10, "Vehicular, Player, and Spectator Access."

10.2b Types of Fencing Material

On most fields, the planner has the greatest range of options for designing outfield fences, because they can be either fully opaque (as in a wooden fence) or see-through structures made of chain-link mesh.

In designing an outfield fence, it is also important to account for the fact that batters must be visually able to distinguish the ball from the background behind the pitcher. For this reason, solid fences (or chain-link fences covered by a solid material such as vinyl sheeting or tarpaulin) are probably to be preferred. Some companies also produce a netting material that improves the batter's ability to distinguish the ball, yet does not suffer as much damage from the wind as solid panels may incur. Before installing any solid material on a chain-link fence, it is a good idea to check with the fence installer to make sure it is strong enough to withstand the additional wind load.

To maximize the batter's ability to see the pitched ball (often referred to as the "batter's eye"), the outfield fence in straightaway center field should be at least 15 ft to 20 ft high, and some fields are built with fences as high as 30 ft. This higher portion of fence should extend 40 ft to 50 ft on either side of a line drawn from home plate through the pitcher's plate to the center field fence.

Solid outfield fences are generally constructed of wood. The use of solid fences was more common in the past, because field owners sold sign space on the fences to sponsors. However, with the advent of inexpensive vinyl signs that can be easily attached to chain-link fences, this reason for wood fences is largely a thing of the past.

Wood fences have a certain nostalgic appeal, but they also have inherent drawbacks. One is their relative lack of durability; even with careful maintenance (which can itself represent a substantial investment in staff time, paint, etc.) wood fences usually do not last as long as chain-link structures. Another drawback relates to safety; solid fences do not "give" as much as chain-link (excepting, of course, the rails and posts that support the chain-link). A further consideration, which may actually be an advantage for the home team, is the ricochet of a batted ball off a solid fence. To ensure player safety, it is wise to have padding on any solid fence surface.

Some diamonds still have brick fences around some portion of the playing area. Where these fences are in use, it is absolutely necessary to have safety padding in place. In addition to the danger of player contact with the fence, the potential for dangerous ricochet is another disadvantage of brick structures. Overall, in spite of their visual appeal, brick fences are too hazardous to be recommended for any sports facility.

A type of fencing sometimes installed for school or recreational fields is temporary or removable fencing. This approach is generally used for outfield fences where a field must serve more than one purpose—for instance, where an adult softball field must also be used for children, or when a field is used for both men's slow-pitch and women fast-pitch competition. Common snow fence is sometimes used for this purpose, but the steel posts used to support such a fence can present a substantial safety hazard for players running into it. Flexible fencing systems available from several manufacturers provide a much safer alternative and should be used for this purpose. It should be noted that these removable fences should not be considered as an acceptable economy measure for permanent installation and should be used only when fencing must be removed to allow use of the field for other purposes.

Foul line fences are almost always made of chain-link fencing, because spectators have to be able to see through them.

10.2c Fence Safety Issues

Safety experts say that fences often present some of the worst hazards on a baseball or softball field. The annual inspection should include a search for any area in which broken or sagging fences may cause injuries to players or spectators who come in contact with them. The jagged edges of fencing (especially chain-link) can cause very severe cuts and gouges, and any damage to a fence should be repaired immediately. (See Figure 10.1.)

Fences should be inspected annually (preferably at the beginning of the season) to detect signs of deterioration. When rust appears on a chain-link fence, paint the fencing with a protective paint. Replace any missing or broken ties to keep the chain-link securely attached to posts and rails.

We also recommend that every chain-link fence have a fence cap to protect players from injuring themselves upon impact with the top, which can have exposed jagged edges. Fence cap is usually supplied as lengths of bright plastic material that is easily installed on the top of a standard fence and can be removed and stored indoors over the winter. The cost of fence cap is quite modest, especially as compared with the potential liability for an injured player. (See Figure 10.2.)

Figure 10.1. This fence should be replaced immediately. The strands of the fence extend out into the playing area and present a safety hazard to players.

Figure 10.2. Fence cap (the rounded plastic material at the top of the fence).

In the construction of all fences, posts should be placed on the outside of the fence surface itself to prevent dangerous collisions with them. Where posts are set in concrete, the concrete should always extend down past the frost line to prevent it from heaving upward past the field surface and presenting a safety hazard.

10.3   BACKSTOPS

Obviously, the purpose of a backstop is to prevent foul balls from flying backward out of the playing area and striking spectators, cars, and so forth. As in the construction of fences meant to protect spectators, the higher the better for backstops; 20 ft to 25 ft is generally observed as a rule of thumb on most fields. If roadways run behind the field, a higher backstop will diminish the possibility of auto accidents caused by foul balls and will also reduce the number of times spectators must cross those roadways to retrieve foul balls.

Professional stadiums typically use netting to protect spectators behind the plate, but most other facilities use chain-link mesh to construct the backstop. Where circumstances dictate, a combination of netting above chain-link provides additional protection.

A cantilevered (tilted-in) top on a backstop cuts down the number of foul balls that go backward out of the playing area. (See Figure 10.3.) Such backstops are used more widely on softball diamonds than for baseball, because home plate is typically closer to the backstop on a softball field. Where the distance is greater, the cantilever has less effect.

(For recommended clearances between home plate and the backstop on various types of fields, see Chapter 11, "Rules and Regulations.")

Figure 10.3. Cantilevered backstop in use on a softball field.

A common problem with the bottom of the backstop is that the chain-link fencing tends to become bent in toward the playing area. This causes a gap under which the ball can pass and creates a safety hazard for catchers looking upward when trying to field pop-ups. For this reason, a bottom rail should be installed with ties 12 in. to 18 in. apart to keep the fence in place. A second rail, 18 in. or so higher than the bottom rail, will provide some additional reinforcement to prevent this problem. (See Figure 10.4.) Another prudent step is to use a heavier-gauge fencing for the bottom 10 in. of the backstop. The typical choice for fencing is 9-gauge chain-link; substituting 6-gauge will help to keep the backstop vertical at the bottom.

Some field managers choose to install an opaque windscreen on the backstop to prevent spectators from watching the game through the backstop, which can present a distraction for players and umpires, and especially for pitchers. This is a step that is appreciated by most players and umpires, which should be considered whenever practical.

We recommend padding wherever the budget allows. Although it is most commonly used with rigid fences, like those of wood or brick, padding also provides extra safety for players when it is installed on chain-link backstops.

The vertical posts used to support a backstop should be Schedule 40 galvanized steel, 3 in. to 4 in. in diameter. Three-inch posts are usually adequate for backstops up to 15 ft high, but 4 in. posts should be used when the finished structure will be higher, to keep the fence plumb. Posts should be anchored a minimum of 4 ft deep for a 20 ft backstop, and deeper for higher structures.

It is important to inspect the backstop at the beginning of each season, to check for damage or deterioration that can present a safety hazard. Check for broken or missing ties, which can allow the fencing to separate from its posts and rails. Most galvanized fencing can be expected to last 20 years without substantial deterioration, but the appearance of rust spots indicates that the galvanizing is beginning to wear away, and it is a good

Figure 10.4. This backstop has been reinforced with horizontal rails and vertical supports to prevent the fencing from bending and causing a safety hazard.

idea to paint the fencing with a rust-resistant paint. Where posts are set in concrete, check for any exposed concrete above the field surface. As we mentioned in regard to fences, any and all damage to a backstop should be repaired at once to prevent injuries to players, umpires, and spectators.

10.4   DUGOUTS

Although the typical baseball fan may visualize professional-style sunken structures when the term "dugout" is used, for our purposes we use this term to refer to any area provided for the batting team and reserves to sit during a game. The primary objective in design and construction of dugouts is to maximize the safety of players and coaches, and they are also typically intended to provide temporary shelter in case of rain. (Dugouts are not meant to provide protection from severe weather conditions such as lightning or high winds, and players should be evacuated immediately from the field area when these conditions arise.)

In the North, where the season may begin when temperatures remain cold, three-sided wooden or concrete block dugouts are popular to provide some measure of protection from the wind. Where these structures are used, openings should be left in the solid surfaces to allow the wind to pass through without damaging the roof. A common method is to leave a 4 in. to 6 in. space between the roof and the top of the wall, or to leave several blocks missing from the top row for this purpose. (See Figure 10.5.)

In the South, where cold temperatures are of lesser concern, open-air dugouts surrounded entirely by chain-link fencing are widely used. (This practice helps to protect the players and coaches from the intrusion of spectators. This construction can be especially appropriate for fields that will be used by children, because it helps coaches keep track of their young players during the game.) Installing an 8 ft fence at the front of the dugout and a 7 ft fence at the rear and sides allows a roof to be sloped backward to provide for runoff of rainwater. (See Figure 10.6.)

Figure 10.5. Cement block dugout, with openings left to allow air to flow through the structure and prevent wind damage.

Chain-link fencing should be installed in front of any dugout, with the top of the fence as high as the roof, and no gaps where a thrown or batted ball can pass through. (See Figure 10.7.) Making the dugout 8 ft from front to back allows for the comfortable movement of players and coaches within the dugout, with space for equipment bags and other gear. A dugout 25 ft to 30 ft long can accommodate players of all ages. As with backstops,

Figure 10.6. A roof over a fenced-in dugout, a design common in the South.

Figure 10.7. Fence in front of dugout. Note that the fence completely covers the front, so that no batted or thrown balls can injure players waiting inside.

the fencing in front of a dugout should have a bottom rail (and preferably a second rail 18 in. higher) to keep the fence in place.

Some planners like the idea of building a solid wall in front of the dugout to a height of 4 ft or so. We do not recommend this design, for the following reasons: The solid wall would still need to be topped by chain-link fence to fully protect players, and the wall itself would then need to be padded on the playing-area side to prevent players from running into it or balls ricocheting off it. Whatever benefits this design may have, the extra expense and safety concerns make it impractical for nearly all fields.

Sunken dugouts are popular where the budget permits their construction, but these structures have several inherent problems. First of all, without proper drainage they can become flooded ponds with each heavy rain. Second, as skinned area or warning track soil is tracked or washed into them, sunken dugouts can develop a layer of dirt on the floor, which is difficult to clean out. (This dirt can also clog the drainage system.) The stairs into the dugout can also present a safety hazard, particularly for children. For these reasons, sunken dugouts are recommended only for professional fields or those with the resources to support the level of maintenance required.

Sometimes players, coaches, and fans have their hearts set on a sunken dugouts, and it is agreed to build one. The construction process is similar to that for a house built without a basement. A floor must be poured, with drains tied into a nearby storm sewer. (Tying the drains into a dry well is not sufficient, because when the dry well fills up, the dugout is flooded.) In the North, a footer must be poured deeper than the frost line. Stairs must be carefully poured to ensure their safe use, and then the walls and roof installed.

Although it is tempting to try to build a major-league-style dugout for school or youth athletes, it is important to keep in mind the two basic functions of such facilities: providing a safe waiting area for players not currently involved in the game, and allowing for minimal shelter against the elements. In the vast majority of cases, these two functions can be performed by a simple structure that is economical to build and easy to maintain.

10.5   BULLPENS

In designing and building a bullpen, three critical factors must be considered: placement, orientation, and construction.

Obviously, in planning for the placement of a bullpen, the object is to create a facility that provides maximum safety for the pitchers and catchers using it, for the players competing on the field, and for spectators nearby. Wherever possible, the bullpen should be located outside the fence around the playing area to isolate those using it from the competition on the field. Under these circumstances, the bullpen can be surrounded by its own fence, to ensure that an escaping ball does not injure spectators nearby. At the very minimum, a fence should be placed behind the position occupied by bullpen catchers. This fence should be at least 8 ft high to prevent a wild pitch from passing over the top, and wide enough to fully protect spectators.

If the bullpen is meant to be used by a single relief pitcher at a time, an area at least 10 ft wide should be provided. Where the bullpen is designed for use by two pitchers at a time, the two pitchers' plates should be placed at least 10 ft apart, with 12 ft to 14 ft providing a greater margin of safety (and less distraction) for the players. This much clearance would require a bullpen at least 20 ft wide.

If the bullpen cannot be placed outside the fence, and must be situated in foul territory, some provision must be made for a spotter to guard the catchers against batted balls and to watch for fielders pursuing pop-ups into foul territory.

In regard to orientation, the bullpen should be laid out so that the pitcher warming up is facing as nearly as possible in the same direction as the pitcher who is actually competing in the game. In most cases, practical considerations dictate that bullpen pitchers are throwing parallel to the foul lines, which vary slightly from the line running from home plate to the mound on the field of play itself. Most fields are oriented so that neither the pitcher nor the catcher is looking directly into the sun, and this principle must be observed for safe bullpen design.

The goal in bullpen design is to match all conditions that will be encountered when the pitcher leaves the bullpen and enters the game. The mound should be of the same height and slope as that on the field, the pitcher's plate should be of the same construction, and even the soil used for construction should be identical to that on the field's mound. Otherwise, the pitcher may encounter distracting variations upon entering the game.

This principle should be carried over to the maintenance of the bullpen; it is important to groom and maintain the bullpen mounds with the same care given to the mound on the field. Daily maintenance practices performed for the field of play should routinely be carried out for the bullpen as well.

Chapter 11

Rules and Regulations

11.1 INTRODUCTION

It is probably accurate to say that few sports fields are more complicated to lay out and construct than baseball and softball diamonds. Distances between bases, home plate, and the pitcher's plate are precisely dictated by each league's rules. The height of the pitcher's mound is established within very close tolerances. Foul territory is a part of the playing area and must be designed and cared for with much greater care than, say, the out-of-bounds spaces of a football field. In fact, the specific requirements are set forth in such detail that a number of common points of confusion arise in the design and construction of these fields. This chapter considers these details in planning a diamond.

11.2 COMMON POINTS OF CONFUSION

Figure 11.1 shows some of the fine points of baseball and softball diamond design that are frequently mistaken. Sometimes such mistakes occur because the appropriate rule book is misinterpreted, and in other cases the rules have been observed by convention but have not been widely printed and distributed.

For example, in taking measurements from home plate, the *white* point on the plate, and not the black point, is the correct one to use. (The black beveled frame around the plate is meant to be covered with skinned area soil.)

Another example concerns the foul lines, which are meant to pass through the outside edges of first and third base and continue to the *outside* edges of the foul poles. These poles (and, for that matter, the foul lines themselves) are probably inaccurately named; they are, in fact, in fair territory.

When it comes to the bases, conventions can be even more confusing. In the case of adult baseball diamonds, the *back edges* of first and third base are to be 90 ft from home plate, but the *center* of second base is 90 ft from the foul lines. The front edge of the pitcher's plate is 60 ft, 6 in. from the white point of home plate, and the center of second base is 127 ft, 3⅜ in. from the white point of home.

In laying out the circled edge of the skinned area (the arc at which the outfield grass begins), the edge is to be 95 ft from the middle of the front edge of the pitcher's plate. In laying out a softball field, however, the arc of the outfield grass does not always have its center at the pitcher's plate; sometimes it is centered on a point several feet behind the pitcher's plate. In designing a softball field, see Table 11.2 or consult the rule book of the appropriate governing or sanctioning body for specifications on the exact center point for the outfield arc.

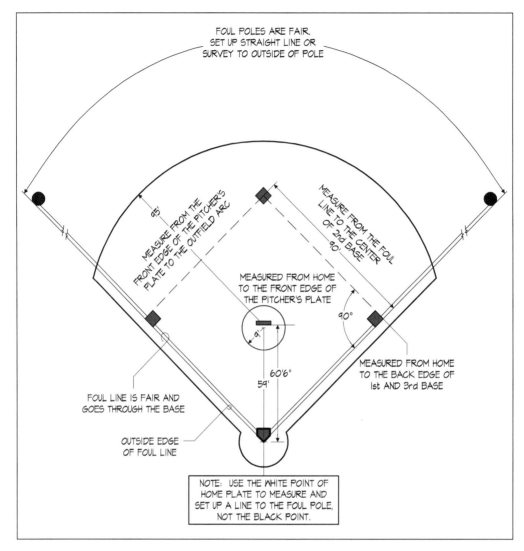

Figure 11.1. Frequently misunderstood points of field design.

11.3   LINE AND BOUNDARY DIMENSIONS

Tables 11.1 and 11.2 show dimensions for the most commonly used baseball and softball fields. Note that some dimensions (like the distance between the bases) are strictly and precisely stated, whereas other dimensions (such as the distance from home plate to the backstop) are stated as recommendations.

Table 11.1. Baseball Field Dimensions

Type of Field	Age	Required					Recommended				
		Base Lines	Pitching Distance	Home to Second	Pitching Height	Backstop from HP[b]	Foul Lines	Center Field	Arc Around Bases/HP	Pitcher's Circle[c]	Outfield Arc from PP
Official Baseball Rules		90 ft	60½ ft	127.28 ft	10 in.	60 ft	325 ft	400 ft	13 ft	9 ft R	95 ft
College—NCAA Rules		90 ft	60½ ft	127.28 ft	10 in.	60 ft	330 ft	400 ft	13 ft	9 ft R	95 ft
High School—NFSHSA Rules		90 ft	60½ ft	127.28 ft	10 in.	60 ft	300 ft min.	350 ft min.	13 ft	9 ft R	95 ft
Pony Baseball, Inc.											
Shetland	5 & 6	50 ft	n/a	70.71 ft	n/a	25 ft[a]	125 ft[a]	125 ft[a]	8 ft[a]	5 ft R[a]	40 ft[a]
Pinto	7 & 8	50 ft	n/a	70.71 ft	n/a	25 ft[a]	150 ft[a]	150 ft[a]	8 ft[a]	5 ft R[a]	40 ft[a]
Mustang	9 & 10	60 ft	44 ft	84.85 ft	6 in.[a]	25 ft[a]	180 ft[a]	200 ft[a]	9 ft[a]	6 ft R[a]	50 ft[a]
Bronco	11 & 12	70 ft	48 ft	98.99 ft	6 in.	30 ft	225 ft	275 ft	11 ft[a]	8 ft R[a]	70 ft[a]
Pony	13 & 14	80 ft	54 ft	113.14 ft	8 in.	40 ft	265 ft	315 ft	12 ft[a]	8 ft R[a]	80 ft[a]
Colt	15 & 16	90 ft	60½ ft	127.28 ft	10 in.	50 ft	300 ft	350 ft	13 ft[a]	9 ft R[a]	95 ft[a]
Palomino	17 & 18	90 ft	60½ ft	127.28 ft	10 in.	50 ft	300 ft	350 ft	13 ft[a]	9 ft R[a]	95 ft[a]
Babe Ruth Baseball, Inc.											
Bambino Division	5 to 12	60 ft	46 ft	84.85 ft	6 in.	25 ft[a]	200 ft min.	200 ft min.	9 ft	5 ft R	50 ft
Babe Ruth League	13 to 15	90 ft	60½ ft	127.28 ft	10 in.	60 ft	250 ft min.	250 ft min.	13 ft	9 ft R	95 ft
16–18 League	16 to 18	90 ft	60½ ft	127.28 ft	10 in.	60 ft	300 ft[a]	350 ft[a]	13 ft	9 ft R	95 ft
Little League Baseball, Inc.	9 to 12	60 ft	46 ft	84.85 ft	6 in.	25 ft min.	205 ft	215 ft	9 ft	6 ft R	50 ft

[a] Authors' recommendation—not in rule book.
[b] The distance from the foul lines to the dugouts are the same.
[c] The center of the circle is 18″ in front of the pitcher's plate.
HP = home plate, PP = pitcher's plate, R = radius

Notes:
1) National Collegiate Athletic Association (NCAA).
2) National Federation of State High School Associations (NFSHSA).

Table 11.2. Softball Field Dimensions

Type of Field	Age	Required			Recommended			
					Home Run Fence		Outfield Arc	
		Base Lines	Pitching Distance	Home to Second	Min.	Max.	Radius	Center[b]
College—NCAA Rules		60 ft	43 ft	84.85 ft	190 ft foul 200 ft center	225 ft	60 ft	43 ft
High School—NFSHSA Rules								
Fast Pitch w/ 12 in. Ball								
Female		60 ft	40 ft	84.85 ft	185 ft	235 ft	60 ft	46 ft
Male		60 ft	46 ft	84.85 ft	185 ft	235 ft	60 ft	46 ft
Slow Pitch								
Female w/ 12 in. Ball		60 ft	46 ft	84.85 ft	250 ft	275 ft	60 ft	46 ft
Female w/ 11 in. Ball		65 ft	50 ft	91.92 ft	250 ft	275 ft	65 ft[a]	46 ft
Male w/ 12 in. Ball		65 ft	46 ft	91.92 ft	275 ft	300 ft	65 ft[a]	46 ft
Amateur Softball Assoc.	Age							
All (Fast & Slow Pitch)	10-Under	55 ft	35 ft	77.78 ft	150 ft	175 ft	55 ft	46 ft
Fast Pitch								
Girls	12-Under	60 ft	35 ft	84.85 ft	175 ft	200 ft	60 ft	46 ft
Boys	12-Under	60 ft	40 ft	84.85 ft	175 ft	200 ft	60 ft	46 ft
Girls	14-Under	60 ft	40 ft	84.85 ft	175 ft	200 ft	60 ft	46 ft
Boys	14-Under	60 ft	46 ft	84.85 ft	175 ft	200 ft	60 ft	46 ft
Girls	15 to 19	60 ft	40 ft	84.85 ft	200 ft	225 ft	60 ft	46 ft
Boys	15 to 19	60 ft	46 ft	84.85 ft	200 ft	225 ft	60 ft	46 ft
Women	Adult	60 ft	40 ft	84.85 ft	200 ft	225 ft	60 ft	46 ft
Men	Adult	60 ft	46 ft	84.85 ft	225 ft	250 ft	60 ft	46 ft
Slow Pitch								
Girls & Boys	12-Under	60 ft	40 ft	84.85 ft	175 ft	200 ft	60 ft	46 ft
Girls	13 to 19	65 ft	46 ft	91.92 ft	225 ft	250 ft	65 ft	46 ft
Boys	13 & 14	65 ft	46 ft	91.92 ft	250 ft	275 ft	65 ft	46 ft
Boys	15 to 19	65 ft	46 ft	91.92 ft	275 ft	300 ft	65 ft	46 ft
Women	Adult	65 ft	46 ft	91.92 ft	250 ft	250 ft	65 ft	46 ft
Men	Adult	65 ft	46 ft	91.92 ft	275 ft	300 ft	65 ft	46 ft
Slow Pitch w/ 16 in. ball								
Women	Adult	55 ft	38 ft	77.78 ft	200 ft	200 ft	55 ft	46 ft
Men	Adult	55 ft	38 ft	77.78 ft	250 ft	250 ft	55 ft	46 ft

[a] Authors' recommendation—not in rule book

[b] The distance from the white point of home plate in a straight line toward 2nd base.

Notes:
1. Pitcher's plate is level with home plate.
2. The distance from home plate to the backstop is a minimum of 25 ft and a maximum of 30 ft.
3. The distances from the foul lines to the dugouts are the same as the distance from home plate to the backstop.
4. A skinned infield is recommended, and for some tournament play is a requirement.
5. National Collegiate Athletic Association (NCAA).
6. National Federation of State High School Associations (NFSHSA).

11.4   GOVERNING AND SANCTIONING BODIES

Among the most important governing bodies for North American baseball and softball are the following:

Official Baseball Rules (published and distributed by):
Sporting News
Post Office Box 11229
Des Moines, IA 50340
(800) 825-8508

These rules are followed by professional baseball, National Baseball Congress, Inc., American Amateur Baseball Congress, Inc., which includes Stan Musial Division, Connie Mack Division, and Mickey Mantle Division, American Legion Baseball, and Babe Ruth League, Inc. For fields used for competition sanctioned by these organizations, contact the sanctioning body for up-to-date rules.

College Baseball and Softball:
National Collegiate Athletic Association
Post Office Box 6222
Indianapolis, IN 46206
(888) 388-9748

High School Baseball and Softball:
National Federation of State High School Associations
Post Office Box 690
Indianapolis, IN 46206
(800) 776-3462

Pony League Baseball:
Pony Baseball, Inc.
Post Office Box 225
Washington, PA 15301-0225
(724) 225-1060

Babe Ruth Baseball:
Babe Ruth League, Inc.
Post Office Box 5000
Trenton, NJ 08638
(609) 695-1434

Little League Baseball:
Little League Baseball, Inc.
Post Office Box 3485
Williamsport, PA 17701
(570) 326-1921

Softball:
Amateur Softball Association of America
2801 N.E. 50th Street
Oklahoma City, OK 73111
(405) 424-5266

About the Authors

Jim Puhalla is the president of Sportscape International, Inc., a firm specializing in the design, construction, renovation, and maintenance of sports fields and related facilities, with operations in Boardman, Ohio; Dallas; and Detroit. Jim has contributed a number of articles to *Sports Turf* magazine.

Jim studied landscape architecture at Ohio State University and accounting at Youngstown State University. He has worked in the sports field industry since 1978, designing, building, or renovating hundreds of fields throughout North America. The company's reconstruction of the Boardman High School field won it a 1995 Baseball Diamond of the Year Award from *Sports Turf*.

Jeff Krans is a professor of agronomy at Mississippi State University in the Golf and Sports Turf Management program. He received his Ph.D. from Michigan State University in 1975, an M.S. from the University of Arizona in 1973, and his B.S. from the University of Wisconsin in 1970. He has taught and advised students in the turf management program at Mississippi State since 1976.

Jeff has conducted research in turfgrass germplasm collection and evaluation, tissue culture and cell selection techniques, and turfgrass physiology. His most recent accomplishments include the development, patenting, and commercialization of turf-type bermudagrass cultivars MS-Pride, MS-Choice (Bull's-eye), MS-Express, and MS-Supreme and the development and production of heat- and disease-resistant creeping bentgrass germplasm. Jeff is a member and former chairperson of the Turfgrass Science Division of the Crop Science Society of America and seminar instructor for the Golf Course Superintendents Association of America.

A native of Springfield, Kentucky, **Mike Goatley** is a professor of agronomy in the Department of Plant and Soil Sciences at Mississippi State University. Mike received his Ph.D. from Virginia Tech in 1988, his M.S. from the University of Kentucky in 1986, and his B.S. from the University of Kentucky in 1983. He has taught and advised students in the Golf and Sports Turf Management program at Mississippi State since 1988.

Mike has conducted turfgrass research in the areas of plant nutrition, plant growth regulation, and soil modification. He serves as secretary and newsletter editor for the Mississippi Turfgrass Association.

An earlier book by the authors, *Sports Fields: A Manual for Design, Construction and Maintenance* (1999) was published by Ann Arbor Press/Sleeping Bear Press.

Index

215